BUT WHAT I
REALLY
WANT TO DO IS
DIRECT

BUT WHAT I REALLY WANT TO DO IS DIRECT

Lessons from a Life Behind the Camera

KEN KWAPIS

ST. MARTIN'S
GRIFFIN
NEW YORK

Library of Congress Cataloging-in-Publication Data

Names: Kwapis, Ken, author.
Title: But what I really want to do is direct : lessons from a life behind
  the camera / Ken Kwapis.
Description: First edition. | New York, NY : St. Martin's Griffin, 2020. |
  Includes index.
Identifiers: LCCN 2020021878 | ISBN 9781250260123 (trade paperback) |
  ISBN 9781250260116 (ebook)
Subjects: LCSH: Kwapis, Ken. | Motion picture producers and
  directors—United States—Biography. | Television producers and
  directors—United States—Biography. | Motion pictures—Production
  and direction—United States. | Television—Production and
  direction—United States.
Classification: LCC PN1998.3.K93 A3 2020 | DDC 791.4302/33092
  [B]—dc23
LC record available at https://lccn.loc.gov/2020021878

First Edition: 2020

10 9 8 7 6 5 4 3 2 1

for Marisa

CONTENTS

BUT WHAT I REALLY WANT TO DO IS DIRECT

>>> >>> >>> >>> >>>

INTRODUCTION

I was bitten by the filmmaking bug when I was ten years old. My parents graciously gave me a Super 8 camera, and I immediately tried to execute a tricky shot. Our house had a pool table in the basement, and I perched the camera on the cushion to shoot a stop-motion shot of pool balls moving under their own volition. I was certain no one in the history of movies had ever attempted such a bold shot, and in my zeal, I managed to elbow the camera clear off the table.

It took two weeks for our local photo store to repair the camera, during which time I combed the public library for books about how to direct. There were none. I found a couple of technical manuals, penned in turgid style, with tips about such matters as the 180-degree rule. There were a few memoirs written by directors, each a litany of triumphs by some aging (and probably unreliable) auteur, with little to no advice for an aspiring filmmaker.

Today, anyone with an iPhone could conceivably make a groundbreaking film, and with the profusion of platforms for short films online, the allure of directing has never been greater. There are plenty of popular manuals for the would-be screenwriter, but there's a marked lack of books about the everyday challenges directors face. For a novice filmmaker, it's exciting to read about directors who enjoy complete control over their work, but it's not particularly useful as you struggle to get a foothold in the entertainment business. It's exciting to read about directors with no financial constraints, but it's hardly helpful when you're fighting to complete a feature on a shoestring budget.

What I'm most often asked by young directors is something you can't find in a textbook or in a film school curriculum—namely, how do you comport yourself as a director? How do you assert authority on the set without being authoritarian? How do you navigate a path in such a turbulent business? How do you pick yourself up off the ground after a major setback? How do you deal with incredibly difficult people? How do you develop a directorial voice?

This is the territory I explore in *But What I Really Want to Do Is Direct*, and here's my game plan for how we'll proceed. The book has three thematic layers. First are autobiographical chapters recounting my experiences as a director of feature films and television. Second are chapters that concern the craft of directing, as well as the personal matters all directors confront, everything from writing a shot list to weathering a blistering review. Third are chapters focused on film images that made a big impact on me, particularly in my early moviegoing years. These layers are interwoven throughout the book, and the thread tying it all together is my desire to be personal and candid about where I've been and what I've learned.

Over the decades, one thing has never changed, and that's the utter excitement I feel making an image. When I returned to that photo store to pick up my Super 8 camera, dented but again functional, the salesman also handed me a little reel of film. It was the very first footage I'd ever shot. Fifty feet of Super 8 film. Two and a half minutes. I honestly couldn't wait to get home to view it. Sitting in the back of my father's car, I unspooled the entire reel into my lap. Like a pile of spaghetti, it was a tangled mess. As the car rolled down our tree-lined street, I held the film up to the light, squinting to see the tiny frames. I was thunderstruck, and I still am.

BEYOND SUCCESS AND FAILURE IN HOLLYWOOD

"Steven calls this the 'wall of shame,'" the production assistant quipped. It was 1986, and I'd been hired to direct an episode of Steven Spielberg's NBC anthology series *Amazing Stories.* My first morning on the job, the gung ho PA gave me a tour of the Amblin Entertainment offices, tucked into a corner of the Universal back lot. A row of one sheets hung on a stucco wall, each from a picture Spielberg either produced or directed that wasn't considered a box office success—this was the proverbial wall of shame. Examples included *1941*, directed by Spielberg, and *Used Cars,* Robert Zemeckis's second feature. "Flops," the PA added helpfully. I was thrown for a loop. These "flops" were films I greatly admired. And studied. The film *1941* is a master class in sight gag construction. And who could possibly be ashamed of the wonderfully unruly *Used Cars*?

As I said, in these pages I want to explore things that film schools won't teach you, and I'm leading off with a whopper: how to measure success on your own terms. You'll certainly get an earful about how Hollywood defines success, particularly at a school that fancies itself a microcosm of the industry. But under the guise of preparing you for a career in the business, film schools often perpetuate Hollywood's worst tendencies. I wish someone had given me tools to survive the toxic ethos of the business. To de-commodify yourself, to actually enjoy the adventure of directing, you need to devise your own measuring stick for success. You should not accept the received wisdom about achievement in Hollywood. You must create your own standard. Your own benchmarks. Doing this is no mean feat, as I can fully attest. The moment I got a toehold in this business, I observed that everything conspires to make you feel inadequate. From headlines in the trade papers to small talk over cocktails, the pervasive message is this: you're not working hard enough, your position in the pecking order is precarious, you're one flop away from needing to look for a new line of work.

The message is often delivered in benign, even encouraging form. Early in my career, I was represented by an agent who proudly decorated his office with one sheets from features directed by his clients. Not all clients were represented; indeed, only films that topped $100 million at the box office earned a place on the wall. It was an exclusive group, a testament to my agent's knack for picking winners—this was his wall of fame. I wasn't on the wall, but I was still an up-and-comer; surely, I'd have a couple of $100 million hits under my belt in no time. Right?

Then as now, social intercourse in Hollywood reinforces noxious standards of success and failure. *Did you catch so-and-so's new show? How disappointing. I'll bet he was a diversity hire. Can you believe the studio gave her an overall deal? Wow, his movie really tanked. Can they take his Oscar back? God knows why they ordered that pilot. Talk about a case of franchise fatigue. She should really stick to comedy. That series sure jumped the shark. I'll bet it drops off 80 percent in its second weekend. I'm not surprised they pulled the plug. She doesn't mean anything overseas.* A steady diet of this palaver, day after day, decade after decade, cannot help but warp your value system.

Unless you're vigilant—unless you maintain a critical distance from this matrix—you will internalize these values in short order. They'll become as natural as the physical environment around you. Not long ago, I spent an afternoon decorating my new office. The task should have been pleasurable. Instead, the question of what to put on the walls, which credits to highlight, which ones to downplay, became fraught. *If you hang that poster on the wall, you'll have to explain why nobody saw the film. Is it pathetic to display memorabilia from a show that got canceled after one season? Will a trophy from an obscure film festival remind people that your film failed to play at a more legitimate one? Why advertise your misfires? Why display defeat? Maybe I shouldn't put anything on the walls. But doesn't that send a signal, too?* As much as I struggle to remain aloof from this way of thinking, I'm not immune. But I'm trying. Here's the good news: when I catch myself buying into Hollywood's version of achievement, or falling prey to vacant flattery and snarky gossip, I step back, shudder a bit, and remember the only criterion of success that matters is the one I create.

Let's get more specific about the matrix, this corpus of shared values I urge you—even if you're still in film school—to resist. There are baseline assumptions in our business that no one refutes, truths so self-evident they seem like natural law. If a film or series makes money, it is a success. If a film or series is loved by critics, it is a success. If a film or series makes money and is loved by critics, it is an unqualified success. How could this not be true? It's as fundamental as night following day. There are corollaries to these essential tenets. If a film or series is hated by critics but makes money, it is a "popular success," a qualification often used to damn crowd-pleasing work with faint praise. If a film or series is loved by critics but no one sees it, it is a "critical success," which is more forgivable in some circles than a popular success. If a film or series is despised by critics and makes no money, it is a special kind of failure. The director of such a failure contracts the show business equivalent of leprosy and is consigned to an imaginary island. "Movie jail" is the popular parlance, though it hardly does justice to the kind of ostracism practiced in Hollywood. A leper colony seems more appropriate. I've known more than a few talented people who, while languishing in detention, simply threw in the towel. What they failed to see was that they were stuck in an exile of their own making, the result of buying into bogus beliefs.

Your goal is to be in the business but not of it. Of course, Hollywood's value system is really no different from the one that rules every American business. What distinguishes Hollywood's pursuit and veneration of success is how unapologetically over the top it is. The preposterous perks that quantify success are too numerous (and silly) to delineate here. All I'm saying is this ethos pervades all facets of American life. It's how we are raised. Teachers and parents may occasionally remind us to follow the Golden Rule, but mostly they teach us . . . to succeed. That's the headline, and the bottom line. The marquee names of American success are not celebrated for their kindness or gentility. I'll leave the last word on the matter to philosopher William James: "The moral flabbiness born of the exclusive worship of the bitch-goddess success. That—with the squalid cash interpretation put on the word 'success'—is our national disease."

In show business, you can't control how your work is received. Ticket buyers and TV viewers have minds of their own. Critics have agendas. It's hard to accept, but the fate of the product is completely out of your hands. The sooner you embrace this, the sooner you can focus on the one thing you can control—namely, the process. My private yardstick for directorial success is whether I improve the process each time I get up to bat. The more process-oriented you become, the easier it is to weather all manner of show business calamity, be it an indifferent audience or a critical shellacking. In fact, if "process" becomes your watchword, there will come a day when such indignities simply lose their power to rattle you.

Here are seven ways I keep focused on the process, all of which I'll explore in more detail down the road:

1   **Do I invest the work with my personality?** With each directorial effort, I look for new ways to personally connect with the material. Four girls who share a pair of pants.

Two oldsters walking the Appalachian Trail. Inuit people fighting to protect their whaling traditions. A real estate saleswoman who becomes a flesh-eating zombie. What do I have in common with zombies, apart from feeling like one after a fourteen-hour workday? Pardon the fleshy metaphor, but a director needs to get under the skin of each scene, even if that means putting yourself in the shoes of the undead. The show in question, *Santa Clarita Diet,* is chock-full of witty dialogue, and for a director, it's tempting to glide across its polished surface. Instead, I try to understand the story on a cellular level, and that requires bringing your own life experience to bear on a scene or character. I have never eaten another human being; however, I have been a slave to out-of-control cravings. I have never enlisted my spouse to murder another human being for food, but I have occasionally demanded that we eat Italian takeout rather than Japanese, and the ensuing argument raised a lot of dormant marital tension. There is no action so outlandish that you can't find some corollary to it in your own life.

2 **Do I create an atmosphere that encourages people to contribute their best work?** Among the many myths enshrined in film lore is that you need to be a tyrant to succeed as a director. Tales of angry eruptions on the set, working a crew to death to achieve a shot, and putting actors through on-screen torture are legion. Otto Preminger, for instance, is not remembered for buying each of his cast members a wonderful thank-you gift. But he is known for literally burning an actor at the stake to get a good performance. Many in the business truly believe that cast and crew do their best work under extreme duress. I prefer a different leadership style, and I measure the success of a particular job by how much I've improved the working vibe on the set. For example, is it really that difficult to learn the names of the people on your crew? You don't need an esoteric mnemonic device. Simply come up with a reason to address someone by name (saying a name out loud is the easiest way to commit it to memory). Start with department heads and work your way through the crew. You'll be shocked what a simple acknowledgment can do to boost team spirit. F. Scott Fitzgerald famously wrote, "The test of a first-rate intelligence is the ability to hold two opposed ideas in mind at the same time and still retain the ability to function." I feel the test of a first-rate director is the ability to hold twenty-five opposed ideas in mind at the same time, among them an appreciation for the mental health of the crew. Such a holistic approach, I promise you, is not on the syllabi at most film schools. If I can improve morale on my set by 10 percent, if only by learning the names of a few more production assistants, that qualifies as success.

3 **Did I forget to bring my passion?** Among Winston Churchill's more quotable lines is one I keep in mind on the set: "If you find a job you love, you'll never work again." After twelve hours on location in the blistering San Fernando Valley, with your dehydrated cast and crew snapping at each other, it's easy to forget that directing is your passion. Once upon a time, you would brave a blizzard to be first in line to buy a ticket for a movie you'd seen three times already. Once upon a time, you'd hang from the roof of your house with your trusty Super 8 camera in hand, risking death to get a shot. It's important to carry your original passion with you, tucked in a tiny, imaginary box. It's equally important to keep your eyes open for signs that remind you of that passion, things that transport you back to less jaded days. Not long ago, I was slogging through a scene on a soundstage at Warner Bros. I had crossed the border between exhaustion and catatonia. My lower back was threatening to mutiny. A production assistant brought me the umpteenth cup of black coffee. He excitedly asked, "Mr. Kwapis, did you know *Casablanca* was shot on this stage?" Looking around, I conjured the image of Michael Curtiz on the set of Rick's Café Américain in the summer of 1942, exhausted, his back aching, giving a line reading (in a thick Hungarian accent) to a recalcitrant Bogart, from a script that didn't have an ending yet. I realized I was breathing rarefied air and returned to the set invigorated to know I was walking in the footsteps of giants. By the way, I have no idea if Michael Curtiz suffered back pain, but it felt better to imagine he did.

 Do I hold my own when others try to assert control? This may come as a shock, but people on your team actually want you to succeed. Forget about that crotchety crew member who has nothing good to say about any-one. Most of your collaborators are rooting for a win. It's easy to forget this because many of these folks are determined to protect their respective turf. The line pro-ducer resists going into "meal penalty" to finish a deli-cate setup. The sound mixer holds up the proceedings to find the source of a barely detectable hum. The on-set wardrobe person insists on another take because a shirt was improperly buttoned. To do my job, it's important that others adapt to what's best for me. One measure of success is how well I establish boundaries on the set and, by the same token, how flexible I am with the right people at the right time. Balancing the needs of the crew with your own agenda requires a supple mind, but the bottom line is you're the only person who knows what's truly important at any given moment. Your flexibility is something the crew earns. No one is allowed to hijack the director's agenda, and I try to convey this in ways that are subtle yet resolute.

5 Do I exercise new creative muscles? As a director, you are a generalist; you need to know a little bit about every-thing. You need a passing acquaintance with each craft, but you needn't be an expert at any of them. As I embark upon a new project, I try to enlarge my skill set, to become conversant in areas where I don't feel sure-footed. For instance, I feel particularly out of my depth discussing costume design. Growing up, no ritual was more tedious than a trip to buy clothes with my parents. I just couldn't care less. My aversion to clothes shopping was part and parcel of a general suspicion of anyone who attempted to be stylish. Like Holden Caulfield, I was constantly on the lookout for "phonies." Early in my directing career, my sartorial ignorance was hard to conceal from costume designers, and occasionally I would throw up my hands and say, "Oh, you decide." Trying to rectify this gap in my knowledge is one way I measure the success of a project. Am I more conversant about costume design? Can I hold an intelligent conversation about makeup and hair? Can I not embarrass myself with the visual effects supervisor? Simply put, did I exercise creative muscles I normally don't use?

6 **Do I reframe problems as opportunities?** Throughout movie history, there are great examples of directors turning lemons into lemonade. A defective mechanical shark famously spurred Spielberg to create chilling effects through suggestion and indirection. The ability to think on one's feet is probably the most important weapon in your directorial arsenal. It's axiomatic that if something can break, it will. Halfway through a long exterior scene, it will certainly rain. After signing an ironclad contract, a cranky landlord will kick you out of a location. Complaining about what you don't have is the mark of a second-rate director. Standing in the pouring rain, don't grouse about the poor weather service. Just come up with a new plan. After the landlord gives your crew the boot, it's up to you to create some rationale for playing a private scene on a public street. There's no question that, at some point during production, you will be forced to abandon your brilliant plans and improvise, and for me, the mark of success is whipping up a backup plan that actually exceeds your original. It's pulling a rabbit from a hat.

With no rabbit. And no hat.

7 **Do I trust the process?** Geoffrey Rush, playing the Elizabethan-era impresario Philip Henslowe in *Shakespeare in Love,* has a brief but significant line, one he repeats three times. Faced with perpetual backstage calamities, the Rose Theatre Company always manages to pull it together at the last moment, and the show goes on. When asked to explain this phenomena, Henslowe shrugs and says, "I don't know. It's a mystery." As a director, there's no logical way to explain why, at the moment everything seems to be conspiring against you, all the elements suddenly come into focus and—voilà—the scene works. I once directed a scene with Jeff Goldblum that was particularly vexing. After a take in which everything that could go wrong did go wrong, Jeff joked, "You realize that if we were the Flying Wallendas, we'd all be dead now." I fancy myself rather unflappable, but in that dire moment, my thoughts ran something along these lines: *This is a disaster. I'm not cut out for this line of work. As soon as this job ends, I quit.* Of course, the scene came together, I didn't quit, and over the years I've come to learn that when everything is about to implode, just trust the process. If your scene is a shambles, don't react by tightening the reins, digging in your heels about a particular point, or locking in to an approach that's not productive. Better to loosen your grip and let the elements fall into place, and they will. If this all sounds vaguely mystical, well—as Mr. Henslowe affirms, it is. By the way, trusting the process will not eliminate anxiety, but it might allow you to think of anxiety as just another tool. Some directors welcome panic. They feel it produces wonderful ideas. They fully expect to hit a wall of massive doubt during every scene; indeed, they're disappointed if they don't. (Just to clarify, embracing inner turmoil is not the same as being a "panic merchant"—that is, someone who inflicts their anxiety on the cast and crew.) Personally, panic is not my partner. For me, trusting the process means knowing when to get out of your own way, and it's a skill I try to refine from job to job.

You cannot control the outcome, but you can control the process, and my barometer for success is how much I manage to improve the process with each new film or show. Some may reject my viewpoint as hopelessly naive. After all, there's no ambiguity about numbers. A $42 million opening is absolutely better than a $24 million opening, and 89 percent fresh is undeniably better than 68 percent fresh. I would counter that if numbers define your self-worth as a director, then you are truly no more than a commodity. If you believe that you're only as good as your market value, then—to cite the tired adage—you are only as good as your last picture. It's imperative to unshackle yourself from the way the business defines you. It takes persistence to tune out the static and internalize your own values, but once you do, you'll hear the refreshing sound of your own voice again.

CRUISING FOR EPIPHANIES

During my formative years, certain film images affected me so deeply that I'm still unpacking their power to this day. I'm not talking about shots that are technically daunting, flashy Steadicam moves beloved by film buffs ("My favorite long take is longer than your favorite long take"). Rather, the images that got under my skin are pretty basic. They don't call attention to themselves, but if you look closer, you'll discover the entire theme of the film crystallized in a moment, a glance, or a gesture. In some cases, the shot is so understated that it took years before I realized how impactful it was. Such is the case with an inconspicuous reaction shot in George Lucas's *American Graffiti,* which I saw at the Westport Twin Cinema in the St. Louis suburb of Maryland Heights during its initial run in the fall of 1973. (Movie theaters, for me, are secular houses of worship, and it's important to be specific about where I experienced cinematic revelations.) While some images opened up worlds of aesthetic possibility (I'll get to a couple of those later), I can safely say that this particular shot in *American Graffiti* opened up the world to me.

Like a guide holding a lantern in the dark, the shot seemed to declare, "This is the way."

Before getting to this quietly profound moment, I need to set the scene by introducing you to the constant companion of my adolescent years: my 1973 Ford Pinto wagon.

My first car cost my father a hefty $6,000 in the fall of '73, the same year *American Graffiti* was released. The Pinto wagon had a putrid yellow-green paint job, and if I'd had any sense of style, I would've balked at the choice, even if my father was writing the check. Style, however, took a back seat to what was in the front seat of the Pinto: a decent FM radio and a working cassette player. During the puke-green Pinto's six-year tour of duty, the cassette player developed a mind of its own and would spontaneously devour any music it deemed mediocre. It's a miracle I didn't kill myself extracting accordion-mangled tape while steering the car with my left elbow.

Speaking of getting killed, let me clarify that Pinto wagons were not the models that notoriously burst into flame upon impact, even a low-speed impact. Those were the Pinto sedans. It took nearly thirty people dying in Pinto fires and over one hundred lawsuits before Ford acknowledged the car's poorly designed fuel tank and rear end. On the rare occasion I took a girl out on a date, I hastened to assure her that my Pinto was "not the exploding kind." Usually, my date had no clue about the rash of fatal rear-end Pinto collisions, and my reassurance had the opposite effect of casting an anxious pall over the evening.

The commute from my home in Belleville, Illinois, to the Catholic high school in St. Louis I attended was approximately eighteen miles, passing through my birthplace of East St. Louis, which, in the early 1970s, was well on its way to earning top honors in the urban decay sweepstakes. The route snaked around a foul-smelling stockyard before crossing that ribbon of sludge, the Mississippi River.

Urban blight, fetid water, malodorous meatpacking. Hardly picture-postcard fare. But with the windows rolled up and prog rock piping from the Pinto's obedient speakers (will somebody please explain "Siberian Khatru" to me?), I was a happy sixteen-year-old.

The Pinto didn't simply ferry me to and from school. It accompanied me on every adventure. That poor car waited patiently outside many all-night diners while my Jesuit high school compatriots and I would wolf down cheeseburgers and rhapsodize about aesthetics and philosophy. These heady debates continued in the Pinto proper as my pals and I balanced steaming to-go cups of coffee while we thrashed out the meaning of life. By the way, there were no cup holders in the '73 Pinto. Shifting gears while cradling hot coffee (and occasionally smoking a cigarette) required the dexterity of a Vegas plate spinner. Of course, the Pinto also bore witness to occasional pot use and my blundering attempts at necking, but mainly it was a highly caffeinated think tank. Rolling through St. Louis in the wee hours on a weekend night, we weren't cruising for girls. We were cruising for epiphanies. We were reinventing the wheel. On four wheels. Indeed, so much serious-minded chatter took place in the Pinto that it does a disservice to even call it a *vehicle*. That word suggests a simple function: movement from point A to B. It implies that driving/riding formed the interstitial portion of my teenage life, the "filler" between more important events. In fact, the opposite was true; the Pinto was the main event.

I don't mean to leave *American Graffiti* hanging, but before taking our deep dive, I need to give the word *epiphany* its proper due in my development. As a Catholic boy, I knew the word from the holy day in January commemorating the visit of the three Magi to baby Jesus, but I'd never heard it used in a nonreligious context. In the fall of 1973, my English teacher, Mr. Conley (even at this late date, I don't feel comfortable referring to my teachers by their first names), put James Joyce's *Dubliners* on the syllabus and introduced the idea of "epiphany" as a literary device. In his essay "Epiphany in the Modern Novel," Morris Beja sums up Joyce's use of this tool: "The Joycean epiphany has been defined as 'a sudden spiritual manifestation, whether from some object, scene, event, or memorable phase of the mind—the manifestation being out of proportion to the significance or strictly logical relevance of whatever produces it.'" Many characters in *Dubliners* experience epiphanies prompted by mundane events, none more famously than Gabriel Conroy, the hero of "The Dead," for whom an overheard melody causes a profound reassessment of his life and place in the universe.

So, a serendipitous convergence: the word *epiphany* enters my life around the same time the puke-green Pinto makes its appearance, and shortly thereafter, I find myself driving to the Westport Twin Cinema on the outskirts of St. Louis. It was a thirty-mile drive from my house to the theater, but I had no choice; it was the only one playing *American Graffiti* (we had not quite entered the "Now Playing Everywhere" era). Inexorably pulled westward, I was on a mission to see a little movie about . . . people in cars.

Curt Henderson (Richard Dreyfuss) is about to leave for an unnamed college "back east," but at the eleventh hour, he's getting cold feet. He has a hard time explaining his reluctance to leave for school, but throughout *American Graffiti*, there are clear signs that he no longer belongs in the one-horse town of Modesto, California. For starters, he's the only major character who doesn't drive an American car. This is no small thing. In the published screenplay of *American Graffiti*, here's how screenwriters George Lucas, Gloria Katz, and Willard Huyck describe Curt's entrance: "Now a grey, insect-like Citroën deux chevaux putters into the parking lot." Granted, Terry the Toad (Charlie Martin Smith) sports a Vespa, but mainly *American Graffiti* teems with wide-ass American gas guzzlers and ear-piercing muscle cars. For example, when Bob Falfa (Harrison Ford) revs the engine of his '55 Chevy, it "sounds like a cross between a Boeing 707 and a Super Chief." Curt, however, motors around in a strange-looking French import, the car you'd expect a tweedy professor to drive. During this decisive night, Curt rarely even drives his Citroën, another fact that underscores the sense that he doesn't have a place in this town. He rides in the back seat of his sister Laurie's '58 Edsel, he reconnects with ex-girlfriend Wendy in the back of her friend Bobby Tucker's VW, and he makes the mistake of planting his butt on the hood of a local hood's De Soto, which results in an anxious joyride in the back of the gang leader's '51 Mercury. It's as if he's a tourist on the main drag of his hometown or, more to the point, an exile on Main Street. He only retrieves his

Citroën late in the story, when it's time for his appointment with destiny.

The critical encounter is spurred by a vision, one that occurs early in the evening. From the back seat of Laurie's Edsel, Curt spies an unnamed blonde (Suzanne Somers) tooling around in a white '56 Thunderbird. While the Modesto girls are a pretty homely lot, the blonde seems to have stepped from the pages of a glamour magazine. Her beauty is incandescent—it's almost surreal.

Convinced they are fated to meet, Curt fixates on the blonde all night, once or twice crossing paths with her T-Bird but never connecting. Finally, he gets behind the wheel of his insect-mobile, but instead of stalking her on the busy streets, Curt heads for the darkness at the edge of town.

His destination is a radio station, where gravel-voiced Wolfman Jack spins 45s and lays a bit of knowledge on his teenage congregation. Curt carries a handwritten dedication to the blonde that he hopes Wolfman will read over the air.

Curt doesn't know her name, let alone her phone number, but he's certain he can reach her via the airwaves. As the screenwriters describe it, Curt drives "along a lonely dirt road, winding its way through dark peach orchards and wizened grape vineyards." The finished film has neither peach trees nor grapevines, but there is a feeling that Curt has left the realm of the ordinary and is partaking in a mystical pilgrimage. As he arrives at the station, "an isolated white frame house sitting in the moonlight," the on-air music is Sonny Till and the Orioles' cover of "Crying in the Chapel." The song's final verse sets the stage for a revelation, inviting us into the sanctuary where, "Your burdens will be lighter / And you'll surely find a way." Entering the station, Curt locates the "dimly lit control booth. A figure inside is barely visible through the reflections in the double glass windows. The figure turns and walks up to the window." This is our first glimpse of Wolfman Jack, seen through two panes of glass, and it's a striking shot because we also see Curt's double reflection. Visually, it's like his sense of self is breaking apart. It's a preview of his transformative moment—the moment you realize you can't look at the world (or yourself) with the same old certitude.

Wolfman Jack fools Curt into thinking he's merely the station manager, and he certainly looks the part with his potbelly and tacky Hawaiian shirt. He invites Curt into the booth and inserts a tape into the machine; it's a bumper featuring Wolfman's patented howl. Curt is devastated: "He's on tape. The man is on tape." In the screenplay, the moment is beguiling: "The manager leans forward and picks up a spool of tape. He holds it up as a magician would for audience inspection, then puts it on a machine." Grilling Curt about his reluctance to leave Modesto, Wolfman urges him to expand his horizons, but Curt remains unconvinced, sinking deeper into his existential funk. Sensing this, Wolfman promises to "try to relay this dedication and get it on the air for you later on." Leaving, Curt retraces his steps down a dark corridor. Hearing Wolfman launch into a rowdy song intro, he turns: "Through the maze of glass, shifting like prisms, he sees the station manager sitting by the mike—howling." In the film, the shot of Wolfman at the microphone is simple; it mainly features the back of Wolfman's head. Curt's reaction, the moment he realizes this unkempt-looking schlub is the legendary Wolfman Jack—is also simple. There's no ham-fisted push-in to underline Curt's realization. A dolly move would simply reduce the moment to one of mere recognition. It's a much bigger event, a tectonic shift for this character. He may not know it, but he's not the same person he was a minute ago. As originally scripted, Curt says to himself, "Wolfman . . ." Happily, in the final film, there's no dialogue, only a soft smile on Curt's face, tucked away in the shadows. The filmmakers (Lucas and cinematographer Haskell Wexler) had the good sense to keep Curt in the dark at the very instant things truly come to light. Far from hindering our involvement, the moody lighting does the opposite. It allows us to stand in for Curt—his dimly lit face becomes the screen on which we get to write our own story. We don't know it yet (neither does Curt, I suppose), but with that subdued smile he has made the decision to leave home. He never states it, except in a wonderfully offhanded way near the climax of the film. After Wolfman makes good on his promise to get Curt's dedication on the air, the blonde calls him (Curt gave her the number of the payphone at the diner). After Curt declares that she's the most "beautiful creature" he's ever seen, she announces, "I cruise Third Street every night. Maybe I'll see you tonight." Wistfully, but with no ambivalence, he replies, "No . . . I don't think so." He doesn't really need to say it; everything in the film points to the fact that his path is heading elsewhere.

After 110 minutes of nonstop music, *American Graffiti* ends in eerie silence as we learn in a postscript the fates of the four main characters. We're informed that "Curt Henderson is a writer living in Canada." At age sixteen, I found this addendum rather cryptic, but soon I understood that Curt probably fled the country to avoid the draft. I also came to believe that Curt, now a writer, is the real author of *American Graffiti*. And like other writers who created memorable portraits of their hometowns (Dante and Florence, Joyce and Dublin), Curt could only write this story in exile.

I walked out of the Westport Twin Cinema, climbed into the Pinto, and drove home. I'm sure the radio was on, but I wasn't listening. I was trying to process what I'd seen. I was disarmed by *American Graffiti*. It wasn't weighty, but I knew there was *something* bubbling beneath its unassuming surface. I just couldn't put my finger on it. I drove back across the river, past the stockyards. Continuing east, I mulled over the film, trying to fathom its mysteries, not for a moment guessing that, like Curt Henderson, my path would soon lead elsewhere. To the west.

HOW TO TAKE A MEETING

I made my professional debut in 1983, directing an episode of the *CBS Afternoon Playhouse* entitled "Revenge of the Nerd" (no relation to *Revenge of the Nerds,* the feature 20th Century Fox released one year later). *Afternoon Playhouse* was CBS's attempt to compete with ABC's popular *Afterschool Special.* To get the job, I had to interview with the executive producer of the show, Bob Keeshan, known to millions of baby boomers as Captain Kangaroo. I spent my preschool mornings glued to *Captain Kangaroo,* a surreal grab bag of skits featuring such immortal characters as Mr. Moose, Dancing Bear, and Mr. Green Jeans. The series ran nearly three decades, from 1955 to 1984. In its waning days, Keeshan added the *Afternoon Playhouse* to his repertoire. It was odd to realize that a man I spent countless hours watching while sucking my thumb was now the gatekeeper of my burgeoning career.

I arrived early at Keeshan's Manhattan office. He wasn't there yet, and his fiftysomething assistant, a dead ringer for Thelma Ritter, had me take a seat on the sofa, where I was surrounded by Captain Kangaroo memorabilia. My nerves getting the best of me, I asked the assistant to direct me to the men's room. She insisted I use Bob Keeshan's private bathroom. This gave me pause. There was something unseemly and vaguely transgressive about using Captain Kangaroo's toilet. I'm sure a Freudian would have a field day with this. When I emerged, the Captain was waiting behind his desk, sporting his signature bowl cut but not his fire-engine red jacket with white braided trim. I was determined to make a good impression, but I quickly sensed the Captain was determined to do the same; in fact, I wasn't sure who was auditioning for whom. From his questions, it became clear the Captain didn't have a clue how to interview a director. On the *Captain Kangaroo* set, I doubt there was much debate about, say, which lens to use on Mr. Moose. After a particularly awkward lull, the Captain asked, "So, Ken, how were your grades in school?" I certainly didn't expect that question, and it stopped me in my tracks. For the record, I left graduate school before completing my MFA, not bothering to finish a handful of classes. Was this some kind of trap? What dirt did the Captain have on me? Not wanting to admit the truth, lest Keeshan conclude I lacked basic follow-through skills, I lied. "Uh, mostly As," I stammered. I couldn't believe it: I'd just lied to Captain Kangaroo.

Imprinted in the deep recesses of memory, I'm sure there's some skit in which the Captain reprimands Mr. Moose for telling a fib (it's impossible to imagine Mr. Moose guilty of anything more heinous than a fib). I was on edge, certain the moment I left the Captain's office he would ask his stony assistant to phone my school and request a transcript. Decades later, I see the meeting in a different light.

Perhaps Bob Keeshan, at age fifty-six, sensed that his time on the playing field was coming to a close. Maybe CBS was merely throwing him a bone, soft-pedaling the fact they were really putting him out to pasture. Faced with an eager twentysomething, he may have felt a pang of obsolescence—"aged out" in his midfifties. In that adrenaline-charged moment, however, I wasn't inclined to consider Captain Kangaroo's emotional subtext. I just wanted one thing. "Mostly As, huh?" Keeshan finally replied. "Good for you." And he hired me.

That was the first of countless meetings I've "taken" in my career. Before we proceed, a grammatical note. In the entertainment business, William Safire reminds us, "Nobody meets, has a meeting, or convenes a group of colleagues: the omnipresent verb is to 'take' a meeting, as if to snatch its minutes from the jaws of time or industry sharks." With rare exception, every director must occasionally march into the office of a producer and/or studio executive to sell themselves. You might be vying to direct a studio feature or a network pilot, hoping to entice a financier to back a project of your own, or trying to land a television commercial. You might be meeting a star with "director approval," or having a "general" to introduce yourself to a potential employer—or remind that same person that you're not dead.

Over the years, I've developed a few rules for surviving this often disagreeable ritual. First, I remind myself that every job interview is a two-way street. For instance, if I'm meeting with a showrunner on a television pilot, part of my job is to gauge whether I want to work with this person. The showrunner may not realize it, but he or she is auditioning for me. Second, I try to find that sweet spot between passionately wanting the job and not giving a damn whether I get it at all. I'll return to "passionately wanting" in a bit. "Not giving a damn" doesn't mean I'm aloof or playing hard to get. What it means is not letting the outcome of any meeting define me. Needless to say, wanting and not wanting at the same time calls for a Zen warrior mind-set, but in a business as capricious as this one, you could do worse than keep a little Zen in your back pocket.

Even with that coolheaded mind-set, you'll no doubt suffer more than your fair share of painful meetings. I've endured so many that I took it upon myself to break them down into categories, to create a taxonomy of bad meetings, as it were. Here are six examples guaranteed to make you squirm:

The Bloviator Meeting: In this situation, your interviewer loves the sound of his or her own voice, eating up valuable time pontificating about the business or, heaven forbid, aesthetics. I once took a meeting with a legendary TV comedy impresario, and he spent the bulk of our time conducting a tutorial about what makes something funny. Two young assistants sat beside him, nodding so continually I thought they were engaged in a prayer ritual. The impresario's thesis was simple: naturalism is the enemy of comedy. "Do you know when Groucho Marx's career started going downhill?" he asked. I shrugged. "Uh, no, I don't." "It was when Groucho stopped painting on his mustache and started growing one instead." Part of me wanted to offer other factors that may have contributed to Groucho's decline (e.g., lousy films), but I chose to keep my mouth shut.

The Pity Meeting: In such an interview, it's fairly obvious to all parties that the only reason you're even in the room is because someone owes your agent a favor. In a Pity Meeting, your interviewer will stare off into the middle distance, perhaps thinking about changing a dinner reservation or wondering how the Dodgers' doubleheader is going. The most disheartening moment in a Pity Meeting, ironically, is when your interviewer sits up and pays attention. This might mean you just pitched a decent idea, one your interviewer will quickly co-opt, representing it as his or her brainchild after not hiring you. But you soldier on, reasoning that if your ideas are good enough to steal, perhaps you'll be invited back for another demoralizing get-together down the road.

The Kamikaze Meeting: This is a rare variety of the genus I've only experienced once in my time. In a Kamikaze Meeting, about halfway through the pitch, you realize you really don't want the job. And you sabotage the interview. In the early 1990s, midway through pitching my heart out to direct a run-of-the-mill studio comedy, I was seized with dread at the prospect of actually getting the job, and I put the brakes on the meeting. "I'm sorry," I announced. "I don't feel I'm the right person to direct this film." The studio executive in charge of the project, along with his assistants, were incredulous. How could I *not* want to direct this film? I suddenly found myself in an absurd pickle. The tables had completely turned: the executive, on the defensive, began pitching the project to me. How dare I cast any doubt on the value of this lightweight comedy! I tried to ameliorate the situation by insisting it was my abilities, or lack thereof, that were the problem. The project had all the hallmarks of a hit—a classic, even—but they'd be so much happier if they just found someone else to direct it.

The Formality Meeting: Your agent tells you the job is in the bag and the meeting with the studio is a mere formality. This is the kiss of death. You walk into the room with a spring in your step, but somehow over the course of the interview you manage to convince your would-be employer not to hire you. Bottom line: If someone tells you the meeting is a formality, don't believe it for a second. We may not care to admit it, but every meeting is an audition.

The Quicksand Meeting: Ten minutes into a pitch, you suggest an idea that goes over terribly. You can see from your interviewer's frozen smile that the meeting is effectively over, and every attempt to rescue it causes you to sink deeper and deeper. Worse, you've still got another twenty minutes of material to pitch, so you swallow your pride and press on. Often, the idea that sends your meeting off the rails is actually quite brilliant, and later, over a cocktail, you can rationalize the whole debacle by repeating, "They just didn't understand the kind of film I wanted to make."

The Be-Careful-What-You-Wish-For Meeting: This is the flip side of the Kamikaze Meeting, in which you deliver a thorough, imaginative, heartfelt pitch for a project for which you have little to no enthusiasm, and your listeners love it. Instead of elation, you leave the room with a sense of foreboding: *Oh my God. Now I have to make the damn thing.*

If this litany of miserable meetings makes you want to throw in the towel, don't despair. Every feature film and television pilot I've directed required me to pitch my wares. None were offered to me sight unseen. There are ways to command the room, instill confidence, and spur your listener to imagine an amazing film or television show. Whether you're an eager newbie or a hardened veteran, what your interviewer wants to hear is that you're passionate, that you're hell-bent on winning the job. It doesn't matter if the project is an adaptation of a Nobel Prize–winning novel or a thirty-second spot for Crest White Strips. Passion wins the day every time. "The world would be a much better place if more people had whiter teeth." I know it might be tough to deliver that line and keep a straight face, but that's what you must do. Anyone can say, "I really want to direct this film." When I interviewed for *He's Just Not That into You,* I said to the producer, "I really need to direct this film." The script was an adaptation of a popular advice book about how men and women perennially misread signals from one another, and I argued that I was the perfect choice for the job because I am terrible at reading signals from people. "I need to direct this film because I know the subject from painful personal experience." I wasn't just being cheeky (well, maybe a little). I wanted to make abundantly clear that my passion for the material was not technical (i.e., I know where to put the camera), but entirely emotional (i.e., been there, done that, put foot in mouth, etc.). I'm the right person to tell this story because I've made every single mistake these characters have, and then some.

Another tactic I employ is to imagine what my perceived weakness is and address it head-on. When I met the producer of *The Sisterhood of the Traveling Pants,* I opened my pitch by announcing, "I am not a teenage girl." This story, about four sixteen-year-old girls, was aimed squarely at a demographic to which I clearly don't belong. I was certain that chief among the producer's concerns was: Why should we hire a guy in his forties to direct a film about teenage girls? The challenge: how to credibly establish my teen girl bona fides. Well, I decided not to even try. Instead, the thrust of my pitch was that I recognized the emotional content of each character's story from my own experience.

For example, in *Sisterhood,* Blake Lively's character, Bridget, has a misguided fling with her soccer coach. That's the story line, but if you scratch the surface, you find that the real subject is grief and how, if untended, grief can cause a person of any age or gender to act out irresponsibly. Giving Bridget's story a broader emotional context convinced my listeners that having "teen cred" was not as important as knowing how to put truthful human behavior on the screen.

One final thought: it can be very effective in a meeting to admit what you don't know. Far from being a weakness, revealing what you don't understand actually shows splendid self-confidence. Put another way, being honest can be quite disarming. When I interviewed with writer-producer Greg Daniels for the job to direct the pilot of NBC's *The Office*, he asked me what I thought of the original UK series. I told him I loved it, but I was confounded by one thing. A not-unimportant thing. "For the life of me," I said, "I cannot figure out the layout of the office itself. Where the characters sit in relation to each other makes no sense. It's a confusing jumble to me." This might have sealed my fate; after all, part of the reason you hire a director is for their visual sense, and here I was admitting to being spatially challenged. It turned out that being candid was the right move. "I'm confused about that, too!" Greg exclaimed. Grabbing a couple of pens and some paper, we sat on the floor like kindergarten kids and scribbled images of the paper company office, trying our best to discern its layout. We bonded over our mutual confusion, and a collaboration was born.

MEMORIES OF BIRD

The interview with Captain Kangaroo was merely a warm-up for my first meeting to direct a feature film for a major studio. While waiting for this one to begin, I was seized with a sinking feeling. With a couple of television shows for kids under my belt, wasn't it time to switch gears and make something weird, idiosyncratic, and edgy? My filmmaking heroes, after all, specialized in dark, inscrutable, provocative stories. I'd been on a steady diet of cheerless art films for years. I glanced around the posh Lennox Hill townhouse. What was I doing here? Why was I not—

An assistant popped her head through a door. "Jim will see you now," she said warmly. I gathered my notes and entered the office where, on a couch, in blue jeans, sporting his familiar bushy beard and mustache, sat Jim Henson. I was twenty-six years old, here for the job of directing *Sesame Street Presents: Follow That Bird,* the first feature film starring Cookie Monster, Grover, Bert, Ernie, Oscar the Grouch, and, of course, Big Bird.

The first thing I noticed was that Jim was quite wiry. I

would later come to learn how remarkably flexible he was, that he could turn himself into a pretzel to puppeteer from a tight space. The second thing I noticed was a clump of green felt planted on the coffee table between us. I didn't give it much thought.

After some pleasantries, I took a gamble and admitted to Jim that I'd never directed a puppet before. Would this bring the interview to a crashing halt? Or would Jim appreciate me being up front about my lack of experience? Happily, he did just that. "Just think of puppeteers as actors," Jim said. Then he picked up the clump of green felt, inserted his hand, and I was stunned to discover that the clump was none other than Kermit the Frog.

"It's good to meet you, Ken," said Kermit. In that moment, all my ambivalence about the project vanished. Gazing at Kermit in wonder, it was as if my four-year-old self were sitting in the room. My film school fantasy of becoming the next gloomy *wunderkind* suddenly seemed trivial compared with the opportunity to be part of this magic.

"You don't direct my hand," Jim said. "You direct me." Only later did I realize that Jim had just given me the job; moreover, he was entrusting me with characters he himself created. Who knew Kermit the Frog better than Jim Henson? Yet here he was turning over the reins to a novice. None of this occurred to me in the moment because I was simply too mesmerized by that frog. By the way, unlike many Muppet characters with foam-core heads (e.g., Bert and Ernie), Kermit was all about Jim's knuckles, and I was stupefied by Kermit's range of expression, not to mention the downright simplicity of it.

Now, let me back up and set the stage. The PBS series *Sesame Street* premiered in 1969. Fifteen years later, Warner Bros., in conjunction with Henson Associates and the Children's Television Workshop, decided it was time for the *Sesame Street* ensemble to make its big-screen debut.

The initial philosophy of the series was that young viewers lacked the attention span to follow a long-form story; therefore, the format was a fast-paced sketch show, with educational segments stylized as commercials ("Today's episode is brought to you by the letter A"). *Follow That Bird*, in contrast, was a full-fledged narrative; indeed, it was an odyssey, in which the main character, Big Bird, undergoes a journey of self-discovery.

Here's the story in brief. Avian social worker Miss Finch, described in Tony Geiss and Judy Freudberg's screenplay as "a six-foot bird of conservative hue, with rimless glasses, a do-gooder's hat and an iron will," has decided that Big Bird would be happier living with their own kind. She tracks down BB on Sesame Street, and the following exchange occurs:

                    MISS FINCH
        You know, Big, you shouldn't live
        here all alone.

                     BIG BIRD
        I'm not alone. There's Gordon and
        Susan and Sally—

                    MISS FINCH
        But they're not birds like we are.

Swayed by Miss Finch, Big Bird agrees to leave Sesame Street and move in with a foster family of dodo birds in Ocean View, Illinois. Quickly discovering that the dodos are insufferably stupid, Bird sneaks away, embarking on an epic trek back to Sesame Street.

Big Bird must leave home to find home and in the process discovers there's strength in diversity, a theme that could not be more relevant in our era, when leaders actively encourage distrust of outsiders. Would small children grasp any of this? Could the preliterate set even follow the contours of a feature-length story?

There were a lot of cooks in this kitchen, and landing the job required five separate interviews. First, I met producer Tony Garnett and his associate Amy Pascal. With their approval, I met with Lucy Fisher, the vice president of production at Warner Bros. After that, I flew to New York to meet Joan Ganz Cooney, the head of the Children's Television Workshop and cocreator of the PBS series. With her nod of assent, I met Jim Henson. There remained one final hoop to jump through, which I'll get to momentarily, but let's return to my interview with Jim and Kermit.

Jim made only one request of me, and he was quite firm about it. He asked that, on the first day of principal photography, I gather the entire crew and instruct everybody to raise one hand in the air and hold it there for a solid minute. He was insistent that everyone understand how taxing it is for a puppeteer to hold up his or her puppet while crew members make umpteen lighting and camera adjustments. I assured Jim I would carry out his demand, and with that, he welcomed me aboard.

By 1984, Jim's range of creative endeavors was quite immense. With Frank Oz, he directed *The Dark Crystal* (1982) and was in early preproduction for the fantasy film *Labyrinth*. Frank himself had just directed *The Muppets Take Manhattan* (1984). Clearly, *Follow That Bird* was not a burning priority for either man, but both agreed to perform their signature characters in the film, and both were incredibly gracious toward the youngest member of the crew, yours truly.

Frank played Cookie Monster, Grover, and Bert. Jim performed Ernie and, of course, Kermit.

The puppet cast included every creature in the Sesame Street stable, including such stalwarts as the Count (his formal name: Count von Count) and Snuffleupagus. Not having grown up on the series, many characters were new to me: Gladys the Theatrical Cow, Telly Monster, Buster the Horse, Prairie Dawn, Grundgetta, Forgetful Jones, Barkley, Herry Monster, Captain Vegetable, Sully, Dr. Nobel Price, Biff the Hard Hat, Two-Headed Monster, Mumford the Magician, and various Honkers. Created for the film was Big Bird's foster family: Daddy Dodo, Mommy Dodo, and Donny and Marie Dodo.

The fifth and most critical audition was with Caroll Spinney, known to most of the planet's population for his eight-foot, two-inch avian alter ego, Big Bird. When we met in the spring of 1984, Caroll was fifty-one years old, but he seemed as spry as a twentysomething Olympian. He was also the gentlest soul I'd ever met. With three decades of hindsight, having endured more than a few appalling and pompous stars, I realize how spoiled I was to have such a kindhearted collaborator on my maiden voyage as a feature director.

As Muppet aficionados know, Caroll's other iconic character is Oscar the Grouch, who lives in a trash can near Big Bird's nest. At our meeting, Caroll warned me that if he spends too much time in the bird suit without a break, Big Bird will start sounding a lot like Oscar the Grouch. Before *Follow That Bird*, I never made much distinction between the words *trash* and *garbage*. I was quickly schooled about the difference by Caroll himself. Oscar loves trash (e.g., a broken toaster) but hates garbage (e.g., a rotten banana peel). Plus, Oscar truly dislikes kindly people, and I was struck by the irony that the most famously misanthropic character since Ebenezer Scrooge was created by such a genial man. I also learned that, in addition to describing Oscar's temperament, "grouch" is a species designation.

Caroll then gave me a basic tutorial about Big Bird. Species: canary. Gender: indeterminate. Age: No older than six. Inside the bird suit, Caroll wears a tiny video monitor strapped to his chest. It shows Caroll what the camera sees, effectively giving Big Bird "eyes." Among many challenges, Caroll had to perform a "mirror image" of his every action.

Big Bird has a gawky walk, but Caroll was as graceful and athletic as Gene Kelly. In the film, Big Bird is introduced roller-skating down Sesame Street. I can barely walk three steps with my eyes closed, and here was a man in an eight-foot bird suit, one hand extended in the air (to operate the beak), his eyes glued to a miniature monitor, nimbly gliding across the set, spinning and slaloming through various obstacles. I'm still mystified.

Throughout production, I was dumbfounded by the puppeteers' ability to perform in the most constricted spaces.

Here are a few memorable examples. When news reaches Sesame Street that Big Bird is on the run, all the residents depart en masse to take up the search. Bert and Ernie scour the countryside in a biplane, and production designer Carol Spier built one scaled down to puppet size. Frank Oz and Jim Henson crawled into the fuselage of that pint-sized plane, but not before much deliberation about how to best tuck their limbs inside, while still allowing each man enough elbow room to operate his puppet. In another scene, Frank had the daunting task of performing Cookie Monster from the back seat floorboards of a Volkswagen Beetle, which required what I can only describe as an extremely advanced yoga pose. At least Cookie wasn't at the wheel. Count von Count, on the other hand, drives a vintage purple roadster named—what else?—the Countmobile (New York license plate 12345678910). The built-to-scale automobile had room for one puppeteer, lying on his back, performing the Count while free-driving with the aid of a video monitor. The coordination involved was mind-boggling. Crowd scenes featuring dozens of Muppets demanded the puppeteers be crammed together like sardines. Actually, it more resembled a New York subway at the peak of rush hour, with each rider holding a puppet instead of the grab rail. Snuffleupagus, descended from the nineteenth-century pantomime horse, required two performers. Marty Robinson played the front half (Marty was renowned for his performance of the people-eating plant in *The Little Shop of Horrors*). Puppeteer Bryant Young played what I'll affectionately call the "ass end" of Snuffy, and he was usually ensconced in the suit by the time I arrived on the set. In fact, I don't believe I met Bryant face-to-face for weeks; instead,

I spoke to him through a little patch in Snuffy's posterior. I certainly didn't have any "notes" for Snuffy's rear end. Mostly, I'd ask, "How are you holding up in there?"

We shot for forty-four days in Toronto, where Henson had groomed a fleet of young puppeteers for his HBO series *Fraggle Rock*. Given that *Follow That Bird* was a coproduction of Warners, Henson Associates, and the Children's Television Workshop, you might guess there was a pileup of producers on the set. In fact, the opposite was true. I had a free hand to try whatever cockamamie idea came into my head. There's a scene in which Bert and Ernie, piloting their biplane, spot Big Bird in a cornfield. I thought, *Cornfield? Biplane? Of course, let's re-create the crop duster scene from* North by Northwest. And we did. Shot for shot. No one questioned the logic of including a Hitchcock homage in a *Sesame Street* film, one that would go completely over the heads of the target audience, not to mention many of their parents.

For this neophyte, there were some notable revelations along the way. I was surprised, for example, by how much I learned about character development from the Muppets. In the intervening decades, I've directed a fair share of stories (comedies in particular) with unfocused characters. A string of one-liners, no matter how clever, is no substitute for a character driven by a clearly defined need. A strong comic character not only has a point of view but is fanatically committed to that point of view, often to the exclusion of good sense or sanity.

Cookie Monster does not want to eat a cheeseburger. He does not want caviar. You can argue that Cookie Monster has no emotional range, that he simply represents the impulsive eater in all of us or that he's an emblem of our desire for instant gratification. I would counter that Cookie is simply a character with a clear motivation, and I only wish more of the human characters I read were as sharply drawn. Consider Telly Monster, who is ambivalent about everything. Telly is fully committed to doubt and uncertainty; as a result, he's a nervous wreck. You might say Telly's point of view is that he's incapable of having a point of view. In his constant vacillation, though, he's every bit as single-minded as Cookie Monster, or the Count with his fixation on figures.

The biggest surprise for me was the emotional depth of the story. I certainly knew the script from top to bottom, but as both a rookie director and—I'll admit it—an emotionally unevolved young man, my initial approach to the story was superficial. I imagined scoring points with cineastes by quoting from other films.

In fact, I fancied myself elevating *Follow That Bird* into an existential road movie à la Wim Wenders's *Paris, Texas*. Instead of Harry Dean Stanton wandering across the panhandle, my existential hero, Big Bird, was hoofing it across the heartland. I recall lining up a shot of Big Bird trudging down an endless country road and found myself musing, *How would Wenders shoot this?* I was enamored by the trappings of favorite art films and wholly unprepared for the discovery of just how painfully human this tale was. Big Bird's loneliness, sense of dislocation, and desire to find the right tribe—I didn't grasp the gravity of this journey until I was well on the road with Bird. Once I recognized the heart of the matter, the film really came to life. To do this, I had to put myself in Bird's proverbial shoes. I had to contemplate my own search for identity, my own yearning to find my people. There was no grand epiphany. No eureka moment. But at a certain point during production, I stopped thinking of Big Bird as an object and started thinking of BB as a subject. Instead of attacking each scene with formal strategies, I began to work from the inside out. The irony, of course, is that it took an eight-foot bird for me to learn that my job—as a director and a storyteller—was to become a student of human nature.

As my connection to Bird deepened, my work with Caroll grew less technical and more emotional. The low point of BB's adventure, without a doubt, is the scene in which our desolate hero performs the ballad "I'm So Blue." It's perhaps the saddest scene I've ever directed. Here's the setup: Big Bird, en route to Sesame Street, is abducted by the Sleaze Brothers (Dave Thomas, Joe Flaherty). Sensing a cash cow in this bird, they transform BB into a carnival attraction. Dyed blue and billed as the "Bluebird of Happiness," Big Bird sings a sorrowful lament, which ends with a blue teardrop sliding down Bird's cheek. Did it ever occur to the powers that be that dyeing Big Bird blue might be construed as child abuse? I've met more than a few people who claim this scene traumatized them as toddlers.

Needless to say, Bird manages to escape the Sleaze Brothers and return home. Upon arrival, he's miraculously yellow again. Don't ask me why or how. Every Sesame Street resident is on hand to greet the prodigal bird. When the misguided Miss Finch appears and promises to place Bird with a more suitable foster bird family, Maria (Sonia Manzano) steps forward to deliver the film's climactic speech: "We're very happy on Sesame Street. And we've got every kind . . .

people . . . monsters . . . birds . . . honkers . . . cows . . .
horses . . . grouches . . ." This declaration, pretty much the
mission statement of the series, deserved special cinematic
treatment, so I staged the first and only 360-degree pan in
my career, featuring every single human and puppet character in the show's vast ensemble. This shot was singled out by
the *Cahiers du Cinéma* as "*une matrice symbolique oú toutes
les races et toutes les especés vivent ensemble dans la paix et le
contentment*" (a symbolic matrix where all races and all species live together in peace and contentment). By the way, deep
in the background of this shot, there's a small, furry red creature poking its head through a window. Near the bottom of
the puppet cast list, that creature is identified as Elmo Monster. Like Ruby Keeler plucked from the chorus in *42nd Street,*
Elmo Monster would shortly become a top-billed Muppet.

During postproduction, Warner Bros. and the Children's
Television Workshop left me alone. In fact, we never had a single research screening for the film. Nobody at the studio felt it
was worth the trouble. Compared with WB's tentpole pictures,
Follow That Bird was not a high priority for the company. I
asked a Warners executive, "Don't you think we should show
the film to some children?" The executive shrugged. "Sure, if
you want. Just don't expect the studio to pay for it."

On that encouraging note, we invited one hundred children to watch *Follow That Bird* at a plush screening room.
On the day, I entered the screening room from the back and
was shocked to find it empty. Turning in panic to the projectionist, I asked, "Where are the kids?" He replied, "Are you
kidding? The place is packed." I walked down the aisle and,
sure enough, each seat was occupied by a very small person.

The high chair backs completely hid them from view. Unfortunately, those high chair backs also prevented the children from seeing the screen. To my mind, there was only one remedy. I instructed the children to stand up on their rather bouncy seats. They were delighted to comply, and the screening room quickly turned into a trampoline park. As the lights dimmed, it seemed clear this audience was mainly interested in bouncing. A few children actually fell off their seats but quickly clambered back to continue springing up and down. Over a sea of bobbing heads, my feature debut unfurled.

For the life of me, I couldn't tell if the children were enjoying the film or not. Many turned away from the screen, preferring to gaze at the children bouncing behind them. In the midst of this hurly-burly, I suddenly recalled my very first meeting with the head of physical production at Warner Bros. The purpose of our meeting was to finalize *Follow That Bird's* budget, and I argued that it was woefully inadequate in certain areas. In a brazen moment, I insisted on a crane for a picturesque establishing shot. The executive just laughed in my face, saying, "Ken, don't you realize we could shoot a ninety-minute shot of Big Bird going around and around on a Ferris wheel, and the audience for this film wouldn't care less?" I was nonplussed. Were Hollywood people really this sour? (Little did I know . . .)

To the executive's credit, he gave me the crane, and I used it for a couple of eye-catching shots, but standing in the back of that screening room, watching my big preview devolve into a school recess period, his words came back to taunt me. Clearly, no one in this group appreciated my crane shot.

When the film reached its heartfelt conclusion, the children rushed out of the screening room like a pack of wild puppies. Obviously, they had better places to be. The projectionist even stopped the film before the end credits finished. As I sat alone, sinking into despair, the projectionist emerged from the booth, lugging film cans. "Well, what did you think?" I asked with forced perkiness.

Tongue firmly in cheek, he replied, "It's *Citizen Kane* for the preverbal crowd."

"Ha ha," I mumbled and quickly repaired to a nearby watering hole. Maybe the Children's Television Workshop was right, I mused while nursing a cocktail. Maybe that sourpuss at Warner Bros. was right. This audience can't follow a story. Were they even watching? Were they paying attention at all?

Lest you think I'm going to end this chapter in a puddle of self-pity, I'm happy to report that *Follow That Bird,* the runt of the litter among the studio's releases, a film that barely made a dent at the box office—indeed, less than a nick—went on to enjoy a long and happy afterlife. As a wise songwriter once wrote, "Children will listen." And I guess they did. Quite a few did, it turns out. One of those children, Odie Henderson, penned this online appreciation thirty years after the film's release: "Director Ken Kwapis shoots his avian star as if he were human, never once fearing any cracks in our suspension of disbelief. He bestows upon Big Bird the kinds of close-ups invented for Lillian Gish, and one swears that there really is something going on behind those fake Muppet eyes, something alive and relatable."

A few years ago, I met with an up-and-coming director at my Studio City office. It was a hellish morning—projects running aground, calls unreturned. I had agreed, as a courtesy, to meet a newcomer with but one music video to his credit. The budding filmmaker took a seat on my couch. After the usual pleasantries, I asked, "What kind of films do you want to make?"

The twentysomething shifted in his seat, weighing his reply. "I'd like to make a movie like that one," he answered, pointing to the *Follow That Bird* poster on the wall behind me.

Suddenly the frustrations of the morning melted away, and I was back in Jim's office, meeting Kermit for the first time. "That film was a big deal for me," the young director said.

I nodded. "It was for me, too," I replied.

BREAKING IT DOWN: A DIRECTOR'S CHECKLIST

Over the years, I've devised my own personal way of breaking down a scene—analyzing its emotional content, pre-visualizing the action. Before sharing my to-do list, let me state categorically that there is no right way to prepare a scene.

Awesome work has been done by directors who carefully consider each detail. Equally great work has been achieved by directors who refuse to plan anything. Indeed, there are more than a few impressive films by directors who were completely stoned on the job. Personally, my psychoactive drug of choice is caffeine, and I tend to skew toward the more meticulous end of the prep scale—all right, I can be downright anal-retentive at times.

I'm also a compulsive list-maker. I often make lists of lists. Of course, I don't always accomplish everything, but the lists sure look great. The following checklist is one I'm continually refining: ten aspects of the directing craft that I keep in mind when prepping a scene. Some are quite fundamental, while others are too often overlooked.

1 **The Emotional Road Map:** As a director, you need a clear understanding of every character's journey, and it's your job to remind an actor where his or her character is on that journey. Most narratives, whether long-form or episodic, are usually shot out of order. To ensure there's emotional continuity, I create a road map for the character. Some people prefer the term *through line,* but I like the topographical image. Before digging into a specific scene, I step back to survey the map: Does the character have an overarching goal? What circumstances shaped this character? What do I know about this character's life prior to the story? A good script will offer plenty of clues to answer these questions. And if a clue doesn't lead to a clear-cut answer, it will certainly inspire you to invent circumstances that will enrich your storytelling and fire up your actor's imagination.

After reviewing the map in general, I zero in on the particular scene. Does the character have a specific goal in the scene, and is it related to his or her overarching goal in the story? What tactics does the character employ to accomplish that goal? Does the character succeed or suffer a reversal, a setback along the way? What circumstances directly precede the scene? What baggage does the character bring to the scene? What roadblocks are waiting for him or her? Not to overdo the cartographical metaphor, but does the path get treacherous? For your character, is this scene a straight stretch of smooth road or a switchback trail down a steep mountain? Is the obstacle external (e.g., another character), cultural (e.g., societal expectations), or internal (e.g., fear)? If you can't pinpoint the obstacle, there's probably not much at stake for your character, and the odds are this scene could end up on the cutting room floor.

2 **Playable Notes:** In my prep process, I not only rehearse the scene in my head, I rehearse the rehearsal. I act out the parts (thankfully, in private) and jot down notes designed to help actors discover something essential about their characters. My goal is to deliver notes an actor can actually play. When in doubt, many directors simply say, "Try something different." This may not be the worst thing to tell an actor, especially if their approach feels set in stone, but it's hardly the most creative note to offer. Basically, you're saying, "Limber up." Certain writer-directors get quite persnickety about their words. And punctuation. "I put that comma in the line for a reason. Try it again, and observe the pause." Well, unless you can explain why you put in that comma, it's not a playable note. Certain old-school comedy directors believe the success of a joke depends on putting emphasis on the right word. "Try it again, but this time really land on the word *spaghetti*." Sure, it's a playable note, but it's pretty mechanical, as if your actor is a dialogue-spewing robot. Other directors offer an intellectual analysis of the action. It may be scintillating, but it's usually not something an actor can translate into behavior. "The Industrial Revolution created a population increasingly alienated from nature itself—that's what this scene is about." I don't envy the flummoxed thespian asked to "play" that note.

Good notes are contextual. Remind your players where

they are on their arc. Be specific about the stakes; stress how critical it is for the character to accomplish a goal. Turn negatives into positives. If a character is described as *miserly*, it doesn't help to lean into words like *greedy* or *selfish*. Tell your actor the character is the only one smart enough to sock away cash for an emergency. Use evocative imagery to stoke your actor's imagination. When the "mean girl" enters the high school cafeteria, tell her to walk in like an empress arriving at court. *Imperious* is stronger than *mean*—it's a word an actor can hang her hat on. With a comic character, avoid giving notes that are outcome-oriented (e.g., "This bit will be funnier if you do . . ."). Better to arrive at that outcome (laughter) with a character-specific note. Emphasize how committed your character is to a particular point of view. Above all, notes should open up possibilities rather than aim for a predetermined result.

Ideally, the actor will use your note as a springboard to do something you didn't anticipate. I'd rather see an actor take a crazy risk than make the expected adjustment. Like a crafty poker player, a good actor will see your note and raise you. Even if you penned the script and put every comma in its proper place, you want the actor to shine a light on aspects of the character you didn't imagine. Much more about playable notes in a later chapter.

3 **Tell the Story with Pictures:** As an exercise, imagine your scene with no dialogue, and try to communicate every story point visually. Can you express character dynamics (e.g., who has the high status in the scene) with imagery? Can you reinforce point of view (e.g., whose story we are following) with pictures? If I'm stuck on a long flight, I often watch films and television episodes with the sound turned off to see how much information about plot and character is conveyed solely through images. When pre-visualizing a scene, I prefer to use the word *image* rather than *shot*. The latter is simply the means to convey the former. For now, forget focal length, image size, or whether the camera is moving or static. Concentrate on the image—the picture—that tells your story. If your hero is a lonely man, walking to his dreary job in the city, what image establishes his loneliness? If your heroine is a lawyer, entering the courtroom and eager to win her case, what image establishes her confidence? To nurture your picture-storytelling skills, I urge you to get acquainted with the great accomplishments of the silent era. As Charlie Chaplin succinctly put it, "Just when we got it right, it ended." Before his death in 1947, Ernst Lubitsch said, "We have become so engrossed in dialogue that we have neglected to take full advantage of the expressive power of the silent approach. In my next picture . . . I will take full advantage of dialogue and speech, but I also would like to leave room enough for the valuable things we learned and have partly forgotten from the silent days." I encourage you to take up Lubitsch's challenge: when prepping your scene, strip out the dialogue and let pictures do the talking.

 Body Language: Use physicality to tell your story. The way a character opens a door, turns her head, or handles a prop could be more telling than a line of dialogue. For instance, I am a big proponent of "back acting." Seeing a character tense his or her back can be more impactful that a facial reaction. When you invite the audience to imagine a character's facial expression, the viewer participates in the storytelling—the audience fills in the gap with their own imagination.

Here are a few of my favorite examples of body language in action. In Steven Spielberg's *Saving Private Ryan,* an army chaplain arrives at the Ryan home with the heartbreaking news that another of the Ryan boys has been killed in action.

As Mrs. Ryan (Amanda Boxer) opens the front door, the mere sight of the chaplain causes her to slump to the floorboards. Spielberg keeps the camera behind Mrs. Ryan, and her ungainly collapse conveys the tragedy more eloquently than any close-up of her face could.

In the final scene of Lewis Milestone's *All Quiet on the Western Front,* German soldier Paul Bäumer (Lew Ayres) spies a butterfly just outside the trench he's guarding. Reaching for it, he inadvertently gives away his position and is shot by a sniper. In staging the death, Milestone focuses entirely on Paul's hand. The hand inches toward the butterfly, then recoils from the gunshot, finally drooping to the mud. Body language tells the whole story.

I can't resist one example from the Lubitsch canon. In *The Shop Around the Corner,* two quarrelsome employees at a Budapest tchotchke shop are, unbeknownst to each other, romantic pen pals.

When Alfred (James Stewart) discovers that the object of his affection is actually his adversary, he cuts off the correspondence. When Klara (Margaret Sullavan) checks her post office box, she finds it empty. Lubitsch films the moment with a close-up of Klara's hand vainly searching for the letter from her beloved. Klara's sense of anticipation, and her deep disappointment, are conveyed entirely through Margaret Sullavan's hand.

There are rare films in which body language is a major building block of the story; chief among them is Jane Campion's extraordinary third feature, *The Piano*. The director's expressive use of hands and fingers pervades every scene. The mute Ada (Holly Hunter) and her daughter, Flora (Anna Paquin), communicate with sign language. To lull her daughter to sleep, Ada recounts meeting Flora's father, and her hand gestures are silken and rapturous. Ada's beloved piano keys are like extensions of her fingers. Even when not playing, we see her lovingly stroke the piano frame. When Baines (Harvey Keitel) caresses Ada's shoulder while she plays, Ada responds by fiercely pounding a Chopin prelude on the keyboard. An oddly intimate encounter between Baines and Ada occurs when he spots a hole in her stocking and places one finger on her bare thigh. Their growing intimacy is an impossible situation, and Ada vents her frustration by wildly slapping Baines in the face. When her jealous husband, Alisdair (Sam

Neill), spies his wife and Baines making love, a dog approaches and licks Alisdair's hand—it's like a perverse stand-in for what he's witnessing. Not surprisingly, hands play a critical role at the story's climax: Alisdair commits an insane act of vengeance, chopping off Ada's index finger with an axe. Without the benefit of a single line of dialogue, you can discern the shifting dynamic between the three main characters by simply watching their hands. Part of your job as a storyteller is to involve all five senses, and it's hard to imagine a more tactile film than *The Piano*.

5 **Shot Selection:** Now let's break down the scene into grammatical units: shots. We'll devote an entire chapter to the process of writing a shot list. In the meantime, here are a few things to consider: Does your story have an overall visual concept? Are you deliberately using the same visual strategy in scene after scene? There's nothing wrong with that, by the way. Perhaps your story calls for a feeling of repetition. The conceit of Harold Ramis's *Groundhog Day* is well served by repeated shots. The stifling monotony of basic training in Stanley Kubrick's *Full Metal Jacket* is reinforced by a lack of visual variety. On the other hand, perhaps you want to create energy by employing an array of visual styles. A scene staged as a fluid master, for instance, might be followed by one with a fast-paced cutting pattern. A scene dominated by close-ups might be followed by one favoring wider shots. How do you decide to stage a scene as a fluid master?

What about the content of the scene demands that it be staged in this way? Does every scene need close-ups? Can you explain why a certain shot choice (e.g., moving the camera) supports the scene? Why move the camera at all? When is an over-the-shoulder shot preferable to a single? When is a profile better than a frontal view of a character? Is there a key moment to highlight a particular point of view? Should the camera be shaky? For my money, if you need erratic camerawork to add energy to your scene, it's possible you don't trust the material, and you're applying an effect to compensate for something that's not on the page (or something you've yet to discover on the page). All these questions really boil down to one: How will your shot selection strengthen a character's emotional arc?

 Color and Light: There are many stylish-looking films in which a controlled color palette and carefully sculpted lighting are merely decorative, with no meaningful connection to the emotional content. Can you start to think of color and light as storytelling tools? Can you design ways for color and light to not only create mood but reveal character, bolster the subtext, or even illuminate a thematic idea? In Bernardo Bertolucci's *The Conformist*, Marcello (Jean-Louis Trintignant) and new bride, Giulia (Stefania Sandrelli), are in Paris for their honeymoon. In their hotel room, Giulia wears a black-and-white-striped dress and is framed against a wall shadowed by the slats of a venetian blind. It's not a big stretch to suggest that the riot of crisscrossing lines graphically defines Giulia as a prisoner—specifically, a prisoner of bourgeois conformity.

Even color temperature can help tell your story. In her adaptation of Louisa May Alcott's *Little Women,* writer-director Greta Gerwig uses a flashback structure to tell what originally was a chronological story. Viewers unfamiliar with the adventures of the March sisters might initially be thrown by the leaps back and forth in time, but Gerwig uses color temperature to cue us. Scenes from the past are bathed in a warm glow, as befits the girls' idyllic adolescence. The present-day scenes, featuring Jo March struggling to launch her career as a writer in New York, and culminating with the death of Beth from scarlet fever, are imbued with cool tones, appropriate for the challenges the four sisters face as adults. Even if we're not cognizant of it, the color scheme—the contrasting color temperature—keeps us perfectly oriented. We're never unsure of our place in Gerwig's story.

Warm tones often evoke a nostalgic view of the past, but they can also be employed to a decidedly darker effect. In the historical drama *Selma,* director Ava DuVernay stages the horrific bombing of Birmingham's 16th Street Baptist Church in 1963, in which four young girls were killed while donning their choir robes in the church basement. In a series of shots, we watch as six children, dressed in their Sunday finery, descend the stairs of the church. The girls chat amiably, and DuVernay bathes the scene in a warm, welcoming glow. It almost feels like a flashback, but anyone familiar with history quickly realizes how grimly ironic the color scheme is. And, for any viewer who doesn't know about the tragic event depicted, DuVernay's use of color temperature, with its suggestion of a sweet and innocent time, is a masterful example of deliberate misdirection.

7 **The Objective Correlative:** Can a prop have its own through line? Can a piece of wardrobe suggest the theme of a picture? Yes, and yes. A good picture-storyteller knows that an object (a hat, for instance) or an ordinary space (a doorway) can reinforce the subtext of the story. I'm going to hit the Pause button on the subject for now; consider this a teaser trailer for an upcoming chapter devoted entirely to the concept of the "objective correlative."

8 **Off-Screen Space:** In addition to arranging what's in front of the lens, a visually adept director knows how to manipulate what's outside the frame. Often, what we don't see is more compelling (or funnier) than what we do. In *The Graduate,* Benjamin Braddock (Dustin Hoffman) lies in bed after another assignation with Mrs. Robinson (Anne Bancroft). He stares blankly at the TV while Mrs. Robinson dresses. Director Mike Nichols (at the suggestion of master storyboard artist Harold Michelson) plants the camera, aimed at the indolent-looking Benjamin. Mrs. Robinson crosses in and out of frame, and with each reappearance she's a little further dressed. In less imaginative hands, there might have been a routine establishing shot of the hotel room. Nichols, however, uses off-screen space to create a ballet; Mrs. Robinson's continual movement in and out of view, juxtaposed with Benjamin's inertness, captures their soulless tryst before a line of dialogue is spoken.

Sam Mendes's *1917* is justly celebrated for creating the illusion that we are witnessing an unending shot (two shots, to be precise). Equally notable, for me, is the fact that the turning point of the story takes place off-screen. Two English soldiers, Blake (Dean-Charles Chapman) and Schofield (George MacKay) are commanded to deliver a message by hand to Colonel Mackenzie (Benedict Cumberbatch), ordering the colonel to call off an attack that will undoubtedly prove catastrophic. En route, Blake and Schofield witness an aerial dogfight, and a German plane crash-lands at their feet, bursting into flames. After dragging the burned pilot from the plane, Schofield goes to retrieve water from a nearby well, and the camera follows him. Hearing a scream, Schofield turns, horrified to discover that the German pilot has knifed his compatriot. It's shocking in no small part because the camera, which has dutifully tracked Blake and Schofield's every move, seems to be in the "wrong" place for the most critical moment of the story thus far. The choice to stage Blake's stabbing off-camera reinforces the sense that in this war, particularly on the chaotic and punishing Western Front, nothing is predictable.

In *Raiders of the Lost Ark,* Steven Spielberg creates an ingenious bit of physical comedy that depends entirely on what's outside the frame. Indiana Jones

(Harrison Ford) has infiltrated a Nazi submarine dock. He's accosted by a uniformed guard. Spielberg frames the confrontation as a close-up of Indy, over the guard's shoulder. Indy kicks the Nazi in the groin. The Nazi doubles over, dropping out of frame. Indy then knees the off-camera Nazi in the face, causing the guard's hat to fly into frame, which Indy casually grabs. Lewis Milestone, in *All Quiet on the Western Front,* creates a similar shot with a decidedly different effect. A German soldier waits for the signal to go "over the top," to clamber out of his trench and join the battle. Milestone shows us only the soldier's boots (the quest to find a decent pair of boots is a small but important story point). At the signal, the soldier climbs out of shot, and Milestone holds on the empty frame as we hear off-camera gunfire. A moment later, the just-killed soldier plunges back through frame; now, all we see are his upside-down boots jutting into shot.

9   **Rhythm and Tempo:** Here's another exercise—I know it may strike some of you as rather abstract. Try to imagine your scene as if it were a piece of music. I'm not saying imagine the musical underscore that may eventually accompany the scene; rather, think of your scene as having a musical quality. Does it have a pulse? Does that pulse change over the course of the scene? Does the action start legato and grow agitato? Does it have a cacophonous texture? Or is there a simple melody line? Can you imagine conducting the scene instead of directing it? There are many great examples of scenes with no music that nevertheless have a musical character. The climactic scene of Alfonso Cuarón's *Roma,* in which the housekeeper Cleo (Yalitza Aparicio) wades into the treacherous surf to rescue two children, has an intrinsic musicality without the benefit of one note of music. The waves breaking on the shore give the scene its pulse, but they provide a truly glacial tempo. As the emotional intensity builds, the waves grow louder, but never change speed. There's a dissonance between the human activity and the natural world; indeed, it's as if the sea is indifferent to the human drama. The scene behaves like a passacaglia, the musical form in which an unchanging bass line repeats as other musical lines develop over it.

10 **Transitions:** Most transitions, I'm sorry to say, are unplanned and haphazard, creating a sense that the directing is flabby and unfocused. A well-designed transition, on the other hand, sends a clear signal to the viewer that someone—you, the director—is in control. In *2001: A Space Odyssey,* when the prehistoric hominid Moon-Watcher tosses a bone into the air, and Stanley Kubrick match-cuts to a spaceship circling the globe, there is absolutely no question who is in charge of the storytelling. Early on in David Lean's *Lawrence of Arabia,* T. E. Lawrence (Peter O'Toole), an archeologist stationed in Cairo, receives orders to proceed to the Arabian desert on a reconnaissance mission. He holds up a lit match—Lean frames Lawrence in a tight close-up, and the moment he blows it out, Lean cuts to an extremely wide shot of the Arabian desert at dawn. It's the quintessential shock cut. By the way, I borrowed this transition for *The Sisterhood of the Traveling Pants*. On the verge of going their separate ways for the summer, the four main characters inaugurate their "sisterhood" with a candlelit ceremony. They blow out their candles in unison, and I cut to the bright morning sky over the island of Santorini, where Lena (Alexis Bledel) begins her adventure. There are plenty of memorable transitions designed for comic effect, among them the climax of Alfred Hitchcock's *North by Northwest*. Eva Marie Saint dangles precariously from the edge of Mount Rushmore. As Cary Grant pulls her to safety, Hitchcock match-cuts to Cary Grant pulling Eva Marie Saint into the berth of their private train car, where an intimate interlude will no doubt follow.

Not every transition needs to be a pair of linked shots. One of my favorite images in Steven Spielberg's *Jaws* is a wide shot of the fishing boat *Orca*, heading off to sea in search of the monster shark. Spielberg frames the boat's departure through a set of shark's teeth hanging in the window of shark hunter Sam Quint's dockside office. It's a witty visual that also creates a perfect sense of foreboding.

BREAKING IT DOWN: *THE SISTERHOOD OF THE TRAVELING PANTS*

Needless to say, not every scene I direct boasts a clever transition or an expressive use of body language, but I do consult these pointers when prepping. Here's how I put the aforementioned list to work in a scene from *The Sisterhood of the Traveling Pants*, one featuring a very emotional exchange between Carmen (America Ferrera) and her father, Al (Bradley Whitford). Here's the setup: sixteen-year-old Carmen lives with her mother in Maryland but eagerly looks forward to spending the summer with her divorced father, Al, in North Carolina. Upon arriving at Al's new home, she is stunned to discover that he's living with a new fiancée and her three children. Needless to say, it's quite a gut punch.

Instead of giving Carmen a proper heads-up, he allows her to be blindsided by the news. Unfortunately, it's a typical move from this emotionally clueless father. Carmen valiantly tries to fit in with her soon-to-be stepmother and stepsiblings, but her efforts backfire, and she hightails it back home. At the urging of her best friend, Tibby (Amber Tamblyn), Carmen finally summons the courage to confront her father—on the telephone.

I'm choosing this scene because, on the surface, it's very simple. There's nothing visually dynamic about people talking on the phone. It's exactly the kind of quotidian activity directors often cover in ho-hum fashion. Getting a truthful performance from the actors was my top priority, of course, but I also wanted to shore up the emotional content with expressive imagery. Not cinematic panache for its own sake but something to make the scene more impactful.

Initially, I worried that Carmen unloading her feelings via telephone would never be as compelling as a face-to-face confrontation. But after putting myself in her shoes, I decided that the phone actually gave her the courage to stand up for herself. Speaking as a conflict-averse person myself, who wouldn't prefer the buffer of a telephone for a difficult conversation?

Screenwriters Delia Ephron and Elizabeth Chandler set the scene:

```
Tibby and Carmen sit silently at the
kitchen table, where a phone rests between
them. Tibby pushes it toward Carmen, who
stares at it, then looks up at Tibby. Tibby
gives her a nod of encouragement. Finally
Carmen lifts the receiver, dials. After a
few RINGS O.S., Al answers.

                    AL (O.S.)
            Hello?


                    CARMEN
            (hesitating)
            Dad? . . .

There's silence on the other end.
```

In the original script, Al remains off-camera throughout the conversation. This might seem apropos for a parent who's emotionally "off-screen" in his daughter's life, but I decided we should stage his end of the conversation in the kitchen of the suburban home he shares with his fiancée, Lydia (Nancy Travis).

Color and Light: I told production designer Gae Buckley to create as much contrast between the two kitchens as possible. Carmen's has orange walls—almost tangerine, and there are splashes of color everywhere. It has a vibrancy that reflects her spontaneity and emotional immediacy. She is someone who leads with her feelings; her father, on the other hand, actively shies away from confrontation. Emotions are messy, and Al prefers to keep them at arm's length. Appropriately, his kitchen is white, modern, and spotless. It doesn't look like human beings actually live there.

Cinematographer John Bailey and I decided that the image of Al on the phone should be *completely white*. Apart from Bradley's skin tone and wardrobe, every inch of the frame would be white. Just before shooting, I checked the shot.

Through the lens, I was surprised to discover, sitting on the table in an otherwise perfectly white room, a bowl of lemons. Clearly, someone made a mistake. I pulled John aside and asked why there was a bowl of lemons in the shot. "Everything's supposed to be white," I reminded him. John replied that the burst of yellow in the middle of the frame is the very thing that enables the eye to perceive the room as white; the lemons are, effectively, the exception that proves the rule.

Body Language: Al starts the scene on his feet—we find him conferring with Lydia and a wedding planner. Carmen starts the scene seated at the table. When Al answers the phone to find his runaway daughter on the line, he assumes she's calling to apologize for her unceremonious departure.

                    CARMEN
          I . . . I wanted to . . .

                    AL
          It's all right. You don't have to
          apologize, sweetheart. You were
          upset, I know.

He's oblivious to the pain he's caused her, and she can no longer hold back her anger.

                    CARMEN
          No, you don't know, Dad. That's
          just it—you've never known.
          Because I could never tell you.

At this point, Carmen stands, and Al sits. It's a simple switch—nothing earth-shattering, but it neatly suggests a change in the power dynamic between them. The daughter is about to school the father; moreover, she's about to throw a grenade into his complacency:

                    CARMEN
          You should have warned me, but it's
          more than that. It's . . . It's the
          fact that you found yourself this

```
new family, and I feel like some
outsider who doesn't even belong to
you anymore. It's like you traded
me and Mom in for something you
thought was better, and I want to
know why. Is it because you're
ashamed of me? Or embarrassed? Just
tell me—what did I do wrong? Why
wasn't I good enough? Why did you
move away and promise me we'd be
closer when it wasn't true?
```

As Carmen takes him to task, Al sits still, framed in profile. He doesn't try to defend himself, and I wanted to physicalize his sense of shame. I told Bradley Whitford to place one hand against his cheek, covering his face, preventing us from seeing it at all. My thought was that Al, in some ineffable way, is hiding from the audience. I chose not to shoot any frontal shot of Al, nothing that would give us a traditional facial reaction. I wanted Al's hand, tensely draped against his cheek, to convey his guilt and self-disgust at having treated his daughter so thoughtlessly.

Shot Selection: In contrast to Al, his face hidden from view, Carmen is framed in close-up, an uncomfortably tight close-up. I wanted the viewer to feel cornered by Carmen, forced to deal with her outpouring of emotion. In my original notes for the scene, I planned a shot of Tibby leaving the room to give Carmen some privacy, but on the shooting day, it seemed more compelling for Tibby to remain deep in the background, like a sentry protecting Carmen's space. Amber Tamblyn has no dialogue in the scene, but her presence is critical. She sits motionless, like the kuroko of Kabuki theater—stagehands dressed in black, onstage but invisible.

Emotional Road Map: America and I discussed Carmen's overall journey at length. Her super-objective: get her father back in her life. The news that he's creating a new family arrives like a bombshell, and, adding insult to injury, it feels like he's trading his Latinx family for a white-bread one. Carmen tries to negotiate this daunting obstacle, but the pain of his original abandonment is never far from the surface. That wound never healed. She struggles to squash her anger at this new betrayal, but compartmentalizing is not Carmen's strong suit. Finally, refusing to play a bit part in Al's story, she throws caution to the winds and tells him exactly how she feels. Carmen's goal in the scene is crystal clear: demand to be acknowledged.

Playable Notes: What tactics should Carmen use to get her father to understand her pain? Should she reason with him? Cajole him? Should she remain levelheaded or try to destroy him? What obstacles are in her path? I suggested that each time Al pauses—each time he fails to step up and tell her he loves her—is a replay of the night he abandoned Carmen and her mother, leaving without a goodbye. I repeated my mantra that there was no definitive way to play the scene, that each take would tell its own story. I encouraged her to try a different approach each time. "Your goal is to remain composed, and you succeed." Or "You steel yourself, but the moment you hear his voice, you want to hang up." Or "Your own anger surprises you, and you're afraid it will drive him away." Or "You rehearsed everything you want to say, but when he says hello, all the words go out the window and you're flying blind."

America had a limitless supply of honest emotion and an intrepid sense of adventure about the scene. We shot fifteen takes, each with its own shape, all of them crushingly real. At one point, my producer pulled me aside, concerned that America's intensity was "over the top." There's an old adage that if the character holds back tears, the audience will supply them. What did my producer fear?

Namely, that Carmen sobbing would make the audience cringe or, worse, laugh uncomfortably. With that seed of doubt firmly planted, I resumed shooting. In the next take, America was just as effusive and unconstrained, and I simply couldn't bring myself to ask her to tamp it down. I couldn't justify it to myself; it struck me as a spineless move to cover one's backside. The whole point of the scene was to witness a catharsis, a dam breaking. After all, shouldn't we occasionally strive to make the audience uncomfortable?

Months later, I got my answer when we screened the film for a test audience in Phoenix. The packed house was dead silent as Carmen began to reprove her father. As her feelings rose, spilling over in waves of anger and hurt, two teenage girls in the audience did start laughing. Instantly, I recalled my producer's warning. It was a white-knuckle moment as I waited for the laughter to spread.

Instead, from the opposite side of the theater, two other teenage girls yelled, "Shut up!" To my amazement, the sniggering

stopped on a dime, and the audience resumed its rapt engagement with the scene. The moral of this story isn't that "more
is more"; rather, if an honest emotion unsettles the audience,
you're probably doing something right.

America does the heavy lifting in the scene, but I don't
want to neglect Bradley's work. Part of my job was to resist
the urge to think of Al as a villain. Every villain, of course, is
the hero of their own version of the story. I subscribe to Jean
Renoir's oft-quoted line from *Rules of the Game*: "The awful
thing about life is this: everybody has their reasons." Why
didn't Al inform his daughter he was getting remarried and
starting a new family? Was he afraid the conversation would
circle back to the failure of his marriage to Carmen's mother?
Again, as someone who's a bit conflict-averse, it wasn't hard
to put myself in Al's shoes. Rehearsing the scene with Bradley,
I shared moments from my own life when, given the chance
to confront a situation head-on, knowing it would entail a
difficult conversation, I opted for a diversion—I did an end
run around the situation. Shining a light on my own foibles
was strategic; I wanted to signal that I was in Al's corner, that
I was here to understand him, not judge him. Bradley and I
also spoke about that inevitable moment when a child discovers that her parents are neither monsters nor gods, just
flawed people. And what is Al's biggest flaw? Perhaps it's a
life spent choosing the path of least resistance. With these
ideas, Bradley brought dignity, humanity, even vulnerability
to a character that could easily have been played as a one-
dimensional heel.

I'm sure I'll revamp the checklist as I face new directorial challenges, but the goal will never change—namely, to

make sure I don't arrive on the set armed with a bunch of routine choices, ones that simply "fell off the truck." I want a visual approach that's truly connected to the inner journey of the characters, not style for style's sake. If you work from the inside out, I'm confident you'll also come up with ways to reinforce the emotional architecture of the scene, choices that will make your audience relax in the knowledge that someone's at the wheel.

HAL'S READY FOR HIS CLOSE-UP

Dr. David Bowman (Keir Dullea) and Dr. Frank Poole (Gary Lockwood), hurtling across the solar system on a mission to Jupiter, have a problem. Their ship's computer, known as HAL, has misdiagnosed a minor malfunction in the ship's engine, which is unnerving because HAL is, for all intents and purposes, incapable of making an error. Actually, Bowman and Poole have another problem. There is no place on the massive spaceship for them to discuss problem number one without being overheard by HAL. With monitors strategically placed throughout the ship, HAL "sees" and "hears" everything. So, on the pretext of discussing some routine maintenance, Bowman and Poole clamber into a small space pod, whereupon they shut the door and disconnect the pod's communication system. They can see HAL through the pod's glass portal, and feeling assured they can speak privately, the men candidly discuss the grave implications of a central computer error, even a minor one. In short order, Bowman and Poole conclude there's really only one course of action . . .

Outside the pod, HAL cannot hear a word of their scheme,

but he doesn't have to; he can read their lips. The insert of HAL's "eye," a dot of red light housed in a lens, lasts about three seconds, but it's one of the most haunting images in the film. Wait a minute. According to traditional film parlance, an *insert* refers to a close view of an object. A *close-up* refers to a close view of a character. Does HAL qualify as a character or an object? It's more than a semantic issue. How you answer might reveal your bias regarding artificial intelligence or raise bigger questions about the nature of consciousness itself. For instance, no sane person assumes that a virtual assistant like Siri has a consciousness. But is it conceivable that one day Siri might spontaneously express her feelings without any request on your part?

What makes this shot breathtaking is that we are by now so invested in the human drama between these three—HAL, Poole, and Bowman—that an insert of what's essentially a flashlight with a red bulb feels like a close-up of a character in the throes of a crisis—namely, he realizes his crewmates are about to betray him. I am awed by anyone who can craft a film that elicits such a complex response to an inanimate object. Oh, by the way, the film is *2001: A Space Odyssey*.

Many films that captivated me as a youngster have completely lost their luster. Radical experiments so relevant in the moment now seem like quaint relics, while their unassuming peers carry the day, slow and steady. As with all relationships, there are films I count as reliable pals, dependable in a pinch. Others are fickle friends I can't rely on for cinematic consolation. In a few cases, my emotional attachment to a film has gone full circle, from head-over-heels infatuation to outright rejection, only to return with a more seasoned appreciation.

And then there's *2001: A Space Odyssey*. There's no film with which I've had a rockier relationship than Stanley Kubrick's eighth feature.

I was ten years old when the film opened in April of 1968. It took several months for *2001* to wend its way to my hometown, where it played at the Lincoln Theater, a former vaudeville house that once played host to the Marx Brothers when they were billed as the Three Nightingales. (An irresistible side note: it was during the Three Nightingales' stint at the Lincoln that Harpo introduced a bulb horn into the act.) On a Saturday night in late '68, my father and I sat among a sold-out crowd of local hippies, all of them primed with recreational narcotics for what MGM would thereafter bill as "the ultimate trip." One-hundred and forty-two minutes later, when the lights came up, I was truly gobsmacked. I was baffled and thrilled. My dad, on the other hand, was furious. He wanted his money back—all $1.50. He'd been game for a good yarn about space exploration, and he took the film's head-scratching finale as a personal affront. Needless to say, as we left the Lincoln, I secretly planned to see the film again as soon as humanly possible. Which I did. The next day.

During its initial run, I saw the film over and over and over again. I committed large stretches of it to memory, and HAL's dialogue in particular was eminently quotable. At the dinner table, for no particular reason, I would announce, "This conversation can serve no purpose anymore," and leave the room. I drove everyone batty blasting *Also Spach Zarathustra* from the Magnavox record player in our living room. I meticulously assembled a plastic model of the Moon Bus, courtesy of Moebius Models kits. I reveled in the fact that people my father's age found *2001* incomprehensible. The film's obtuse ending was a convenient cudgel I used against my parents. "Of course you don't understand the film. You're old!" Never mind the fact that the director himself was pretty much the same age as my parents. And never mind that if you put a gun to my head, I couldn't explain *2001* to save my life. But it was 1968. Things didn't need to make sense for me to love them. I mean, *now they know how many holes it takes to fill the Albert Hall,* right?

Once in college, I switched cinematic gears, and, enchanted by the controlled chaos of directors like Robert Altman and the uncontrolled chaos of filmmakers like John Cassavetes, I began to turn on *2001*. Kubrick's anal-retentive attention to detail, the cold formality, his mania for one-point perspective composition, the stultifying pace, the too-cool-for-school Nietzscheanisms—the whole spectacle now struck me as bloated and self-important. It had been the perfect film for a pretentious teenager like me, enamored with sleek symmetries and cosmic bombast. But now its high-flown themes and obsessively manicured surface seemed like the work of, well, an arrested adolescent.

I broke up with *2001,* but the film wouldn't go away. It just lurked in the background, standing quietly, neither challenging nor welcoming me. Just standing. Like a sentinel—okay, you win, like a monolith. Time passed. In the post–*Star Wars* era, movies got faster while attention spans grew shorter. As a hired gun in Hollywood, at the helm of studio fare, I learned firsthand how impatient viewers had become and how utterly fixated the powers that be were on pumping up the volume and tightening the pace of every story. To even suggest that a scene needed to "breathe" was to risk being pegged as difficult. Moments that lagged could always be propped up by a pop song. Coherence took a back seat to energy. A random barrage of shots became the norm for action scenes, so much so that a pithy pundit christened a new genre: "chaos cinema."

By the year 2001 itself, I was a successful worker bee in the dream factory, fully conditioned to believe that Hollywood films should all play at an amphetaminic pace. When I heard that *2001* was screening at a local revival house, my initial reaction was, *How quaint*. With perhaps a tinge of guilt (it was I, after all, who jilted *2001*), I decided to catch the show. As the lights went down, I was all but certain the film would feel doubly lugubrious given the current state of the art.

Instead, 142 minutes later, I was gobsmacked all over again. Richard Strauss's grandiloquent fanfare aside, I was struck by the film's radical *quiet*. Critical scenes have no music and barely any sound effects.

Silence as a storytelling tool is almost unthinkable in modern cinema. Today's films are crammed with layer upon layer of sound effects; it's the aural equivalent of baroque architecture, with a cornucopia of details, one sculpted curlicue atop another. By contrast, the sound design of *2001* is stripped down, minimalist even.

I was also struck by the film's radical *stasis*. One decade after the original release of *2001*, with the birth of the Steadicam, elaborate moving shots became de rigueur. Armed with this new toy, directors seemed hell-bent on outdoing one another with byzantine camera moves. In the 1980s, after suffering through the umpteenth music video featuring an out-of-control Steadicam shot, I worried that camera movement itself might lose all currency. Reconnecting with *2001* reminded me that a truly great director knows when *not* to move the camera.

Another thing I found arresting was the film's radical *pace.* Its stubborn refusal to quicken the pulse was like a refreshing slap in the face to purveyors of movie sugar rush. It was a pleasure to luxuriate in images that simply lingered on the screen, hushed and immobile.

Seeing the film again was like reconciling with a spurned lover. How could I ever have doubted you, *2001*? Will you forgive me for straying?

Let me set aside *2001*'s formal qualities—pace, sound design, camera movement (or lack thereof)—for a moment. What really affected me anew was the film's emotional content. It's commonplace to label Kubrick a cold-blooded ironist, but I found the story of *2001*, specifically HAL's moral dilemma and his ultimate "termination," to be surprisingly moving. Of course, I was watching the film with forty additional years of life experience under my belt, and I was definitely viewing it through a sadder-but-wiser lens. There are more than a few people in my life suffering cognitive decline, some more precipitously than others. When Bowman dismantles HAL's brain, one memory module at a time, HAL beseeches him to stop, and the spectacle of HAL's memories disappearing actually brought me to tears. This is not how you're supposed to respond to Stanley Kubrick—the analytical, methodical, calculated Kubrick. You're supposed to be wowed by his technique or cackle at the dark comedy, not get emotional over a computer being "put down." Yet, with each of HAL's pathetic pleas ("I'm afraid. I'm afraid, Dave. Dave, my mind is going. I can feel it.") I became more and more choked up. I thought of loved ones losing their sense of self, their consciousness slipping away like sand through a sieve. It was painfully relatable, and I was heartbroken . . . for a machine.

All of which brings us back to HAL's big close-up. There are plenty of spectacular images in *2001*. The sudden, surreal appearance of the monolith in the ape-men's den and Dr. Poole jogging in the zero-gravity centrifuge are two of many that come to mind. The close-up of HAL as he reads Bowman's and Poole's lips, by contrast, is an ordinary shot. But it delivers a dramatic punch in inverse proportion to its plainness. On the soundtrack, there's no dialogue or music, just the white noise of the pod bay itself. And yet, the entire plot turns on this simple, unadorned image. We don't know HAL's thoughts or, I daresay, feelings at this moment, but no doubt he's experiencing the sting of betrayal.

Have you ever inadvertently overheard someone speak ill of you? I still wince at a decades-old incident: Someone I was on the phone with assumed the call was over when, in fact, the line was still connected. I listened while that person made a cutting comment about me, one I was not supposed to hear. I could easily put myself in HAL's place the moment he realizes his team has turned against him.

A rationalist (like my father) would argue that HAL is only capable of whatever feelings were programmed into him at the computer plant in Urbana, Illinois, where HAL "became operational." Yet, as Bowman disconnects the computer's brain, HAL repeats, "I'm afraid." Why program a computer to experience such existential dread, to fear for its life?

I would argue that HAL experiences a range of feelings,

among them guilt. He's the only member of the team who fully knows the nature of the mission. One can only imagine what a burden it was for HAL to possess such privileged information. By way of analogy, it would be as if I were hired to direct a television series that I knew was already canceled, and it was my job to keep the cast and crew in the dark. By withholding critical information from Bowman and Poole, HAL is effectively living a lie. At one point, HAL coyly muses about the mission to Bowman, speculating about things he actually knows good and well. Did they program HAL to be disingenuous? Also, did they program him to feel doubt?

Clearly, HAL suffers anxiety about the mission itself. He ultimately concludes that the humans on board are incapable of carrying it to fruition, prompting HAL to make a choice that's irrational and immoral—namely, to murder the crew. But perhaps eliminating the crew is not so immoral. After all, wouldn't you do anything to protect yourself from annihilation? And even for a computer, is self-defense an emotional reaction or a logical choice?

For me, this intricate web of emotions is fully contained in a three-second shot of a light bulb. It's not the first image of HAL in the film, but it's the closest view we've seen to this point. The conventional wisdom about close-ups is that you keep them in reserve until it's time to highlight a moment of intensity. That a shot of something as banal as a light bulb could convey such intensity is, for me, a bit of a miracle. No pyrotechnics. No flamboyant movement. But with the right shot at the right moment, you're suddenly 365 million miles from Earth, where a computer floats in space, worried.

HE DIRECTED, SHE DIRECTED

"How did you two meet?" our dinner companion asked. It's a simple enough question, right? We'd only been dating for two years. The event was no doubt fresh in our minds. Yet as Marisa Silver and I answered the question, our stories diverged, the details clashing to a noteworthy degree. There was no dispute about where we met. It was at the birthday party of a friend. How hard could it be to recall who said what to whom? Clearly, one of us misremembered the occasion. Or did we both?

It was 1989, and we were seated in a small booth at Musso & Frank Grill, the venerable Hollywood establishment that first opened its doors in 1919. If the walls at Musso & Frank could talk, the stories they'd tell would be juicy. On this night, however, the walls were witness to a young couple, both film directors, arguing the fine points of their first meeting. Most couples embellish their origin stories with colorful details or enshrine the moment in myth ("We were fated to meet"). The event becomes family lore passed down to one's progeny ("Your father had to borrow his brother's suit for our date, and it was three sizes too big!"). As for our foundational story, there was a marked lack of consensus. At issue, among many things, was the question of whether my fitful attempts at small talk were intended as flirtation. I won't rehash the debate, but we were rescued by the arrival of our entrées. By the way, I recall with absolute certainty that I ordered liver and onions, a fact with which Marisa would have no quibble.

Later, I proposed we make a film based on our conflicting accounts of that decisive day. Marisa took the baton and ran with it. "We'll call it *He Said, She Said*," she announced. Now, let's cut to the chase. I want to go on record and credit Marisa for coining this phrase, though there have been variants in the past. In 1966, John Lennon penned the song "She Said She Said," about a woman trapped in a stifling relationship. A decade later, sociolinguists Nancy Henley and Barrie Thorne wrote a scholarly analysis of communication between the sexes entitled "She Said-He Said." In 1948, big-band singer Marion Hutton recorded the Roy Jordan ditty, "He Sez, She Sez." But that evening in the late 1980s, Marisa offhandedly came up with the epigram that would become ubiquitous in characterizing conflicting stories between men and women.

William Safire explored the etymology of the phrase in his On Language column in *The New York Times,* noting how its original application had changed:

> The idea was that when a woman says, "I have a problem at work," she means "Listen to my problem"; a man takes that same phrase to mean "Tell me how to solve the problem." That theme was picked up in the 1991 movie *He Said, She Said,* written by Brian Hohlfeld and

given its title by co-director Marisa Silver. "The phrase gained popularity during the Anita Hill–Clarence Thomas hearings," Hohlfeld recalls. "Our film was about gender differences, but now the phrase seems to be more about who is telling the truth and who isn't." He's right. The latest meaning has nothing to do with dialogue (he said and then she said) and no longer refers to missed communication. Now the phrase most often means "testimony in direct conflict," with an implication that truth is therefore undiscoverable.

But I'm getting ahead of myself. Continuing to brainstorm, we quickly decided to codirect the film. *He Said, She Said* would be as much about directorial point of view as it would be about the opposing points of view between two characters—"he" and "she."

Our goal was to make a romantic-themed film that was partly autobiographical, explore gender difference without slipping into stereotypes, create a script with a bifurcated structure ("he said" followed by "she said"), employ a circular storytelling strategy (each half begins in the present, unfolds in flashback, then loops back to the present), use a variety of means to express point of view (e.g., imagery, shot selection, performance, music), and showcase two distinct directorial styles. Needless to say, it was a tall order. The first question: Who would possibly fund such a crazy project?

Marisa's second feature film, *Permanent Record*, was a drama focused on a teenager's suicide. It's noteworthy for many reasons, among them a compelling, nuanced performance by twenty-four-year-old Keanu Reeves and a scrappy musical score by post-Clash Joe Strummer. *Permanent Record* was produced by Frank Mancuso Jr., who oversaw the successful *Friday the 13th* franchise. Frank was drawn to dark material, whether a science fiction–horror tale like *Species* or an intense *policier* like *Internal Affairs,* and I was initially skeptical that he had the temperament to guide a project about falling in love. Our first meeting, however, dispelled any concern on my part. The three of us had an animated and often irreverent debate about the differences between men and women, and I was heartened by Frank's desire to tell the story in a nontraditional way. Under Frank's wing, we pitched the project to the powers that be at Paramount Pictures. I girded myself for a cool reception and was surprised when the executives in attendance launched into a litany of their own "he said, she said" moments. As we discovered, the mere mention of the film's concept was an open invitation for people to bring their own stories to the table. Everyone, it seemed, had something to say about "cross-gender discourse," to use Deborah Tannen's phrase from her popular 1990 book on language and gender, *You Just Don't Understand.*

To provide cohesion for a film with two potentially incongruent directorial styles, we opted for a single voice in the screenwriting department. We enlisted Brian Hohlfeld to pen the script and mediate between our different points of view. For me, it was an easy choice. Brian and I had been friends since 1971, when we met in St. Louis as high school freshmen. We survived four years of Jesuit indoctrination, we were preoccupied with the same girls, made the same romantic missteps, and most important, we became devoted cinephiles. In an earlier chapter, I reminisced about my puke-green Pinto station wagon; Brian often rode shotgun as we prowled the streets of St. Louis, arguing the merits of various girls and films. Among many shared cinematic epiphanies was one key moment in *Day for Night*, François Truffaut's 1973 valentine to the filmmaking process. In the film, the hopelessly infantile actor Alphonse (Jean-Pierre Léaud) poses a question to the director of the film within the film, Ferrand (François Truffaut): "Are women magical?" To our feverish teenage minds, it was not a hyperbolic question, and the answer was unequivocal. Yes, women are magical. They actually cast spells. Needless to say, Brian had the perfect sensibility for the project, but would his knowledge of my checkered romantic history bias his telling of the story? I didn't give it a second thought. Indeed, given our mutual blunders as would-be Lotharios, it was likely Brian would give more credence to the woman's side of the story.

And it's a simple story: two writers for a Baltimore newspaper, conservative-minded Dan Hanson (Kevin Bacon) and left-leaning Lorie Bryer (Elizabeth Perkins), compete for a chance to have their own opinion column. The editors instead publish their op-ed pieces side by side, and readers are charmed by the pair. As their public persona as a battling duo grows (they eventually graduate from newsprint to television), the two fall in love, but Dan's inability to commit to the relationship (okay, I promised there was an autobiographical element) precipitates a crisis, one that forms the inciting incident of the film. During a live taping, Lorie hurls a coffee cup at Dan, beaning him in the forehead.

As Dan recovers from the shock of being targeted with a flying mug, the film moves backward in time to recount Dan and Lorie's courtship from his point of view, leading up to the moment when, just before that fateful broadcast, Dan breaks up with Lorie. Having come full circle, the inciting incident is replayed from Lorie's point of view. We are no longer shocked by her intemperate act; if anything, given our feelings about Dan's obstinance, we await it eagerly. After banging him on the noggin (it seems to hurt worse the second time), Lorie beats a hasty retreat from the studio, and the film flashes back to tell the couple's story from her point of view. The final portion of the film is told from an "objective" perspective, leading to a traditional denouement: Dan realizes he's happier with Lorie than he could ever be alone, or—depending on your point of view—Lorie wears down Dan's resistance and he capitulates.

Marisa and I came up with ground rules for how to work as a codirecting unit. Most important, except for the "we said" section of the story, we directed separately. I told the story from Dan's point of view, and Marisa told the story from Lorie's. There are many paired scenes in the script, one from each character's perspective. A few are repeated word for word, while others are deliberately inconsistent, some wildly so. In preproduction, we planned our separate approaches in detail. With cinematographer Stephen H. Burum, we pre-visualized each version to create as much contrast between Lorie's and Dan's personalities as possible. For example, I often show Dan's *literal* point of view of Lorie, while Marisa uses camera movement and choreography to underscore how Lorie feels about herself (i.e., insecure). With identical scenes, we decided that I would direct the "he said" version first. The chief reason is that it occurs first in the story, but it also gave Marisa a chance to monitor what I was doing and fine-tune her approach to the corresponding scene, enabling her to create a more striking variation. Neither version represents the "truth," though one could argue that the last witness in a courtroom often has the most influence on the jury.

Let's examine the inciting incident, from each directorial point of view. In my version, on the heels of delivering Lorie his heartbreaking decision, Dan takes to the stage, clueless about how devastated she is. He basks in the glare of the television lights. He carries himself like a a star.

Visually, there's nothing to suggest anything amiss between the couple because, on a subtextual level, Dan is brilliant at compartmentalizing his feelings. I chose to minimize shots of Lorie during the scene, the better to heighten the shock of her walloping him with the ceramic mug. (By the way, we built a lightweight mug, but Elizabeth has an excellent pitching arm, and during a few takes Kevin definitely felt her fury.) Conversely, Marisa's version of the scene concentrates on Lorie's inner turmoil. Marisa designed a labyrinthine path for Lorie's dramatic exit. The camera tracks her as she zigzags through the studio, underscoring how completely unmoored she now feels. Marisa turned the television studio into an obstacle course, a great example of how production design itself can be a tool for illuminating point of view.

Another key ground rule was that we only talked to the actors during our respective scenes. When I directed a scene between Kevin and Elizabeth, Marisa sat at a distance from the camera. She no doubt had thoughts about what the actors were up to but would not offer suggestions. Likewise, when Marisa stepped in to direct her version of events, I kept my distance, ensuring that Marisa had a direct, unmuddied line of communication with the cast.

Each of us had different strategies for eliciting performance. My notes to Elizabeth Perkins, for instance, were quite different from Marisa's. I wanted Elizabeth to play an *objectified* version of Lorie. I wasn't particularly interested in Lorie's inner life, because I didn't feel Dan had the emotional maturity to understand her. He didn't so much *listen* to her as *look* at her. For Dan, she is a glorious, beguiling, confounding, alluring, and—yes—magical object. During rehearsal, I often took Elizabeth aside and said, "In this scene, you are beautiful." Or "In this scene, your hair looks great." Or "In this scene, you have an amazing smile." The fact that Lorie's smile masks a bedrock insecurity does not help me tell the story from Dan's perspective. I would argue that adding that level of nuance weakens Dan's story.

I'm sure I gave an active note now and then, but mostly I directed Elizabeth to play Lorie as the object of Dan's desire. To her credit, Elizabeth was game to embrace notes that, in a different circumstance, would be appalling. Marisa, on the other hand, turned the spotlight on Lorie as she sees herself, emotionally attuned if sometimes painfully vulnerable. She reminded Elizabeth that all the obstacles in Lorie's path were ones she placed there herself. A different actress might have suffered whiplash trying to navigate such wildly different approaches to one role, but Elizabeth tuned in to both ends of the spectrum, creating wonderfully subtle differences between Lorie the object and Lorie the subject.

While prepping any feature, I design a curriculum related to the story I'm telling, my own private survey course of films that cover similar territory. For the rescue adventure *Big Miracle*, I watched everything I could get my hands on set in the Arctic, from Robert Flaherty's *Nanook of the North* to Nicholas Ray's *Savage Innocents*, featuring Anthony Quinn as the hunter Inuk ("Mighty Quinn the Eskimo," as celebrated in the Bob Dylan ditty). For *He Said, She Said*, Marisa and I wanted to soak up the many ways other directors manipulate point of view. We watched films with different accounts of the same event (e.g., Akira Kurosawa's *Rashomon*, Stanley Kubrick's *The Killing*), along with stories featuring multiple narrators (e.g., Orson Welles's *Citizen Kane*).

Our arsenal of storytelling tools included shifting perspective between foreground and background. A minor character in one version of the story becomes a major character in another. The effect is ironic, forcing us to recognize there is no definitive version of any story, as Tom Stoppard demonstrated by elevating two bit players from *Hamlet* into the leads of *Rosencrantz and Guildenstern Are Dead*. My favorite comic example of shifting between foreground and background is a bit from *Monty Python's Life of Brian*, directed by Terry Jones. The Sermon on the Mount, the story from the Gospel of Matthew in which Jesus delivers the Beatitudes to a crowd ("Blessed are the peacemakers, for they will be called children of God"), is told entirely from the point of view of the attendees at the farthest edge of that crowd. Unable to hear Jesus clearly, they continually misunderstand his proverbs:

                    Man #1
I think he said, "Blessed are the
cheesemakers."

                  Mrs. Gregory
Ahh, what's so special about
cheesemakers?

                    Gregory
Well, obviously, this is not meant
to be taken literally. It refers to
any manufacturer of dairy products.

In the "he said" section, Anthony LaPaglia plays Mark, a production assistant at the television station where Dan and Lorie tape their weekly "point/counterpoint" program. His role is minor; indeed, Dan barely knows he exists. As "she said" unfolds, we quickly realize that Mark is completely smitten with Lorie. He couldn't be happier that she clobbered Dan with the mug and secretly hopes she'll wake up to the fact that there's a better prospect waiting in the wings—namely, himself.

At many points during the story, Dan and Lorie are unreliable narrators. Either they can't remember the facts of a given event, or they've deliberately altered the facts to suit their interpretation of that event. Likewise, Marisa and I have either misremembered our first meeting or fabricated the details. (There is, of course, the remote possibility that Marisa recalled everything perfectly while I embroidered the truth, but I doubt it.) In Dan's version, his first dinner with Lorie is interrupted when sometime girlfriend Susan (Ashley Gardner) approaches their table. After a bit of small talk, Susan makes her exit, but not before asking Dan to give her a call. In Lorie's version of that dinner, Susan saunters over, and while shamelessly flirting with Dan, her breast unaccountably pops out of her low-cut dress. Is this really what happened? Or is Lorie's imagination working overtime, framing any female friend of Dan's as a floozy? Or is Dan conveniently forgetting the moment an old girlfriend had an embarrassing wardrobe malfunction? More likely is that both accounts are unreliable, and, as William Safire wrote, "truth is therefore undiscoverable."

One device Marisa and I avoided was outright fantasy, which we decided was the least compelling way to illustrate point of view. It felt like a cheat, a way to cut corners. It was more exciting to explore the disparity between Lorie's and Dan's stories than to plunge into either character's fantasy life. The one exception, a scene that blessedly hit the cutting room floor, was a full-blown revenge fantasy in which Lorie imagines herself at a bowling alley. The setup: Lorie believes that Dan still pines for ex-girlfriend Linda (Sharon Stone). In the bowling fantasy, Lorie lifts her bowling ball, only to discover that it's Linda's disembodied head—and it's alive! After Linda makes a snarky wisecrack at Lorie's expense, our heroine cocks her arm and sends Linda's head sailing toward the pins. This perverse idea came at the suggestion of some studio executive who felt the film needed to be more outrageous. During postproduction, cooler heads prevailed, and the scene was relegated to the scrap heap.

We also used music to distinguish Lorie's and Dan's stories. Composer Miles Goodman wrote an effervescent theme for "he said," lushly orchestrated, as if Dan fancies himself the lead in a Rock Hudson / Doris Day vehicle. The same theme is arranged with more introspective coloring for Lorie's story, reflecting her self-doubt and uncertainty about Dan's love. Marisa and I were neither trying to reinvent romantic comedy nor destroy it, just tell a familiar story in a fresh way. But we were mindful of the genre, and as an affectionate nod to romantic comedy tropes, we featured a little-known tune by George and Ira Gershwin, a parody of love song conventions called "Blah Blah Blah." We invited Mac Rebennack (a.k.a. Dr. John) to cover the tune, and his swampy growl was a perfect match for such dazzling lyrics as these: "Blah blah blah blah moon / Blah blah blah blah croon."

Marisa and I were proud of our efforts, but there were bumps in the road during postproduction, some inevitable, some surprising. Despite a pair of enthusiastic preview screenings, a top Paramount executive suggested we throw out the entire "he said, she said" concept and recut the film as a straightforward narrative. This executive shall remain nameless, but it still boggles my mind that people who make such pronouncements actually draw a paycheck. On top of that, the Paramount marketing department, in its inimitable wisdom, designed a campaign for the film using clichés about men and women that were tired in the 1930s, let alone the 1990s. The advertising department pitched taglines that reduced the film to a ham-fisted battle of the sexes. I won't resurrect any of these for public display, but it fell to Brian

Hohlfeld, our screenwriter, to pen the simple, elegant tagline the studio ultimately chose: "The story of true love . . . both versions." An unexpected blow came from our own union, the Directors Guild of America, which decreed that Marisa and I were forbidden to share a codirecting credit. Appealing our case to the guild's board of directors, we argued that this was a personal project, one we conceived together, planned together, and executed as a team. The DGA overruled us, insisting on a clumsy title card in which one name followed the next.

Despite these setbacks, the most important outcome of the film was that the two directors survived the production intact. They never came to a consensus about the details of their first meeting, but no matter. If you can survive making a movie as a couple, how hard could it be to spend the rest of your life together?

BEING PROACTIVE ON YOUR OWN SET

I've observed a lot of young directors at work. Some are boisterous and cocky, others nervous and withdrawn. Some conduct the set like a cruise ship captain, eager to make everybody happy. Others sit grim-faced, advertising their pain, as if directing were the equivalent of passing a kidney stone. Many carry themselves with a sense of entitlement, while just as many feel singularly out of place, as if they were chosen to direct by mistake. Some assume their job is to tyrannize the set; they test their powers by torturing an underling. In all cases, I've noticed a common issue. Whether tempestuous or timid, too many directors are not proactive on their own set.

It's tempting for an inexperienced director to simply let things happen. Overwhelmed by options, why not take the passive route and let others make decisions for you? This applies to directors of all stripes. *Cocky* is not the same as *proactive*. You may have a big mouth but nothing to say. I've watched directors equivocate with utter command. A stentorian clamor masks the fact they're just dodging one decision after another. A common avoidance tactic is to fixate on the wrong things. For instance, while the tyrant is lobbying to fire a production assistant, others take up the slack and ready the next shot. While the cruise ship captain mingles with producers, the cast is left to its own, puzzling out how to perform a scene. If you're too busy micromanaging a needless detail, the show will go on without your input. If you're hell-bent on reminding everyone you're in charge but never actually make a choice, the crew will smile and trudge ahead. If you're too tortured to make a decision, trust me—someone will relieve you of that burden.

The key to being proactive on the set is to remind yourself of a fundamental fact: you are the only person entrusted to tell this story. No one else. Perhaps you're directing your own screenplay, which might be wholly autobiographical. In that case, you have an added degree of authority; this is your story. On the other hand, you may be directing the umpteenth episode of a popular television program. If you think of yourself as a hired gun, a guest worker, you're well on your way to passive directing, to phoning it in. The cast and crew of a long-running series may seem intractable, completely set in their ways. When tackling the 186th episode of a series, you may have the urge to let the show run itself. But in the process, you've relinquished your role as the designated storyteller in favor of being a traffic cop.

I directed two episodes of the medical drama *ER,* which, in its sixth season, was astonishingly successful. Clearly, whatever they were doing was working, and I'd never witnessed a more well-oiled production. The actors knew their characters inside out, and a few pointedly warned me against giving notes—why try to improve on success? Similarly, the camera crew welcomed my ideas but made it clear there was nothing new under the sun. I was told, in effect, "There are only so many ways to photograph someone pushing a gurney through the emergency room, and we've done all of them." A medical consultant pre-rehearsed the surgery scenes, giving each actor specific business (e.g., administering anesthesia, tying off an artery). I was amazed by the massive machine in action and more than a little insecure about my own credentials, having directed mainly lighter fare. Hey, I've worked with Kermit the Frog; that makes me the perfect person to direct a quadruple bypass operation, right? The challenge: how to quickly become a member of an insular group while asserting my authority over that group. Again, the key was keeping in mind that, despite having the least amount of experience on the show (in my case: zero), I was the only person authorized to the tell the story.

I approached the task by imagining I'd been invited to a dance. I choose a dance partner, escort them onto the floor, and do the moves they're most familiar with; only then, having gained his or her confidence, do I try out a few new steps. And it worked. It soon became abundantly clear that the stars of *ER,* particularly ones who professed to be set in their ways, were desperate for fresh ideas. Even the medical consultant was game to adapt surgical business to my directorial needs. And as for that gurney, let me state categorically: there will always be a new way to photograph someone pushing a gurney down a hall.

Asserting authority on the set is often misunderstood to

mean lording over the cast and crew. Needless to say, establishing authority and acting authoritarian have nothing to do with one another. The history of the world is filled with despots, and the history of cinema and television is no less littered with legions of autocrats. As is the case with most bullies, their bark is worse than their bite, and more often than not, behind all the bellowing is nothing more than a person uncomfortable in their own skin. When I was a fledgling filmmaker, I once phoned my agent to complain about a famously combative actor who'd given me flak on the set. Citing a director well known for brooking no dissent of any kind, my agent said, "He would never take shit like that from anybody." The implication was clear: I was a softie. I needed to run roughshod over people who challenged my authority. I joked to my agent that perhaps the time was ripe for the Directors Guild of America to hold seminars on how to be an asshole. He didn't laugh. It was no joking matter. For my agent, and he was hardly in the minority, the proper way to gain respect was to instill fear, pure and simple.

Clearly, if you're reading this book, you know that I didn't follow his advice, which brings us to another way to be proactive on your set. Forget being a fearmonger. You can assert great authority by valuing each crew member's expertise in his or her respective capacity. It takes nerves of steel to be a crack focus puller, a painter's eye to be an inspired gaffer, the grace of a ballerina to be a master dolly grip, and enviable core strength to execute a tricky Steadicam move. I am awed by these and countless other skills that, together, form the heartbeat of a crew. And I believe it's possible to acknowledge each and every craftsperson, sometimes without saying a word. That sense of regard will be palpable—it's part of the atmosphere you create, and it will make all the difference when you urge your focus puller to be more precise or insist the dolly grip hit a mark more crisply.

That bedrock of respect will enable you to get what you need to tell the story. Unlike the autocrat who leads by belittling the team (or ignoring them), your crew will happily reimburse you for the regard you pay them. Pretty elemental, right?

Well, you'd be surprised how many directors consider their crews to be basically invisible.

I have syntactic strategies to help me assert control while encouraging teammates to bring their A game. The first maneuver is what I call "Feeling, not Thinking." I've found that giving a note couched in *feeling* terms—to an actor, crew member, or producer—is more effective than framing it as a *thought*. For example, after a less-than-satisfying camera rehearsal, I know in my heart something needs to be scrapped. We need to reconceive the shot or throw out the blocking. If I address the group and declare, "I don't think this shot is working," I'm operating on an intellectual and argumentative plane. Using the word *think* can put people on the defensive, as anyone who's ever been in a romantic relationship knows. Just consider the difference between "I don't think you love me anymore" and "I don't feel you love me anymore." A feeling is inarguable. No one can tell me what I feel. It's also nonjudgmental—that is, I didn't arrive at this conclusion by a rational process; it's just what I feel. Getting back to the set, if I announce, "I don't feel the shot is working," or "I have a gut feeling the shot isn't right," there will be a markedly different response from the team. My feeling is an unimpeachable fact, and by framing my note in this manner, I'm effectively inviting the cast and crew to uncover the source of my feeling rather than engage in an argument.

The second tactic is to present a note in the form of a question. Consider this a Socratic method of directing; instead of making decrees, I pose questions and draw ideas from the dialogue that ensues. This approach is not just reserved for directors with luxurious schedules. Even on a punishing episodic schedule, you can do more than just issue edicts. Why is it worth opening a dialogue? Because I want my colleagues to have an ownership stake in the process. Also, a note delivered as a question will spur the team to tackle something they might otherwise resist. Consider the following directive:

"I want the camera to dolly through this doorway." You're aware the doorway is narrow but confident the shot can be achieved. By posing it as a demand, however, you invite objection (e.g., "Can't be done," mumbles the grip). Alternately:

"Is it possible for us to dolly through this doorway?" The doorway may be too narrow, but if you frame it as a hypothetical, the crew is more inclined to make it work, even if the operator's posterior gets grazed in the process. Also, by substituting *us* for *I,* you dispense with the hierarchy and remind everyone you're all in this together.

If you're a director with no experience pre-visualizing the action, you could find yourself hamstrung by a cinematographer who's eager to create shots that are "interesting" (i.e., shots that call attention to themselves). You may not have the skills to translate your vision into *images,* into concrete pictures that convey the story's emotional thrust. Rather than acquiesce to a cinematographer who may have an ulterior motive (e.g., add impressive shots to his or her reel), you can be proactive by articulating what's important in the scene (e.g., our hero is ill at ease and grows more rattled as the action unfolds). You can pose your note in the form of a question: "Can we visually show how unnerved the hero is? Can we create images that reinforce how frantic he becomes over the course of the scene?" This applies to all phases of directing, but it's especially critical in production, when time is scarce and you must guard against a cinematographer getting sidetracked by an idea that doesn't speak to the heart of the matter. It's not important whether you can talk the language of lenses. The emotional content of the scene is where your authority lies.

I often think of the set in terms of a family dynamic. It doesn't matter if you've been hired by a top-tier producer or showrunner. It doesn't matter if you have less experience than every member of the crew. For the set to be creative and efficient, you are effectively the head of the household. Inasmuch as I want to embrace everyone's input, some voices will be distracting, or even destructive, and it becomes necessary to draw a line.

Like a parent.

Of course, in any family, some children are wont to push your buttons just to test their powers. They're eager to prove they can exist and thrive independently of your guidance. Yet they simultaneously yearn for the opposite; they want the security of knowing you've got their backs. They want a boundary. I once worked with celebrated acting coach Sondra Lee, who coached such luminaries as Marlon Brando. I asked her, "What's the most important thing a director can tell an actor?" She didn't hesitate for a moment. "Tell them where to stand," she replied. "They need to know where they are." There's no question that certain actors put directors through a testing period before trusting them. It's hard not to feel insecure, but it's less a referendum on your abilities than an index of their need to feel grounded—they just want to know where to stand.

Screenwriters may feel particularly vulnerable and require special care; having birthed the script, they are essentially turning over their baby to you, the adoptive parent. I'll try not to drive this analogy into the ground, but an adoptive parent soon comes to know their child's mind better than anyone else. A gifted screenwriter will create a story full of truthful behavior, but he or she may not see the multiple meanings in their own work or the untold possibilities for bringing it to life. It's your job to use the script as a springboard to discover layers of meaning the writer did not envisage. The writer is an essential resource, but there may come a moment when, for the story to blossom, it's necessary for the adoptive parent, as it were, to set a limit with the original parent.

Plenty of colleagues require a clear boundary now and then, but there's a whole other class of character you will no doubt encounter. Defiant and unruly for no obvious reason, these are Very Difficult People. There are many categories of Very Difficult People, but the common denominator is that their obstreperousness has nothing to do with you. Very Difficult People behave as disruptively at the grocery store as they do on the set. The entertainment industry is a magnet for people who would be considered sociopaths in any other line of work. Examples abound. The man booted out of anger management class gets hired to be your production manager. The woman who honks one millisecond after the light turns green ends up being your showrunner.

Over the years, I've compiled a list of exceedingly difficult people who fall under the heading LTS: Life's Too Short. Some collaborations are simply not worth the price you pay in mental duress, sleepless nights, and so on. Of course, you don't always enjoy the privilege of choosing your colleagues. You may find yourself saddled with not one but two or three Very Difficult People on the job.

There's nothing to gain by indulging a rageful person. At the same time, butting heads is a losing proposition. It may tempt others to test their powers to enrage. When faced with a tantrum, I find that acknowledging someone's anger is 80 percent of the battle. You don't have to solve a problem. Just give the Very Difficult Person a little space to vent. You don't have to understand the real source of the anger (a job best left to a therapist), but in my experience, Very Difficult People share an inability to articulate the tiniest grievance. They sit on their complaint until it mushrooms into a full-blown rant. Faced with such ferocity, I nod sympathetically and thank my lucky stars that I don't have to deal with whatever demons are fueling this outburst.

One last parental responsibility is to monitor sibling rivalries within the cast and/or crew. Everyone needs a pat on the back now and then, but make sure not to pat the same back over and over again. If your leading man keeps forgetting his dialogue, requiring extra attention on your part, be mindful of the leading lady delivering one flawless take after the next. Your job is to simultaneously manage his insecurity and her impatience. There may be a problematic member of the ensemble demanding all your attention. Just know the other actors are painfully aware which squeaky wheel is getting all the grease.

Setting limits. Delivering a note in question form. Couching a suggestion in "feeling" terms. Deflecting the pique of a Very Difficult Person. There's plenty in the arsenal to help you become more proactive, but none of the tools mean a thing unless they unburden you to make choices—to embrace the adventure of *making a choice*. Down the road, you may look back at some choices and shake your head. *What was I thinking? Why didn't I shoot a close-up? Why did I insist on so-and-so wearing that green dress?* But in the moment, with the clock ticking, when the harried costume designer holds up a red dress and a green one—even if you don't trust your sartorial instincts—you take your pick. "My gut tells me to go with the green one," you declare, and because your directive is based on a feeling, no one challenges you. Save your second thoughts for another day. You can rue the green dress in years to come. All that matters is this precise moment. There's a fork in the road, and the cast and crew need your guidance. If you dally, the team will have no choice but to blunder down one road, unsure of itself, with you following in their wake. The world will not stop turning if you pick the green dress. So . . . decide.

And when vexed with doubt, just take two aspirin and recite these lyrics from Stephen Sondheim's "Move On," in which the singer recounts the moment she stood at the cross-roads, faced with a decision more momentous than a dress color. After making a choice that irrevocably changes her life, she concludes: "The choice may have been mistaken / The choosing was not."

GARRY SHANDLING'S HOUSE OF MIRRORS

"I'm not an asshole," Garry Shandling insisted. "But I have the potential." This was Garry's answer to a question I posed at our first meeting in 1992. It was a job interview. Garry's follow-up to his wildly inventive meta-comedy *It's Garry Shandling's Show* would be its complete opposite. *The Larry Sanders Show* was conceived as a realistic backstage story about the daily ordeal of putting on a television talk show. I was offered the job to direct the pilot episode and much of the first season, pending this interview with Garry. We talked at great length about the tone of the show and the journey of the titular character. "Could you boil the entire arc of the series down to one simple statement?" I asked. "Can you give me a mantra, something to remind me what our mission is when things get hectic?" Garry liked the challenge and paced the room, mulling the best way to encapsulate his new creation. Finally, he announced, "This is a show about whether or not I'm going to become an asshole." He quickly added, "I'm not an asshole. But I have the potential." Was Garry talking about himself? About Larry Sanders? It wasn't clear, but I sensed that the gray area between Garry and Larry was the true subject of the series.

And, as I soon learned, some days I was working with Garry while others I was working with Larry. No one was more acutely aware of this duality than Shandling himself. Once, during a rehearsal, he became unaccountably testy with me. Then, turning on a dime, he apologized. "Sorry, Ken. That was Larry talking."

Garry used Larry as a means to study, interrogate, and often excoriate himself. The result was a highly personal experiment unique in the annals of film and television, and I was present at the creation. It was a white-knuckle ride.

The first order of business, for me, was to make sure the world of the show felt authentic. Garry wanted *The Larry Sanders Show* to mimic the moment-by-moment workings of a network talk show with pitch-perfect accuracy. Not a mockumentary per se, the series would nevertheless paint a lifelike picture of an intense, embattled, dysfunctional workplace.

Johnny Carson's thirty-year reign as host of *The Tonight Show* was coming to a close in 1992, and among the parade of final guests was Shandling himself, not only much admired by Carson but long rumored to be his likely successor.

Having never attended a talk show taping before, I accompanied Garry to NBC Studios in Burbank for his *Tonight Show* stint. With an hour to go before showtime, Garry and I lingered outside the green room, soaking up the atmosphere. I spied fellow guest George Foreman chatting with a makeup artist. I overheard a staffer mention that Jimmy Stewart, originally scheduled to appear, bowed out at the last minute due to illness.

As Garry and I stood like statues, I suddenly heard a familiar voice at the end of the hall. It was music director Doc Severinsen, walking briskly toward us, flanked by a young production assistant. Doc, sporting a plain T-shirt (not clad in one of his signature flashy suits, he was barely recognizable), complained to the PA about coyotes that had recently infiltrated his property. "I'd like to take a shotgun and kill every one of those fuckin' coyotes," Doc proclaimed as he passed us and disappeared around the corner. Garry nodded sagely and declared, "That's our show." One of Garry's goals was to contrast the way show business people comport themselves in front of the camera with the way they behave when those cameras are turned off. Catching Doc in an unguarded, unexpurgated moment was exactly what Garry had in mind. Equally important for Garry was a storytelling style with plenty of room for throwaway moments like the one we'd just witnessed, inconsequential yet character-revealing. Garry told me he yearned to write a *Larry Sanders* episode with no plot whatsoever, one that takes place in a backstage hallway, consisting entirely of ephemera—banal, fleeting exchanges, nothing that would remotely rise to the level of a story. Doc and those "fuckin' coyotes" fit the bill perfectly.

Shandling's quest for realism was not just confined to the look of the show. He wanted a performance style that was natural and understated. In contrast to much network comedy fare, with its desperate-to-please, pile-driver delivery of jokes, Garry wanted a show in which the comedy was behavioral and well observed, not presentational. To that end, he made a few unorthodox requests. He asked me to come up with a shooting method that would prevent the cast from knowing whether the cameras were rolling or not. I admit, I was stumped.

Larry Sanders belonged to the pre-digital era; we shot on 16 mm, which meant we were constantly reloading film magazines. There was no way to hide that from the cast. The solution I came up with was to stop using the word *action* at the top of each take. Garry liked this idea, and we worked out a system wherein the cameras began turning without the standard announcements ("Rolling!" "Speed!"). I then gave Garry a signal, either a nod or a simple "Go ahead," after which he'd engage in chitchat with the cast before moseying into the scene. *Mosey* aptly describes the casual, conversational quality Garry desired.

Sometimes, it wasn't obvious when a scene actually began; the dialogue just flowed naturally out of the pre-scene banter. Again, this was a radical break from situation comedies in which actors essentially "sell" jokes to an audience. *The Larry Sanders Show* invited viewers to eavesdrop on the lives of its characters. Often, the best directorial choice was to simply be a fly on the wall. After *Larry Sanders,* I dispensed with the word *action* altogether. To this day, I begin each take with an offhanded "Go ahead." Taking my lead from Garry, I feel it makes each take less precious and sacrosanct; in some small, ineffable way, "Go ahead" blurs the line between the scene and real life.

As I hinted at the outset, directing *The Larry Sanders Show* was a crazy ride. From a production standpoint, the show was a mash-up of multi-camera and single-camera shooting styles. The backstage story was shot on 16 mm. The show within the show, in the tradition of programs like *The Tonight Show*, was recorded on one-inch videotape (one of the visual hallmarks of *The Larry Sanders Show* is the bold contrast between formats—grainy celluloid versus slick videotape). Each week, we'd rehearse from Monday to Wednesday, then shoot twenty-plus pages of backstage material on Thursday and Friday. Every third Friday, after a dizzying shoot day, we'd press on late into the evening, taping the talk show itself in front of a live audience.

After *Larry Sanders* premiered and was showered with plaudits, celebrities lined up to do cameos, eager to play unsavory versions of themselves. Before the show gained such cred, however, Garry pored through his Rolodex, calling in favors to stock the show with stars. Often, scenes or whole story lines would be tailored to a particular celebrity, complete with real-life details about that person. Invariably, the moment the script was issued, the celebrity in question would drop out of the show. This process would repeat over and over, resulting in a riot of conflicting scripts. For example, we begin the week with a script built around Julia Roberts. By Monday afternoon, Julia passes, and the draft is quickly rewritten for Sarah Jessica Parker, who passes on Tuesday. Several passes later, Mimi Rogers agrees to appear in the episode, but the script is now littered with remnants specific to all the actors who declined the invitation. God forbid any actor discover that he or she was not the top choice. As you might guess, the process of vacuuming those remnants from the shooting draft was a job unto itself.

Adding to this combustible mix were a few challenging

actors, none more formidable than Rip Torn, playing the role of Artie, the talk show's producer. Rip's reputation for volatile behavior was legendary. Everyone knew about his infamous dinner meeting with Dennis Hopper in 1967, ostensibly to discuss playing a role in *Easy Rider,* which ended with Torn pulling a knife on Hopper. Needless to say, Hopper didn't give him the part. I'd seen Norman Mailer's feature *Maidstone,* with its jaw-dropping brawl between Mailer and Torn, during which Torn surprises Mailer by whacking him with a hammer, to which Mailer responds by biting Torn's ear. I was more than a little nervous about directing this pugnacious actor, and I was hardly reassured at our first get-together. He wore a fishing cap and a scowl and barely looked me in the eye. In situations like this, my default position is to lean into "midwestern nice." Eager to impress Rip with my knowledge of his filmography, I singled out for praise his work in Jean-Luc Godard's *1 P.M.,* a barely comprehensible stew of radical politics filmed in 1968. Rip shot me a paranoid look and muttered something to the effect that he was a nervous wreck during that film because he was convinced Godard had hired a band of Maoists to kidnap him. I nodded and thought it best not to pursue the matter further, but it was not the last time Rip shared stories about people who were "out to get me." (In Rip's defense, he claimed it was Dennis Hopper who pulled the knife on him, which I find highly credible. As for *Maidstone,* I've read accounts that variously describe Rip's weapon of choice as a "toy hammer" or a "tack hammer." In either case, I'm sure there were more than a few people inclined to hit Norman Mailer with a blunt instrument.)

To be honest, Rip's whole relationship to reality seemed

pretty tenuous. One afternoon while shooting the pilot, a production assistant knocked on Rip's dressing room door. "Mr. Torn, we're ready to rehearse," the PA declared, not realizing he'd roused Rip from a deep and troubled sleep. Carelessly throwing on his clothes, Rip marched to the soundstage in a daze. Garry and I were discussing the scene when Rip burst onto the set and began spouting his dialogue in a loud and oddly robotic fashion. It was as if he were in a trance, speaking in tongues. Garry and I just stared, confused and a bit alarmed.

Eventually, Rip snapped out of his stupor. Realizing his entrance didn't have the desired effect, he sheepishly turned and hightailed it off the set. Later that day, I cornered Rip and gently asked him to explain his confounding behavior. He was happy to oblige. According to Rip, the knock on his dressing room door was so startling that he completely forgot where he was. In his stupefaction, he felt certain he was about to miss his entrance in a play. Only after delivering his lines did he realize he wasn't facing a packed house of theatergoers but merely a few puzzled-looking crew members on a television set. He confided all this to me in a perfectly casual way, as if massive psychic dislocation was as ordinary as sneezing. As Rip wandered away, Garry approached me. Having overheard our conversation, Garry quipped, "Just think: this man has a driver's license."

Initially, Rip's approach to the character of Artie worried me, and though I make no great claims, I did offer him a small, useful note. Artie was partly inspired by the charismatic Fred De Cordova, who produced *The Tonight Show* for twenty-two years. In a *People* magazine profile, De Cordova described his job this way: "I'm chief traffic cop, talent scout, No. 1 fan and critic all rolled into one."

Rip's original take on the talk show impresario struck me as needlessly grim, as if he were a general overseeing a military campaign he knew was doomed. One afternoon, I took Rip aside and reminded him that part of Artie's job was to buoy Larry's spirits, to brighten his neurotic star's mood. Glaring at me, Rip growled, "What do you mean?" It was not a question. Knowing I was on thin ice, I gingerly replied, "Maybe you should, I don't know, smile now and then." His glare, if possible, grew fiercer. "You mean, like this?" he shot back and produced something I can only describe as a cross between a grimace and a crazy grin. It was positively scary. "Yeah, something like that," I said, wishing I'd never opened my mouth. Just then, Garry sat next to us and was taken aback by Rip's frozen smile. Garry asked, "What's that on your face?" Rip pointed directly at me and barked, "He told me to do that!" Assuming I would be shortly looking for a new job, I was relieved when Garry began laughing uproariously. Rip relaxed, clearly pleased to have won the boss's approval, and before long he added that pained smile to Artie's repertoire.

Rip taught me a valuable lesson about actors. In retrospect it seems quite obvious, but in 1992, I was still learning on my feet. Highly gifted actors, and Rip was certainly one of them, have the ability to express a character's inner life, but they are often quite hopeless at articulating their own feelings. On a nearly daily basis, Rip would track me down, and within an inch of my face, scream, "*This whole fucking thing sucks!*" Not having any clue what he was talking about, I would nod agreeably. "You're right, the whole thing sucks," I'd repeat. "It sucks. It really sucks. Now . . . what is it that sucks, exactly?" The reason for Rip's explosion usually had to do with something small and easily fixable.

Camera placement, for instance. He might fret that the camera wasn't in the right position to catch one of his favorite lines. Rather than pull me aside when the concern first arose, Rip would let his irritation build and build until he turned into Mount Vesuvius. I quickly learned not to take these eruptions personally; moreover, it didn't take much to calm him down. "I'll make sure the camera's in a better place" was usually enough to lift his colossal gloom. "Thanks, Kenny, m'boy," he'd chirp, patting me on the shoulder. I handily dowsed many a flare-up, but being constantly roared at by Rip—at point-blank, to boot—did take its toll: I noticed a precipitous change in my hair color during my *Larry Sanders* tenure. But I was proud of my status as a crack Rip wrangler.

Equally complicated, though much less bellicose, was Garry himself. Twenty-five years after directing *The Larry Sanders Show*, I had lunch with a well-established comedy writer who introduced himself as "a fellow member of the Garry Shandling survivors network." It's true the casualty rate on *Larry Sanders* was high, and I would eventually join their numbers. At the start of the series, Garry was axing showrunners left and right. The drama behind the scenes certainly reflected the behind-the-scenes drama depicted in the show. Or was it the other way around? Working on *Larry Sanders* was like trying to make your way through a house of mirrors. Garry wanted to hold up a harsh mirror to himself. He could be duplicitous, passive-aggressive, cowardly, self-hating—I'm sorry, I'm talking about Larry, right? As you might expect, giving Garry notes about his alter ego was a treacherous business, particularly any note that probed those darker recesses. I had to tread lightly offering a suggestion that Garry might misread as a note about himself, rather than his creation. At the heart of the whole project was a paradox; Garry wanted to expose his own dark impulses but then felt compelled to punish anyone who helped bring those impulses to light.

In the midst of this self-exorcism, however, there were times when Garry exuded childlike excitement about the process, unfettered joy watching the world he created come to life. There's a scene in the pilot that introduces Larry's writing staff, among them Jerry (Jeremy Piven) and Phil (Wallace Langham). The staff writers kill time, waiting for Larry to appear so they can pitch ideas for the upcoming show's monologue. Bored, the staffers compare notes on their preferred brand of antidepressants. Jerry says, "Imipramine? Nobody's taken imipramine for years . . . Why don't you just put leeches on your head?" Still more bored, they begin trading jokes. Phil pitches the following: "Okay, how about this? Jeffrey Dahmer says to his shrink, 'If you suck a cock and it's not attached to anybody, does that make you gay?'" During the shooting of this scene, Garry stood next to me, wearing a set of headphones. He tried hard not to laugh each time Wallace Langham delivered the Dahmer line. Indeed, he insisted the actor run the line again and again. "Let's do it one more time," he begged with glee.

After far too many takes, I finally put down my foot. "Garry, we need to move on," I urged. He took off the headphones and sighed. "You know, Ken," he said. "We're never going to use this joke." I nodded, assuming what he meant was the joke was in such monumentally bad taste that no network would ever run it. "Yeah," he added wistfully, "by the time our show airs, no one will remember Dahmer." And with that, Garry walked away and resumed the mantle of our anxious, tortured, self-absorbed, vicious, perverse, capricious, and brilliant leader.

THE SHOT LIST CHALLENGE

There are many directors who cannot figure out how to shoot a scene until they see it in rehearsal. Only after blocking the action, deciding how various characters move in a given space, do they feel comfortable breaking it down into a series of shots. There's nothing wrong with this; indeed, many great filmmakers consider the camera a tool for *capturing* action, as opposed to those who choreograph action *for the camera*.

There are directors who plan everything in advance, drawing storyboards and/or writing shot lists. Before the rehearsal even begins, such a director feels absolutely confident about the blocking. Hitchcock famously pre-visualized his scenes so carefully that very little was left to chance on the set. For Hitchcock, conceiving the images was infinitely more exciting than committing them to film. Shooting was simply a matter of replicating the storyboards.

When considering how to shoot a scene, each director brings both skills and limitations to the task. Directors with an acting background might "find" the scene in rehearsal but rely on his or her cinematographer to translate it into pictures. A screenwriter-turned-director may have an easier time hearing a scene than seeing it. Directors who are image-oriented might think of actors as mere pictorial elements, leaving the cast to suss out why their respective characters are moving from point A to B or not moving at all.

At the start of my career, I was woefully ignorant about the acting process. In college I enjoyed a rich diet of film history, theory, cinematography, editing, and sound design. But no acting. I'll dive into this in more detail in a later chapter; for now, suffice it to say this was a big gap in my skill set. As a result, the first day I marched onto a professional set, I came armed with a complicated shot list and fully expected that all the elements would simply conform to my intentions. If I needed an actor to hit a mark to create a symmetrical composition (one that called to mind a supercool shot I'd seen in a supercool film), that cast member should just comply, right? The idea that an actor might question why his or her character would land on that mark seemed, to me, downright rude. That it was my responsibility to give some logic to the blocking, to make it organic, struck me as absurd. Don't these people realize their job is to *perform the shot list*?

If an actor demanded to know his motivation, I grew tongue-tied. *Your motivation*, I thought but never said, *is to help me create a cool shot*. When actors did what they were told, the shot "worked." Soon, however, I discovered that being slavish to one's shot list produced a well-composed and easy-to-edit scene that had no life to it. Like butterflies displayed in a shadow box, my characters were arrayed across the screen in eye-catching formations, but they weren't breathing.

For me, pre-visualizing the action came all too easily. For better or worse, my brain is like a warehouse full of TV and movie images. I would simply conjure up favorite shots and plug them into the scene. Again, I quickly figured out this was a dead end; I knew I had to strike a balance between imposing a visual plan on the scene and bringing it to life from the inside out. I needed to come up with a more dynamic and fluid approach to breaking down the action into shots.

Before we go further, there's a word I'm avoiding, and it's time to confront it head-on: *coverage*. Whether in a classroom or on the job, at some point, every director becomes conversant in film grammar, that set of traditional building blocks used in visual storytelling. Conventional wisdom dictates that you *cover* a scene with a variety of shots, in order to have flexibility in the cutting room. For instance, you might shoot a WIDE SHOT, a MEDIUM SHOT, and a CLOSE-UP of the same action, giving you the chance to choose the best image size during the editing process. What could possibly be controversial about coverage?

Well, I abhor the word *coverage* for two reasons. First, it makes me think of insurance. You buy an insurance policy to protect you against certain risks.

Similarly, many directors cover scenes with risk aversion in mind; in other words, protection against the risk of a bad directorial decision. Unfortunately, for many directors, coverage is a way to sidestep directorial decisions altogether—that is, it's a way to avoid imposing *any* directorial vision on the scene. Certain producers don't help matters when they urge a director to grab every conceivable angle, or "hose it down," a phrase that effectively means "abdicate your position as director, and think of yourself as someone who simply collects data." The data will later be assembled into a story, inevitably by someone other than yourself. Far too many directors buy into the notion that data gathering constitutes good directing.

The second reason *coverage* makes me cringe is that the word suggests an actual cover, like the fabric you drape over a sofa, or curtains to cover a window. I know plenty of directors, especially in episodic television, who feel their job is to *decorate* the scene, to *drape* the dialogue in shots. Some showrunners exacerbate the problem by insisting that every syllable of dialogue be visible to the viewer. God forbid a key line plays on an actor's back, in silhouette, or—horror of horrors—off-screen. Every jaw flap must be captured in frontal close-ups, and if the dialogue is comedic, better make sure it's delivered by an actor who is not moving. (The dictum that comedy is best served by static shots featuring static actors, lit as flatly as possible, is no relic from ancient times; it's still quite pervasive in mainstream film and television.) Rather than urge directors to come up with images that express the inner lives of the characters, we are often expected to create window dressing for dialogue, to prettify it in a style that's sensible and easily absorbed by the audience.

So, here's the shot list challenge: You don't want to depend entirely on the rehearsal to figure out how to shoot the scene. You want to pre-visualize the action but not be bound to your shot list. You shouldn't be so severe about your visual plan that it squeezes the life out of the cast. You want the rehearsal process to enhance what you've already envisioned. And you want to come up with images that truly belong to your scene rather than mimic shots from somebody else's work. You want to give yourself options in the cutting room without feeling obliged to *hose down* the scene. With all this in mind, how the hell do you write a shot list?

For me, a shot list should be readable by anyone, even if they don't understand the difference between PAN and TILT (you'd be surprised how many screenwriters don't know the difference; I read the phrase PAN UP all the time). For starters, here's an example of a convoluted, overly technical shot description:

> Start CLOSE (50 mm) on two feet walking into a bedroom; TILT UP to reveal Joe, and DOLLY in front of him as he walks fifteen feet toward the bed, then PAN as he sits on the bed next to Mary; PULL FOCUS to Mary.

Let's please declutter this description. Unless you're trying to impress your cinematographer, there's no need to include focal lengths (50 mm) in a shot list. Unless there's a compelling reason to note the length of a character's walk (e.g., it's the length of a football field and you'll need just as much dolly track), don't mention it. If you know you're using a dolly and not a Steadicam, it's fine to specify this as a DOLLY shot; otherwise, simply say, "We LEAD Joe" or "We FOLLOW Joe." And, unless your camera operator has recently been sleeping on the job, there's no need to offer a gentle reminder to PULL FOCUS. Finally, unless it's critical to keep the owner of the "two feet" a mystery, better to say, "Start CLOSE on Joe's feet." And, while we're at it, let's give Joe a pair of shoes. Trust me, I have written some spectacularly clunky shot descriptions in my time, ones that no doubt caused a lot of head-scratching. I've learned the hard way that less is more. Here's a cleaner version of the original description:

CLOSE on Joe's shoes as he ENTERS; we TILT UP and LEAD Joe across the room as he sits on the bed next to Mary.

Sometimes I add a tag to suggest the final composition: "Hold as CLOSE on Joe and Mary." Since Joe and Mary are side by side, I might put a finer point on the framing: "Hold as RAKING CLOSE on Joe and Mary," indicating my preference for an image of their stacked profiles rather than a frontal view.

Okay, now your shot description is efficient, but it's rather cold. The next step: add expressive language to make the scene come alive on the page. Wait, isn't that the job of the screenplay? Isn't that what we paid the writer for?

Why should a shot list regurgitate what the screenwriter already established? You're right, it shouldn't, but now it's time to convey your vision of the action. The emotional content of a scene is not set in stone. Ten directors will bring ten distinct approaches to the same moment. Using expressive language in your shot list clarifies how you see that moment. I'm not talking about florid prose, just words that are active, emotive, and character-specific. Here are three versions of the same shot, each suggesting wildly different emotional content:

1. CLOSE on Joe's shoes as he ENTERS; we TILT UP and LEAD Joe as he strides across the bedroom, sitting beside an ecstatic Mary.
2. CLOSE on Joe's shoes as he ENTERS; we TILT UP and LEAD Joe as he staggers across the bedroom, sitting beside a disapproving Mary.
3. CLOSE on Joe's shoes as he ENTERS; we TILT UP and LEAD Joe as he tiptoes across the bedroom, sitting beside an oblivious Mary.

Now your shot description has a bit of oomph, but are you really telling the story with pictures? If a viewer muted the sound, would the gist of the scene be clear? Are there images that can do the heavy lifting? Why start the scene on a pair of shoes at all? What story are you telling with Joe's shoes? If the shot list read, "CLOSE on Joe's shiny new shoes" or "CLOSE on Joe's bloodstained shoes" or "CLOSE on Joe's mud-caked boots," I'd agree the image is pushing the story forward. Short of blood and mud, why open the scene on Joe's footwear? Among the dubious platitudes I learned in film school is this old chestnut: to create a seamless transition, always begin a scene on a visually neutral object (e.g., a waiter's tray as it passes through a restaurant). This maxim has given birth to countless opening shots that are, yes, visually neutral but utterly flat (e.g., Joe's shoes). Dig deeper and you will discover an image that actually gets to the heart of the scene—a picture that talks. Set Joe's shoes aside and look elsewhere. Here, for instance, is a completely different entry point:

> CLOSE on Mary's hands as she twists her wedding ring.

Without a single line of dialogue, the image suggests umpteen story lines, all more intriguing than a peek at Joe's shoes. It's behavioral and neutral to boot. Mary twisting her ring raises the next big issue in our shot list challenge: Are you telling the story from a particular character's point of view? How long has Mary been waiting for her husband, Joe, to come home? Has she decided to admit she's fallen in love with another person? If so, Mary is clearly the emotional anchor of your scene, and a new opening shot may be in order:

> CLOSE on Mary's hands as she twists her wedding ring; TILT UP to reveal a resolute Mary.

Before developing our list further, a quick sidebar. It's important to know who the audience is for your shot list. Your cinematographer needs to translate your intentions into images. Script supervisors appreciate a road map for the scene. The first assistant director relies on your shot list to manage the day. Less obvious, though equally important, is your editor.

Once upon a time, there was a communal ritual at the

end of each shooting day called *dailies*. The crew would gather to screen the fruits of the previous day's labor. Invariably, some takes would prompt a hearty groan from the group, but in my experience, there was never an evening of dailies that wasn't a festive event, a celebration of the collective effort to tell a story. Sitting with your editor, you picked favorite takes and shared thoughts about how to shape the scene editorially. I'm sorry to report those days belong to a bygone era. Today, if crew members watch dailies at all, it's on their laptops, at home or alone in a hotel room on location. My longtime cinematographer John Bailey dubbed this the "balkanization of dailies." Directors no longer enjoy everyday contact with their editor, which is why your shot list must take up the slack and clearly convey an editing plan. With this in mind, let's return to Mary and Joe and build a sequence that represents your preferred cutting pattern:

1. CLOSE on Mary's hands as she twists her wedding ring; TILT UP to reveal a resolute Mary. She sees . . .
2. WIDE on Joe as he pauses in the doorway—ANGLE from Mary's POV.
3. CLOSE on Mary as she steels herself.
4. CLOSE on a fuming Joe; we LEAD him as he advances toward the bed and sits next to Mary. Hold as RAKING CLOSE on Mary and Joe.

Your shot list is now precise without being overly technical. It clarifies that we're telling the story from Mary's point of view. It uses active verbs and emotional cues to convey your interpretation of the scene. And it communicates a simple cutting plan to your editor.

Finally, here's the most important part of the shot list challenge. When you arrive on the set, be prepared to throw the list away. Invariably, the actor playing Joe will challenge your staging. "I'm absolutely sure Mary is seeing another man," he declares. "I'm so angry and hurt, I'd never cross the room, let alone sit next to her." The actor playing Mary concurs. "If he sat down on the bed, I'd move away from him," she insists. In short order, your cast rejects your blocking ideas. As a director, you have two choices. You can bend over backward to justify your blocking (e.g., "Joe and Mary are able to sit next to each other because they're both so good at covering their feelings"). Or you adjust the staging, a subject we'll return to down the road. Setting your ego and shot list aside, there's every possibility the actors' instincts will lead you to a blocking idea that's stronger than the one you conceived in a vacuum. Perhaps Joe plants himself in the doorway for the entire scene. With no less than fifteen feet between Joe and Mary, you have the perfect opportunity for a *wide shot* that places them at either edge of the frame, a composition that highlights the physical and emotional gulf between the two. Don't think of this as a compromise; instead, credit yourself with the good sense to hear a smart idea and use it. Yes, you should do your homework—envision the scene and represent it clearly in the form of a shot list. Then get ready to tuck that list into your back pocket. It's not scripture. Investing time and energy on pre-visualizing the action—and in the process uncovering the emotional core of the scene—is what allows you to be supple on the set. It frees you to think on your feet.

BEEN THERE, DREAMT THAT

According to legend, the germ of Robert Altman's 1977 film *3 Women* came to the director in a dream. It was so enthralling that Altman expanded the dream into a film treatment, then approached 20th Century Fox. As Altman recounts it, "I called Alan Ladd at Fox and said, 'Listen, I read a short story, and I want to make a film of it.' I didn't want to tell him it was a dream. And I kind of made up the story. And he said, 'Great. Go ahead and make it.'" This anecdote knocks me out on several levels. It's remarkable that Altman had sufficient clout in the mid-1970s to get a green light for a notion sprung from his unconscious. Granted, in his pitch to the studio chief, Altman hedged his bets and disguised his dream as a piece of intellectual property (did Alan Ladd Jr. even bother to ask who the author of the "short story" was?). Still, it's amazing Altman pulled it off.

I've never directed a film literally based on a dream, but ever since my career began, many of my dreams—the vast majority of them, actually—focus on one subject: the anxieties of being a director.

Needless to say, the literature regarding dream interpretation is vast, and I am hardly an expert on any school of thought. Many distinguish between a nightmare, characterized by feelings of utter dread and physical oppression (e.g., the inability to move or breathe), and an anxiety dream, characterized by feelings of complete frustration (e.g., the inability to complete even the simplest task). My directorial dreams fall squarely into the latter category, and the "plot" of these dreams usually involves a typical shooting day. Indeed, I've spent far more time directing in dreams than I have in real life. No matter whether I conk out after a cup of chamomile tea or a dry martini, I invariably find myself in the throes of production, struggling against uncanny forces to begin a scene, end a scene, or simply locate the set.

Henry James once offered a warning to fellow storytellers: "Tell a dream, lose a reader." Mindful of the risk, here are three reasons I feel my work-related dreams are worth sharing. First, I know my fellow filmmakers will find them painfully relatable. You are not the only one to wake up at 3:00 a.m. in a cold sweat, fretting over a shot you missed the previous shooting day.

Second, anxiety dreams are a rich vein to mine for a director. Even if there's no dream scene per se in the story you're telling, there may be scenes in which your hero suffers a level of frustration or anxiety that is truly dreamlike. You could do a lot worse than examining the *mise-en-scène* of your own dreams, making notes about camera angles, cutting patterns, even the performance style of the people who populate them. *Uncut Gems*, the sixth feature directed by Josh and Benny Safdie, unfolds like many anxiety dreams

I've endured. Particularly dreamlike is its dense sound design, so thick that it's often impossible to discern any discrete piece of aural information. There's no literal dream scene in this tragic tale of a compulsive gambler, but the filmmaking suggests the quality of a true fever dream, and I can't help but wonder if certain directorial ideas were drawn from nocturnal research.

Last but not least, creative people of all stripes constantly yearn for ways to channel . . . more creativity. What are the conditions needed to unlock fresh ideas? For me, the first thing to do is figure out where the blockage exists, and without getting too deep dish about the matter, I'm convinced the clues are hiding in plain sight—in one's dreams.

TOTALLY UNPREPARED

For someone who prides himself on doing his homework before arriving on the set, I am often unprepared and caught off guard in dreams. Typically, I've forgotten to read the script and must pretend I know what we're shooting. I wander around in fear that my ignorance will be discovered. Everyone else seems to know the script well. Even production assistants have a firmer grasp on the material than I do. My usual goal is to stall, to create a distraction, anything that will buy me time to figure out what I'm supposed to be directing.

Often, I can't for the life of me remember where I put the script, and to the crew's annoyance, I leave the set to track it down. Did I leave it in my car? At home?

Halfway around the world?

In some variations on this dream, I have the script, but none of it makes any sense. One vivid iteration begins with me seated in the back of a production van, heading to our location. The vehicle is full of crew members, chatting amiably, but I soon realize that no one is speaking English. Unnerved, I open my briefcase and pull out the script. The title page reads, "Les Parapluies de Cherbourg." Apparently, I'm directing a remake of Jacques Demy's 1964 musical *The Umbrellas of Cherbourg*. Needless to say, the script is in French, a language I can't speak at all. The van arrives, the crew disembarks, and I'm determined to fool everyone into thinking I'm fluent in French. The trick is how to do it without opening my mouth. Everybody surrounds me, ready for direction. Not knowing a whit about the scene, and with no French at my disposal, I start waving my hands about, hoping that pantomime will provide the *lingua franca* needed to pull the wool over everyone's eyes. But my gestures are ridiculous—I look like a mime school reject—and the assembled group, confused and concerned, mutter to each other. In French, of course.

As we know, the meaning of any dream is camouflaged, and here's how a therapist might decode this one. The most telling detail is the French language itself. Why French? Well, a good many of my filmmaking heroes are French. Perhaps the dream has to do with my fear that I'll never accomplish anything as great as the directors I admire. Fair enough, but with a little free association, maybe there's more to unpack. French, after all, is the language of love. Why is everyone fluent in the language of love except me? A therapist might suggest that the unconscious (the French crew) is fluent whereas the ego (yours truly) is blocked. In other words, a simple dream about being caught unprepared may have deeper implications for the creative process in general.

Here's a version of the "unprepared" dream specific to episodic television directing. The premise: I've been asked to return to a long-running series after an extended absence. During my time away, the series has flourished and expanded, with a host of new characters, locations, and story lines. I have not kept up with the show, and when I arrive, nothing is familiar. One particularly intense dream found me directing an episode of *Malcolm in the Middle*. In reality, I directed nineteen episodes of *Malcolm*, the most I've contributed to any series. In the dream, I was invited back to the show after an absence of nearly thirty years. Remarkably, the series was still on the air. The cast had grown exponentially; the young characters were now middle-aged, with large families of their own. Each of these families occupied homes I didn't recognize. The set was monstrous, spanning the entire back lot of a studio. It was a *Malcolm* megalopolis.

The "show bible," in which all story lines are cataloged, filled hundreds of volumes, each too cumbersome to hold. Not bothering to reacquaint myself with the show—having failed to watch the last seven hundred episodes—I am hopelessly lost. A graph the size of a billboard outlines all the character relationships, but it would take me weeks to read, and I am already late to the set. But which set? The place is overrun with people, hundreds of them, all strangers to me, moving in every direction. To my relief, I spot the familiar—if now wrinkled—face of an original cast member, but he doesn't recognize me and drifts into the crowd. Tailing him,

I shout, "Don't you remember? I used to work here!" I pursue the actor until I find myself on a high precipice, overlooking *Malcolmopolis*. I've lost sight of him; worse, I suddenly realize the structure I'm perched on is fake.

It's a television set, after all. I try to keep my balance, but of course I fall.

Falling is a familiar feature of anxiety dreams and can be read in many ways. It could reflect a sense of being out of control. Work-wise, it could represent failure at not having accomplished a task. In my dreams, falling often coincides with the moment I'm revealed to be an imposter, when I can no longer hide the fact that I didn't do my homework, that I have no clue what I'm doing. When it comes to being unmasked as a fraud, I'm happy to report that I'm in very good directorial company. In 8½, Fellini's alter ego, Guido Anselmi (Marcello Mastroianni), feels artistically bankrupt; he spends most of the picture unsure of the story he's supposed to be telling. Guido's convinced he has nothing to say, and in the celebrated opening scene, he escapes from his suffocating creative block by floating above the world. The freedom from responsibility is short-lived, though, as Guido—his ankle tethered to a rope—is unceremoniously yanked back to earth.

Charlie Chaplin's *The Circus* is not about a film director per se, but it is a very personal story about the nature of comedy, and the climactic scene resembles countless dreams I've had about trying to persuade people that I know what I'm doing. In the scene, Rex, the circus's handsome tightrope walker (Harry Crocker), is late for his matinée performance. With the audience clamoring for a show, the ringmaster sends Chaplin in as a substitute. The property man rigs a device that suspends Chaplin in the air, creating the illusion that he can walk the tightrope. As you might expect, the device fails and Chaplin desperately attempts to maintain his balance (read: avoid being exposed as a fraud). Chaplin the director adds a truly nightmarish touch: a quartet of circus monkeys frolics on the tightrope before climbing onto Chaplin's head. One bites his nose, while another sticks its tail into Chaplin's mouth. It's horrifying. And hilarious.

François Truffaut's *Day for Night* features Truffaut as the director of the film within the film. During the story, Truffaut has a recurrent dream in which a young boy steals lobby cards from a movie theater late at night. The lobby cards are from *Citizen Kane,* and when I first saw *Day for Night* as a teenager, I had a simplistic interpretation of the dream—namely, that it was about young Truffaut's anxiety over getting caught stealing Orson Welles lobby cards. Years later, as a working director, it became clear to me that the dream is about Truffaut's anxiety over getting caught stealing Orson Welles's ideas, that he will be exposed as someone who's only as good as the ideas he pilfers from others.

TOTALLY PREPARED

On the flip side are dreams in which I know exactly what I'm doing. I am focused and articulate; yet, I can't accomplish anything. Every element, from an innocent prop to the weather itself, conspires against me.

These dreams feature a cascade of calamities, surreal versions of the challenges I routinely face on a set. Plus, there's plenty of falling. Stuntmen leap from rooftops before the cameras roll. In a forest scene, a tree falls in the middle of a take. I find myself directing from atop a telephone pole or a Ferris wheel, invariably tumbling from each.

Actors bump into each other because they can't figure out whose marks are whose. Even the law of gravity won't comply; actors are unable to hit their marks because they're hovering in midair. And complaining about it. While on location, the sun unaccountably sets at noon. This dream mirrors a real event that took place early in my career. I was shooting an exterior scene in mid-December in the town of Montclair, New Jersey. At 4:00 p.m., with much of the scene yet to shoot, the sun dipped below the horizon. Darkness quickly enveloped the set, and we erected a battery of HMI lights, designed to simulate daylight. We fired up so many of them, however, that it caused a gigantic power outage—in the middle of a take, the entire neighborhood suddenly went black.

My furious producer quickly laid the blame at my feet. Had I planned my shots better—had I been more prepared—we wouldn't have blown out the power over a three-mile radius. For this fledgling director, a mere six months out of film school, it was mortifying. And I'm sure I've been processing this snafu over the course of many dreams.

DREAM CAST

Starring in my dreams is a crazy quilt of people I've worked with over the years. A bit player I haven't given a waking thought to in decades will appear alongside Robin Williams, with whom I worked on *License to Wed*. A girl I dated in high school will randomly pop up next to Seth Rogen's character from *Freaks and Geeks*. I use the word *randomly* with caution, as dream interpreters argue that no one makes an incidental walk-on in a dream. Jungians, in particular, believe that every person in a dream represents some aspect of the dreamer. In addition to past colleagues, my dreams feature a stock company of authority figures who take turns making my life miserable, among them teachers, priests, and one particular nun. I single out for consideration Sister Clementine, who oversaw my second-grade class. Unlike nuns who doled out everyday abuse (e.g., a rap on the knuckles), Sister Clementine excelled in weird mind games. After several girls complained about my rambunctious behavior during recess (I was chasing them, I admit it), Sister Clementine stood me up in front of the class and announced, "Ken, if you like being around the girls so much, perhaps we should get you a uniform like theirs." The class broke out laughing, but even as a seven-year-old, I knew Sister Clementine's reprimand was a little strange: let's embarrass Ken by threatening to put him in a dress.

Sister Clementine shows up in more than a few of my production dreams, there to stifle me in some new and ingenious manner. Why her? Well, once upon a time, Sister Clementine humiliated me for expressing my boyish self. In that sense, she's no different from the executives and producers I work with who question my instincts and squash my ideas. Again, the Jungian believes that everyone in a dream stands for some aspect of the dreamer. In other words, Sister Clementine doesn't represent other people at all. Perhaps she personifies all those self-censoring mechanisms I've internalized over time, all the constraints baked into my creative process. She's essentially the Standards and Practices Department of my psyche.

META-DREAMS

The dreams I've described thus far focus on the travails of production. I've also had dreams in which the dream itself is the film I'm directing. The phrase *lucid dream,* coined by Dutch psychiatrist Frederik van Eeden, refers to a dream in which you are aware you're dreaming. In my "meta-dreams," I actually have control over the dream. I am aware of the *film grammar* employed in the dream, and my anxiety often stems from the fact that I haven't *covered* the dream sufficiently. My fear is the dream won't *cut.* Conversely, I once had a meta-dream with a long, languorous passage, and even while dreaming, I assured myself that I could tighten up the dream in the editing room. It's as if I'm standing outside the dream even as I'm experiencing it. Of course, "standing outside" my dream produces another kind of anxiety. If, as a director, I'm observing my own dream, perhaps it means I'm not fully asleep. Distressed that I won't get a good night's rest, I try to quit *directing* the dream in order to enter it completely.

One of the greatest "lucid" or "meta" dreams in movie history occurs in Buster Keaton's *Sherlock Jr.,* in which Buster plays a movie theater projectionist who falls asleep on the job, whereupon he dreams of entering the very film he's projecting. Once "inside" the film, he finds himself at the mercy of the *mise-en-scène* itself, as the simplest transition from one scene to the next—a cut—proves treacherous for Buster.

Another great example of a lucid dream about movies is Delmore Schwartz's haunting short story "In Dreams Begin Responsibilities." The nameless hero of the story has a dream in which he finds himself in a movie theater. On-screen, he's shocked to find, is a movie starring his own parents. It's the story of their courtship—specifically, the day the hero's father proposes to his mother. The hero leaps from his seat and yells at the screen, "Don't do it! It's not too late to change your minds, both of you. Nothing good will come of it, only remorse, hatred, scandal, and two children whose characters are monstrous." Unlike my meta-dreams, in which I have some control over the proceedings, the protagonist of Schwartz's story has no choice but to witness the events that will inevitably lead to his own birth. As author Irving Howe acutely noted about the story, "The past revived must obey its own unfolding, true to the law of mistakes. The reel must run its course: it cannot be cut; it cannot be edited." Our hero continues to harangue the screen until an usher finally drags him up the aisle, reprimanding him with beautifully twisted logic. "You can't act like this even if other people aren't around," says the usher as he ejects the young man from the theater, effectively kicking the dreamer out of his own dream.

Unlike the hapless hero of Schwartz's story, I don't want to be ejected from the theater. I want to stay, observe, and take notes. It's like having your own private cinematheque. Night after night, personal issues are revived and reconstituted in wonderfully cinematic form. You don't have to pay for parking, and the admission is free. There are no commercials or trailers, just the main attraction. It's an awfully good resource for anyone in the business of creating collective dreams. So, whether you're planning a comic dream scene (e.g., the delirious bowling dream in *The Big Lebowski*) or designing a nerve-racking set piece (e.g., putting your hero on a tightrope full of monkeys); whether you're exploring the nature of dreaming itself (e.g., Christopher Nolan's *Inception*) or trying to imbue a straightforward story with dreamlike elements (e.g., the assaultive *Uncut Gems*); in every case, try to be mindful of the auteur at work in your unconscious. There's an inspiring feature playing there every night.

WHAT MAKES SAMMY CLIMB?

I wasn't in a great frame of mind as I put on my best suit and drove from my home in the Hollywood Hills to a theater in Century City. The drive wouldn't take long, because it was Sunday morning, which is precisely why I was in a bit of a funk. The powers that be at 20th Century Fox decided to schedule the premiere of my fourth feature, *Dunston Checks In,* at 10:00 a.m. on a Sunday. I felt demoralized. The studio was marginalizing the picture, sticking it in the kiddie corner. Granted, *Dunston* is a film about the friendship between an eight-year-old boy and an orangutan. It's not Ingmar Bergman's *Persona*. But please . . . ten o'clock in the morning? Would it have been so terrible to premiere the film in the afternoon? The executives who made this decision were no doubt at home in their pajamas. Happily, the theater was full, but as the lights went down, I sank into my seat and sent my customary prayer to the movie gods: "Don't let me be embarrassed."

In brief, here's the story that unspooled (yes—*unspooled; Dunston* belongs to the pre-digital era) before that Sunday morning crowd: A debonair jewel thief, Lord Rutledge (Rupert Everett) checks into the Majestic Hotel with his orangutan accomplice, Dunston. After a successful robbery, Dunston flees the clutches of his sadistic master and hides in the hotel, whereupon he befriends eight-year-old Kyle Grant (Eric Lloyd), whose father, Robert (Jason Alexander), manages the Majestic. A prominent hotel critic (Glenn Shadix) is secretly embedded among the guests, and hotelier Mrs. Dubrow (Faye Dunaway) fears that a runaway orangutan will destroy the Majestic's chances for a tip-top rating. She enlists the aid of a demented animal exterminator (Paul Reubens), ordering him to eliminate Dunston by any means necessary.

After the screening, I dutifully shook a lot of hands, fielded a fair number of compliments, and made mental notes about whose kudos seemed genuine. The mood was buoyant, but somehow I didn't trust it. Fox's support for the film felt tentative and middling. It's tough to pour your heart and soul into a project, only to realize the studio considers it a mere programmer. Then, Glenn Shadix—the undercover hotel critic in *Dunston*—approached me with an elderly woman at his side. I had no clue who she was. Did Glenn invite his mother to the screening? I shook the woman's delicate hand, and Glenn introduced her. "Ken, I'd like you to meet my date for the premiere, Eleanor Keaton." I froze. I couldn't believe it. I was shaking hands with Buster Keaton's widow, Eleanor. She was, I learned, seventy-eight years old. Two years later, she would pass away from a long battle with cancer.

But on this crisp January morning in 1996, she was bubbly and full of unalloyed enthusiasm for *Dunston Checks In*. Still clutching my hand, she announced, "Buster would have loved this movie." Let me state for the record that this is the most mind-blowing compliment I have ever received. And Eleanor didn't stop there. "Buster would have been tickled by your reference to *Steamboat Bill, Jr.,*" she added.

Okay, this plaudit needs a quick translation. In Keaton's feature *Steamboat Bill, Jr.,* the foppish title character (Keaton) returns home from college sporting a pencil-thin mustache and an artsy beret. Steamboat Bill Sr. (Ernest Torrence) insists on buying a manly hat for his twee offspring, and Keaton creates a brilliant set piece in which he models a multitude of hats, from a bowler to a boater—there's even a nod to Keaton's signature porkpie hat. In *Dunston Checks In,* the simian title character breaks into a wealthy woman's hotel room, but before absconding with her precious pendants, he is distracted by her hat collection. Dunston plants himself before the vanity mirror and tries on each of her frilly hats. In fact, before I shot this scene, I watched the Keaton version many times.

Flabbergasted, I managed to confirm that Dunston's hat show was a deliberate homage to Eleanor's late husband. As others pressed forward to offer their congrats, Glenn and Eleanor disappeared into the crowd. I never saw her again. The pique I felt at the studio's second-class treatment of my film suddenly seemed irrelevant. The widow of one of history's great comic minds had just given *Dunston* the ultimate seal of approval: "Buster would have loved this movie."

When I first read the screenplay of *Dunston,* written by John Hopkins and Bruce Graham, two things appealed to me immediately. First, the entire story takes place under one roof, a luxury lodging in Manhattan. Not to drag Aristotle into this, but I love stories that observe the unities of time, place, and action, as first expounded in Aristotle's *Poetics*. With *Dunston*, there is a unity of place and action. Single father Robert Grant not only manages the hotel but lives there with his two sons, Kyle and Brian (Graham Sack). The workplace is their home. The workplace is also Kyle and Brian's playground, and the prospect of Kyle and his thirteen-year-old brother having the run of a magnificent hotel, privy to all its secret passages—from the boiler room to the rooftop—enabling the duo to pull pranks on insufferable guests, was irresistible.

Second, the script was jammed with sight gags and physical comedy. It was a great opportunity to get serious about slapstick, the perfect project to pay homage to comedies and comic directors I've admired. Many of those directors were responsible for ingenious comedies set in hotels, among them Peter Bogdanovich (*What's Up, Doc?*), Jerry Lewis (*The Bellboy*), and Jacques Tati (*Monsieur Hulot's Holiday*). The climactic scene in *Dunston* takes place at a black-tie gala in the Majestic's enormous ballroom. The event is hosted by Faye Dunaway's imperious Mrs. Dubrow, a character modeled on the famously tyrannical hotelier Leona Helmsley (a.k.a. the Queen of Mean). Dunston slips into the room, and havoc naturally ensues, building to the moment in which he leaps from a chandelier onto Mrs. Dubrow, and she tumbles backward into a giant cake. I was excited to take a deep dive into pastry-related comedy, from the Three Stooges' *In the Sweet Pie and Pie* to the epic pie fight in Blake Edwards's *The Great Race*, a scene that reportedly utilized no fewer than four thousand pies. With all these comic role models in mind, I had yet to make the Keaton connection. But that was shortly to come.

My only misgiving about the project was its hero. Did I really want to make a monkey movie? Did I really want to follow in the footsteps of such fare as Disney's *The Monkey's Uncle*, starring Tommy Kirk, Annette Funicello, and a chimp named Stanley? At this point, I should mention that I was ignorant about a basic zoological fact. I shared my apprehension about monkey movies with a friend who promptly set me straight: "Ken, an orangutan is not a monkey. An orangutan is an ape." Oh. How did I not know this? Chagrined by this gap in my knowledge, it occurred to me that I didn't know much of anything about orangutans. I barely knew what one looked like. And it was only when I encountered a live orangutan that I made the Keaton connection. An orangutan's face is perfectly deadpan. Totally stone-faced. Like the Great Stone Face himself, Buster Keaton. With that, everything came into focus: Dunston, like Buster, would be the stoic center of a three-ring spectacle, unflappable in the face of chaos, levelheaded and self-possessed while others are hysterical. Most importantly, this would be my first opportunity to direct a silent star.

I quickly learned two things about orangutans, the first of which made me particularly excited to direct one. Orangutans are generally considered the most intelligent of all nonhuman primates. Their cognitive faculties, creative tool-making skills, sophisticated social organization, and linguistic capabilities have been well documented. The second thing I learned gave me real pause.

Orangutans are dying at an alarming rate. They can only be found in the rain forests of Malaysia and Indonesia. The

International Union for Conservation of Nature (IUCN) estimates that one hundred thousand orangutans currently survive in the wild, but by 2025, that number will dwindle to forty-seven thousand. The decimation of the orangutan is the result of several factors, all human-related. The conversion of vast tracts of rain forest to palm oil plantations has shrunk their natural habitat. They are killed for bushmeat, considered a delicacy in some corners of the globe. Orangutans are hunted and sold as pets; in fact, mother orangutans are murdered to sell their babies on the underground pet market. Conservationists have undertaken the near impossible task of retrieving these orphan orangutans and rehabilitating them into the wild, none more celebrated than primatologist Dr. Biruté Galdikas. What Dian Fossey did for mountain gorillas and Jane Goodall for chimpanzees, Biruté does for the critically endangered orangutan.

In January of 1995, the month I began prep on *Dunston,* the Orangutan Foundation International hosted a book-signing event for Dr. Galdikas in Pasadena. She was on the stump, promoting her just-published memoir, *Reflections of Eden: My Years with the Orangutans of Borneo.* Galdikas was a compelling speaker, and her passion for these primates, not to mention her advocacy for rain forest conservation in general, was exhilarating. I felt inspired . . . and stymied. How do I justify making a film with an animal that's well on its way to extinction? Was there a way to honor this imperiled species in a movie otherwise packed with boisterous antics? Could I fashion a moment that hinted at the danger orangutans face? Am I the only director who turns a knockabout comedy assignment into a major moral conundrum?

While wrestling with this dilemma, I met animal trainer Larry Madrid, who arrived for our meeting accompanied by a four-year-old orangutan named Sammy. They walked into the room, hand in hand. A second-generation, captive-bred orangutan born in a Miami eco-adventure park called Parrot Jungle, Sammy had a youthful gait but deep-sunk eyes circled with old-man wrinkles. His face had both the innocence of a cherub and the melancholy of an ancient seer. There were others in the room, but Sammy intuited that I was someone to regard and locked eyes with me. Was he simply curious, or was he sizing me up—was *he* auditioning *me*? Perhaps Sammy considered this a "chemistry" meeting, to determine whether he, the simian star, was comfortable with me, the human helmer. Extending one arm in a languorous reach, Sammy ruffled my hair. I guess I passed the test.

Sammy moved into Larry Madrid's house in Los Angeles for twenty-two weeks of training. Larry had two sons, six and eight years old, which afforded Sammy the chance to socialize with children. Larry spent every waking hour with Sammy. At the dinner table, there would be a chair for Sammy. If Larry was doing yard work, Sammy would climb a nearby tree. Over the course of the training period, they touched on every scene in the script. Each piece of business would be finessed on the shooting day, but what astonished me is how Sammy committed to memory myriad behaviors, including a few stunts. To rehearse Dunston's climactic leap from the chandelier, Larry taught forty-pound Sammy to jump from a tree into his arms, after which Larry would give Sammy a huge hug, signaling that this odd bit of business was a positive behavior. As I described earlier, Dunston dives straight into the doyenne of doom, hurtling her into a massive cake. To refine the stunt, Larry had Sammy jump into his arms, at which point, Larry would quickly sit down in a chair. Once Sammy became accustomed to that modification, Larry would catch Sammy and fall over backward. "Sammy was a sponge," Larry told me, "always curious, excited to learn, and he didn't forget a thing." I asked Larry to rate Sammy's intelligence, and he replied, "Orangutans—they're half a chromosome away from us."

20th Century Fox did not trust that a real orangutan could perform all the action in the script, which included scaling the side of the hotel, crawling through its duct work, donning a ninja outfit, taking a bubble bath, giving an unsuspecting woman a back massage, along with the belly flop into Mrs. Dubrow. The studio demanded that we build an orangutan suit to be worn by a small actor. The costume would feature a sculpted head cast in soft foam latex and mechanized with remote controls for facial movements. The spandex bodysuit would consist of yak belly hair knotted into the material, along with extended arms sculpted in an ape-appropriate walking position. Despite the meticulous craftsmanship, the finished suit looked like, well, a suit.

To comply with the studio's request, we hired a two-foot, eight-inch man—he was one of the shortest people on the planet—to wear the orangutan costume. Over the course of our sixty-day shooting schedule, Sammy was not only game to perform in every scene but his performance grew increasingly polished. In what became a ritual at the close of each shooting day, I apologized to our very patient actor. In the end, we couldn't justify keeping him on the payroll, so one afternoon, I bid a heartfelt goodbye to the fellow who had waited in vain to wear that studio-mandated ape suit. Cut to: three years later. That actor, Verne Troyer, became a movie star, creating the iconic role of Mini-Me, the Lilliputian clone of archnemesis Dr. Evil in *Austin Powers: The Spy Who Shagged Me.*

Among the humans in the cast of *Dunston* was Faye Dunaway. Deserved or not, she has a singularly formidable reputation, but when we met for lunch at the Four Seasons Hotel in Beverly Hills, she positively gushed at the prospect of starring in a slapstick comedy opposite an ape. I reminded the Academy Award winner that the script required her to catch a flying orangutan and plummet into a monstrous cake. She leveled a serious gaze and declared, "Ken, I will fall into that cake as many times as you want." I didn't mention the fact that our budget would only accommodate three cakes, but I couldn't argue with Faye's genuine determination to do a pratfall into a mountain of frosting.

One reason Faye was available to star in *Dunston* was that she had just left the touring company of Andrew Lloyd Webber's musical *Sunset Boulevard*. I had no information about her unceremonious departure, and I had no intention of asking Faye about the matter. It did, however, come into play when we shot the climactic scene. After Dunston upends Mrs. Dubrow's gala, she locks eyes with her simian adversary, with murderous intent. Before her close-up, Faye took our first assistant director aside and handed him a small square of newspaper, folded over several times. "Please stand by the camera," Faye said. "And when I hit my mark, hold this up for me to see." The camera rolled, Faye hit her mark, the first assistant director held up the scrap of paper, and Faye delivered a spine-chilling glare. I called cut and quickly found out what inspired her incomparable reaction: clipped from the newspaper was a photograph of Andrew Lloyd Webber. File under: *Turn Your Pain into Art.*

The *Dunston* ensemble was a wonderfully eclectic lot. Jason Alexander was eager to play a character distinct from his popular role on *Seinfeld.* The studio, however, had a decidedly different point of view. When Jason insisted on a hairpiece, the head of 20th Century Fox called me on the proverbial carpet. "Don't you understand, Kwapis? We didn't hire Jason Alexander. We hired George Costanza!" I calmly replied that the Majestic Hotel would never hire George Costanza as its manager, and after much grousing, the studio chief relented. For the role of Lord Rutledge, Rupert Everett made a style choice that caused another needless kerfuffle. Rather than lean into his naturally dashing good looks, Rupert chose to play Rutledge as a dandified bounder in homage to the various twits and cads created by English comic Terry-Thomas; indeed, he wore a gap in his upper front teeth à la Terry-Thomas. Again, the head of the studio protested, and the gist of his argument was: we hired these people to play types for which they're already known. Why would you muck it up by actually letting them create . . . characters?

During the shoot, Sammy approached each scene like a game, relishing the opportunity to hit multiple marks and perform bits with precision and élan. Was this acting? Well, Sammy was certainly more focused than many humans I've directed. Though I conveyed my notes to Larry Madrid, Sammy listened attentively, seemingly aware that whatever I was blathering about had some relevance to his work. On occasion, I simply forgot that Sammy was an orangutan and delivered my notes directly to him.

Dunston ends happily, with Robert, Kyle, Brian, and the titular hero now ensconced at the Majestic Hotel in Bali. We glimpse Dunston atop a palm tree on the hotel's property, along with his new mate (played by Geri, Sammy's half sister). While not exactly the rain forests of Borneo or Sumatra, Dunston's new home is at least in the right hemisphere.

Sammy retired from acting four years after *Dunston,* but unlike the orphans rehabilitated by Dr. Galdikas, he was too old and too domesticated to acclimate to the rain forests of Southeast Asia. He spent his autumnal years in a primate sanctuary in Wauchula, Florida, called the Center for Great Apes. The preserve is home to primates rescued from the exotic pet trade or retired from show business. I can easily imagine the retirees chewing the fat and trading war stories about their Hollywood years. Half sibling Geri followed Sammy to the sanctuary, where the two became real-life mates, producing a baby named Jam. Years later, I received a photo of twenty-year-old Sammy, and he looked quite majestic. His reddish-brown hair was long, his face boasted wide cheek pads, and his fingers were the size of cigars. Orangutans cherish their solitude, and I trust the center provided an environment where Sammy could at least pretend to be a creature in the wild, even if he knew in his heart he would live out his days in a man-made place. Every so often, he might even have a faint recollection of that wonderful game he played long ago, in front of that odd, rectangular-shaped box.

PLAYABLE NOTES

Some directors have wonderful tricks and devices for pulling performances. Norman Taurog is an expert. When he wanted to make me cry, he'd take me into a corner and ask me to think about what would happen if my little boy was hit by a truck.

—JERRY LEWIS, *THE TOTAL FILM-MAKER*

Godard has a knack for making people around him feel awkward, and then using that to bring out tensions in the script.

—PHILLIP LOPATE, *CONTEMPT: THE STORY OF A MARRIAGE*

I earned a bachelor's degree in filmmaking at one university. I attended another to obtain a master of fine arts in the same. I took umpteen number of film classes over nearly seven years, but not once did I take an acting class. Neither school required me to do so. One film department focused on experimental filmmaking, and learning to elicit a good performance was not just a low priority, it was regarded with suspicion. Acting is about creating and sustaining an illusion, and this school encouraged us to do the opposite: to create films that made the viewer conscious of the filmmaking process. The other curriculum focused on narrative films, but once again, acting got lost in the shuffle. A good performance, we were taught, was less a function of good acting than it was good editing. As you know, I landed a directing job shortly after graduate school, at which point I had the shuddering realization that I didn't have a clue how to talk to actors. I don't want to launch into a grouchy diatribe about this egregious gap in my film school curricula, but this aspect of the director's craft—arguably the most critical one—was something I had to learn on the job.

My most important resource was actors themselves, and over the years, I queried quite a few about their craft, specifically the kinds of notes they welcomed (or rejected) from directors. During a memorable exchange with Peter Falk, with whom I worked on a couple of occasions, I asked about his storied collaboration with director John Cassavetes. He recalled that Cassavetes's notes were exasperating—they made no sense at all. Once, a thoroughly befuddled Falk complained to Cassavetes that his suggestions were, frankly, bonkers.

Cassavetes coolly replied that his goal, indeed, was to keep Falk in a state of confusion. As Falk put it, "John felt that if an actor understood the note—if it made sense—he would no doubt translate it into clichéd behavior." Confounding his actors, for Cassavetes, was a creative strategy. I admit I've confused many an actor in my career, but never with such a shrewd agenda.

I'm always searching for ways to direct with precision, and

a couple of years ago, I was heartened when a cast member took me aside after a scene to offer the following pat on the back: "Ken, you give playable notes." Finding words to unlock your actor's imagination, understanding each character's intention, knowing how that intention fits into the character's overall journey, setting a tone that encourages exploration—ultimately, it's all about finding something . . . to play. To get there, let's start with a process routinely given short shrift during preproduction: the rehearsal.

GETTING TO KNOW YOU

Among the challenges of prep is carving out rehearsal time when you're being pulled in fifteen directions at once—finalizing the schedule, pre-visualizing the film, adjusting the script to accommodate production issues, and scouting locations. In the midst of this chaos, what often gets compromised is time with the actors. Adding to your woes is the fact that busy cast members won't be available until the last minute and the near certainty that your budget won't allow for more than a handful of rehearsal days. I've learned the hard way that it pays to fight for as much rehearsal time as you can get.

What do you do with those measly days? First, you hold a table reading of the script with as many cast members as possible. In addition to the players, it's essential to invite key crew members to the reading, not just to generate esprit de corps but to give everyone a sense of the story's shape and tone.

Staging a reading is a delicate matter. Ideally, the cast

should sit around a table, facing one another. Apart from the director and a designated scene description reader (I often take that job myself and make a point of streamlining the scene description), no one else should penetrate this enclosure. Crew members should sit along the perimeter of the room, outside the circle of actors. I'll stop short of calling it a *sacred space,* but I do consider this a protected area, free of judgment. Many cast members are meeting for the first time, and no one can predict how or whether this ensemble will cohere. The read-through is the first opportunity for a director to establish the tenor of the production, and the first task is to put everyone at ease. I normally give a short speech, which includes three key points:

1 I remind the actors that auditions are officially over; they've got the job. This may sound light and trivial, but the truth is every actor in the room has a lingering fear that the read-through is actually another audition, after which they will no doubt be replaced.

2 I stress to everyone that this is a reading, not a performance. The cast hasn't studied the script yet, let alone memorized their parts. It's possible the script was being revised the previous night. Or even that morning. Insisting that actors refrain from acting is a gift to your cast, but there's a strategic purpose as well. More often than not, your table reading will be attended by studio and/ or network executives, many of whom have agendas that conflict with your own. To be quite blunt, executives don't always have your best interests at heart, and to protect yourself from a lot of nonproductive feedback, it's vital for them to lower their expectations of the reading.

3 The one piece of direction I do give the ensemble is to use the script as a means to get to know one another. I don't care if someone stumbles through a speech. What's more important is that the players enjoy each other's company, that they engage and listen attentively. The reading should feel like a cocktail party without the cocktails. Instead of trading small talk, we read dialogue.

SHOPPING IN CHARACTER

With a less-than-luxurious rehearsal period and no access to actual locations, it's mostly impractical to block scenes. More important is to give actors a chance to build bonds and develop a shorthand. There are, of course, noteworthy examples of actors who felt it necessary to keep their distance from other cast members. In preparing the role of wannabe comic Rupert Pupkin in *The King of Comedy,* Robert De Niro respectfully told costar Jerry Lewis that he didn't want any social contact during the making of the film, the better to engender the sense of alienation that propels De Niro's character to a deranged act of abduction. Those exceptions aside, I feel actors need to spend as much time together as possible, especially if they are playing characters with established relationships—longtime friends, for example.

The Sisterhood of the Traveling Pants tells the story of four lifelong friends, born days apart, now sixteen years old.

The actors, Blake Lively, Amber Tamblyn, Alexis Bledel, and America Ferrera, were new to each other. We had but a few rehearsal days to create the illusion of a tight, unshakable foursome. To quickly form that camaraderie, I designed a couple of exercises. First, I sent them on a shopping expedition to a local thrift store. I instructed each actor to purchase an article of clothing . . . in character. This wasn't a random assignment; a pivotal scene in *Sisterhood* takes place in a thrift store, where the characters discover the eponymous pants. Each actor had a budget of seventy-five dollars, and I told the quartet not to be shy about proffering opinions of their fellow cast members' fashion instincts—in character, of course. Debating how a dress looks on your best friend, defending your own style choices, cajoling a pal into making a bold purchase—the exercise quickly established the dynamic within the group.

In addition to shopping, I gave Blake, Amber, Alexis, and America a writing assignment. In the film, the four friends go their separate ways for the summer, but not before marking the occasion by inaugurating the Sisterhood of the Traveling Pants. I instructed the cast to create a document: the Constitution of the Traveling Pants, a set of bylaws governing the actions of the sisterhood. This document was not part of the story, but I knew that writing it would enrich the way the cast played the inauguration scene. It would be a set of precepts, behavioral guidelines for the "sisters" during their summer apart. I left the foursome alone to create their code of conduct, and they attacked the task with zeal. A bit too much zeal, it turns out. When I returned an hour or so later, the cast had not only finished the document but managed to rewrite all the dialogue in the scene as well. I urged them to trust the original words, but the key takeaway was that the scene now belonged to them. The exercise was a success; the four actors now had a shared history.

JUST THE FACTS

Chief among my goals during rehearsal is to scour the script for simple facts about the characters, ones that help an actor deduce or wholly invent a backstory. This is particularly important for characters who don't have many scenes in a film. During our *Sisterhood* rehearsals, I met with America and Rachel Ticotin, who play Carmen and her mother, respectively. Needless to say, it's a pivotal relationship, though they share little screen time. Rachel's character doesn't even have a name. She's simply "Carmen's Mom."

Although *Sisterhood* is adapted from a novel, I confined myself to the script by Delia Ephron and Elizabeth Chandler, hunting for clues to inspire creative backstory choices. There wasn't a lot to go on, but late in the second act, I found a promising lead. There's a one-eighth-page scene in which Carmen and her mother sing while washing dishes. Here's what precedes the moment: Carmen has returned home after the disastrous visit with her father, and her mother wants to comfort her. In this sliver of a scene, the two luxuriate in a simple, comforting routine. The scene description did not specify a song, which opened up tantalizing possibilities. It's easy to imagine that mother and daughter have sung together before, no doubt in the kitchen while cooking or cleaning. Is this a song Carmen's mother taught her as a child? What associations might the song have? Do they have a repertoire of favorite tunes?

As we explored the possibilities, I was suddenly called away by my producer to resolve a budget issue. I turned over the matter to America and Rachel, instructing them to come up with a tune I could reasonably license for the film. "In other words," I said, "You can't sing 'Hey Jude.'" I hoped for a song that would tell a story. When I returned, I was surprised to find America and Rachel belting a number from *Guys and Dolls*. I wasn't sure how to connect the dots between this mother-daughter duo and Damon Runyon, but the actors were jazzed to discover their mutual love of show tunes. That led to America reminiscing about her childhood dream of performing in musicals. As a young Latinx actor, however, she could only imagine two roles open to her: Maria in *West Side Story* and Morales in *A Chorus Line*. Morales, one of the aspiring chorus members, sings the comic tune "Nothing," about an insufferable acting teacher named Mr. Karp. In the song, Karp asks the class to pretend they're on a bobsled rushing down a snowy hill. Everyone is quick to imagine the cold air and snow on their faces. But not Morales. When pressed by Karp to describe what she feels, Morales replies:

> *And I said . . . "Nothing,*
> *I'm feeling nothing,"*
> *And he says, "Nothing*
> *Could get a girl transferred."*

Without prompting, America launched into the song, Rachel chimed in, and it was like a window opening onto their characters' history. Had Carmen's mother once soothed her daughter's disappointment over not getting a role in a school play—because she was the wrong "type"? Was this their "comfort food" song? "Nothing" was a specific and playable choice, one that would resonate with viewers in a precise way. It was a pricey song to license, by the way, and in the finished film, America and Rachel barely complete a line before a phone call interrupts them, but it was a wonderful example of a seemingly unimportant detail leading to real insight about the characters.

ROOKIE MISTAKES

You've studied the scene and pre-visualized the blocking; now it's time to shoot. Here are a few mistakes I made as a rookie (and occasionally continue to make). First is a time-management misstep that can have an adverse effect on cast morale. If the day's work includes a one-eighth-page scene establishing a location and featuring a bit of shoe-leather on the part of your characters, followed by a substantial three-page dialogue scene, best to take the plunge and shoot the meaty scene first. I've fallen into the trap of dressing up an establishing shot with a complicated camera move, only to discover ninety minutes later that I'm still trying to perfect the shot, one with a better-than-average chance of ending up on the cutting room floor. To be frank, sometimes I dawdle over an establishing shot because I'm apprehensive about the weightier scene. This is more than just a time-management flub. Your cast is geared up for the three-page scene. It's as if you're keeping them seated around a swimming pool, toes dipped in the water, growing anxious. Don't stall; just push everyone into the deep end at the start of the day.

Let's stick with our hypothetical three-page scene. Another common mistake is to block the action before the cast has any sense of the scene. The first order of business is to gather the actors and read the words. No movement. No staging. Just read the dialogue. Actually—wait a moment. I'm skipping a step. The *very* first order of business is to clear the set of all crew members except your first assistant director, your cinematographer, and the script supervisor. These are the only three who should be privy to the rehearsal process. Let crew members grab another cup of coffee; the first assistant director will summon them when you're ready to present a fully blocked scene.

Okay, you've read the words. Without letting things devolve into a marathon discussion, now is the time for you to identify a character's intention, what's at stake, and the tactics he or she might employ to accomplish a goal or negotiate an obstacle (we'll return to tactics shortly). The first assistant director may be breathing down your neck, but it's worth taking the extra moment to ensure that everyone's telling the same story.

Now you get the scene on its feet. As discussed in our chapter on shot lists, when it comes to blocking, a common faux pas is to force the characters to serve the image, rather than create an image that serves the characters. Here's a colorful example. Let's imagine your three-page scene takes place in a villa on the island of Capri. Let's further imagine that you have the wherewithal to bring your entire company to Capri. (If you do, by the way, I'm very jealous.) Your protagonist—we'll call him Giacomo—enters the front door of the villa. On your shot list, Giacomo crosses the room to an open window. In all likelihood, you don't have an organic reason for Giacomo to make that move; you just want him to end up in a place where we can see the Aegean Sea behind him. Face it: the character is serving the image. You have three choices: 1) you admit there's no justification for Giacomo to stand at the window, apart from wanting the production value of the Aegean Sea; 2) you concoct a flimsy reason for Giacomo to cross the room and hope your actor doesn't see through the ruse; 3) you find a collaborative middle ground and the actor freely makes the choice you wanted in the first place. "I'm not sure there's a good reason to end up at the window. Maybe we can find one," would be my opening gambit. If we discover a reason for him to cross the room, but it takes nearly two pages before Giacomo moves, I might add, "It would be great if you weren't stuck in that doorway for most of the scene." If the actor resists moving sooner, you may decide that his motivation for remaining in the doorway is more compelling than your desire to frame him against the sparkling sea. And if the producer upbraids you for failing to exploit the sumptuous backdrop (I have been in this very position, by the way), your counterargument is that overusing the Aegean Sea will diminish its punch—better to save it for the last page of the scene.

Once you finesse the staging, the crew gathers for a blocking rehearsal. Among the crew is the "second team," stand-ins for the cast who replicate the staging so the cinematographer can execute a lighting plan. At this point, the cast is dismissed, and I urge you to take advantage of lighting time to confer with individual actors. There are many things you can accomplish during an intimate sidebar with a cast member. In rehearsal, you already laid the groundwork by establishing a character's intention (e.g., Giacomo wants to persuade his father to loan him money to start a business). But you probably didn't have time to discuss the tactics Giacomo might use to meet his objective. Does he *beg* for the money? Does he *flatter* his father? Does he *coax* him into making the loan? If the stakes are high, Giacomo will use any method to achieve his end. You can break down the action into different stages or "beats"—that is, moments in which the character makes a transition, switches tactics (e.g., from coaxing or joking to demanding or pleading). In a well-written scene, not everything is conveyed verbally, and it's a helpful exercise for an actor to articulate what's not said—to improvise his or her subtext. Looping back to the example of Carmen and her mother, the subtext is based on facts you've discovered and/or extrapolated from the script (Carmen and her mother's longtime love of show tunes). Based on facts gleaned about Giacomo's relationship with his father, you've created a history that forms the scene's subtext. Verbalizing that subtext will help your actor invest the scene with a lived-in reality.

FASTER AND FUNNIER

The cameras are rolling. Your top priority is to guide the cast, to ensure their behavior is honest and compelling. The easiest mistake to make, particularly for a director with no acting background, is to shape a performance with result-oriented notes. "Bring it down." "Make it more intense." "Give me 10 percent less." "Make it faster!" These notes describe a performance level but have nothing to do with the inner life of the character. They are not playable notes. A good actor can translate your result-oriented note into a playable one by substituting an active verb. Let's say Giacomo is coaxing his father into lending him money. If I ask the actor playing Giacomo to "make it more intense," he could mentally replace the verb *coax* with *insist* to create the desired effect. The smarter approach, of course, is for the director to have a ready supply of active verbs, the better to reframe the character's intention in a number of equally valid ways.

For the record, I'm not categorically opposed to result-oriented notes, provided you use them sparingly and choose your words wisely. Instructing actors to "bring it down" is a lackluster way to tell them to stop overacting. My preferred verbiage is: "Keep it simple," or "Keep it conversational," the latter having the added benefit of reminding your player to be an active listener. "Make it faster" is a truly inartful way of telling the cast to energize a scene. After a few takes, I may say, "Don't lose your energy," a note devoid of judgment. Regarding tempo, it's only when the cast has confidently "found" the scene that I suggest, "It's time to pick up the pace." To do so prematurely, before the actors have navigated the beats of the scene, runs the risk of stripping everyone's gears. The cast needs to know what they're playing before they can do it briskly.

My catalog of rookie mistakes includes mood-oriented notes. Yes, characters have feelings, but it's not helpful to ask someone to play a mood. "When Giacomo enters, he's forlorn" is a static note. You may indeed want Giacomo in a particular frame of mind as the scene begins, but try to convert that mood-oriented note into an active one. "Can you enter *as if* you just lost the winning lottery ticket?" Also, I personally steer clear of line readings. If you're an actor-director, giving a line reading may be a legitimate tool. Some directors will argue that a line reading is really a way of explaining the intention of the words to an actor. To my mind, it prevents the actor from truly owning the dialogue. If you need to micromanage a line, syllable by syllable, perhaps you should just cast yourself in the part.

When it comes to notes, remember that one size does not fit all. You must tailor your notes to each player's skill set and temperament. Seasoned actors may insist they need no direction. They do—of course they do!—but it's your job to indulge their need to feel self-sufficient while casually slipping them a suggestion or two. A novice may not have the ability to absorb a note and make the proper adjustment. Up-and-comers often *freeze* their lines—they can only deliver their dialogue one way. It's not your job to teach acting, but it behooves you to loosen things up for that newcomer. Complex notes won't cut it—better to just encourage an untrained actor to listen. The simple act of listening will free his or her mind from a reading that seems hopelessly set in stone.

To keep things loose, I occasionally interrupt the take without calling, "Cut." I'll wander into the shot, make a suggestion—sometimes it's quite arbitrary—then instruct the group to "take it from the top" or resume the scene from a particular moment ("Let's pick it up from Giacomo crossing to the window"). Instead of upholding the take as something inviolable, I try to keep it pliable and playful. Put in a more philosophical way, I don't want the cast to feel compelled to find *anything definitive*. I will never announce, "Circle that take!" or "That's a keeper!" or "You nailed it!" We've been handed a scene and an allotment of time to explore that scene. Let's look at it from different angles, shine a light on it, turn it inside out, then simply move on to another scene.

Lest I forget, while handling crisis after crisis throughout your shooting day, it's easy to neglect actors in minor roles. For example, in our one-eighth-page establishing shot, perhaps Giacomo arrives at the villa and the gardener says, "Good morning." You chose the day player who delivers this innocuous line, and you should instruct that actor to imagine the entire story from the point of view of the gardener. In that version, the gardener is the hero and Giacomo the bit player. By giving the actor one specific note (e.g., the gardener drank too much last night, and he's trying to conceal his hangover from Giacomo), you encourage a day player to create an inner life, adding a layer of reality that—I promise—audiences will feel and appreciate.

KNOWING / NOT KNOWING

The final directorial mistake I want to discuss is a big one, and it applies to far more than your work with actors. When I was fresh out of the gate, I was obsessed with making sure people felt that I knew what I was doing. As I grew more poised and assured, I began to realize that *not knowing* was a kind of strength. I touched on this in our chapter about how to take a meeting. Over time, admitting what I didn't know or wasn't sure about became my secret weapon, particularly when directing actors. "The scene feels flat, but I'm not sure why." Or, "Something's bugging me about this moment, but I can't put my finger on it." Far from being an invitation to a free-for-all, such an admission can bring out the best in actors, who now feel like valued members of the storytelling team. It doesn't undercut your authority in the least; quite the opposite, it speaks to a deep level of confidence. Not only is it inclusive, it also reinforces the primacy of process over outcome. It reminds your cast that the adventure of looking for an answer is ultimately more important than any answer you might find.

WALKING WITH BERNIE

I could tell you I was hired to help launch *The Bernie Mac Show* because I was a Bernie aficionado, that I'd loyally followed his career since the beginning, that while attending college in lily-white Evanston, Illinois, I would routinely hop the "L" for the south side to catch his act at Chicago's Cotton Club. I could tell you that I used to parrot his banter ("I ain't scared o' you moth-afuckas"), that I monitored his rise on the new Chitlin' Circuit, that I was a fan of his early film work, could argue the merits of his performance as Judge Peabody in *Booty Call* to any nay-sayer, and that I had a front-row seat for the record-breaking Original Kings of Comedy tour.

I could tell you this, but none of it would be true. When I read Larry Wilmore's script for *The Bernie Mac Show* pilot, Mr. Mac's substantial career was barely a blip on my radar. My work on *Malcolm in the Middle* recommended me to Larry, but I read his script with some trepidation. I wasn't keen to tackle another family comedy, and who exactly was this Ber-nie Mac anyway? After reading the first page, however, I was completely hooked. Above all, what struck me was the bluntness of the main character, named Bernie.

The script opens with Bernie addressing the audience. Needless to say, breaking the fourth wall is hardly unique in television comedy. George Burns did it week after week; Frankie Muniz, playing the title character of *Malcolm in the Middle,* routinely interrupts the action for a sidebar with the audience. What was different about Bernie was the ballsy manner in which he broke that proverbial wall. Quite simply, his salutation to viewers was: I ain't scared o' you mothafuckas. The moment the story begins, Bernie informs us that he's thoroughly aggravated by the three young children who have come to live with him and that at some point he will probably kill them.

```
              BERNIE
           (to camera)
    I'm going to kill one of those
    kids. Don't get me wrong, I love
    'em; they're my blood; I'd give them
    the shirt off my back, okay? But
    I'm going to kill one of 'em. You
    ever see a chicken get his neck
    wrung? Try me. You little . . .
           (imitates wringing a
           chicken's neck)
    Snap!
```

Clearly, we are not in the Cleaver neighborhood. Equally compelling was the fact that the show's premise was steeped in sadness. In the post-cable/streaming era, there is no shortage of comedies with dark undercurrents. I directed episodes of Tig Notaro's *One Mississippi*; among the cheery subjects it treats are breast cancer and the sexual abuse of children. But when Larry wrote this script, the notion of mixing comedy and trauma was pretty novel, particularly for network television. The inciting incident of *The Bernie Mac Show,* inspired by events in Bernie's real life, is that his sister can no longer raise her children because she's a drug addict. After a Chicago court deems her unfit, the kids are shipped off to live with their uncle in Los Angeles. Aside from being irritated by his young charges, Bernie has absolutely no sympathy for his sister:

> BERNIE
> (to camera)
> America, let's talk, we're family.
> I'm not ashamed to tell you this.
> My sister's a drug addict, okay?
> Some people call it a disease.
> No, it's not. She's weak. She had a
> choice. "Bernie Mac, you cold."
> You damn right I'm cold. But I'm
> not high. How're you gonna raise
> kids high? They deserve better.
> I'm sorry, this is how I feel,
> America. I can't help how I feel.

So, in the first scene of the show, Bernie unapologetically condemns his drug-addled sister and defies anyone to judge him. Many pugnacious characters have graced the small screen (Ralph Kramden and Archie Bunker come to mind), but I'd never encountered anyone quite this bellicose. And this was only page one. It was like opening the front door of your house and having a stranger yell at you. Of course, for a great many viewers, Bernie was no stranger.

To prepare for my meeting with Bernie, I gave myself a crash course in his work. I caught a matinée of Spike Lee's concert film *The Original Kings of Comedy,* which had opened a couple of weeks earlier. Bernie's performance was volcanic, and I had a hard time imagining how it would translate to the intimate format of a single-camera series. I was reassured by the fact that his material was never jokey. He told personal stories, more than a few of which revealed a life of struggle and pain. Still, his high-definition, outsize performance seemed better suited to a multi-camera series, a format that encourages playing to the rafters.

In fact, Bernie wanted none of that. He turned down numerous offers to do a series in front of a live audience. He wanted a different relationship to the viewer, one that was low-key and personal. In the pilot, when Bernie speaks to "America," it actually feels like he's confiding something private to you, his trusted friend. Some characters break the fourth wall with a certain insouciance (e.g., Ferris Bueller, Groucho Marx), but Bernie breaks the wall to unload his feelings. He wanted a rapport with the viewer that seemed more akin to, say, therapy than to vaudeville. The conventional wisdom is that you break the fourth wall to disrupt the illusion, to create an intellectual distance from the material. That was the crux of Brecht's "distancing effect." Bernie, on the other hand, wanted to break the wall to bring you inside, to strengthen your emotional involvement. Call it the *endearment effect.* Paradoxically, the artifice enhances the intimacy, which was exactly what the show's creator, Larry Wilmore, had in mind.

As I mentioned, Larry had seen my work on *Malcolm in the Middle,* with its robust, in-your-face visuals. The performance style of *Malcolm* was equally robust and in-your-face. Everything was pitched at a high-octane level; in other words, the visual approach and performance style were completely in sync. What Larry envisioned for *The Bernie Mac Show* was a series that would be down-to-earth yet stylistically flexible. For example, an understated moment might be followed by a surreal interlude. My job, as the pilot director, was to set a tone that accommodated these divergent—possibly conflicting— approaches. At our first meeting, Larry said he was eager for bold, stylistic strokes, so I went for broke and pitched the idea of using jump cuts in the show. This led to a lively discussion about Jean-Luc Godard's use of jump cuts in *Breathless.* Whether jump cuts became part of the show's grammar was unimportant. What mattered was Larry inviting me to join the hunt for something new. By the way, helping a showrunner discover his or her vision doesn't mean you're not bringing your own to bear on the piece. For me, much of the pleasure of directing a pilot—of setting the house style for a series—is figuring out where my vision and the showrunner's intersect. With Larry, the Venn diagram of our respective instincts really overlapped. Even if we didn't have the answers, we were excited by the same questions. Now, only one question remained: Would the star feel the same way?

I arrived early for my dinner with Bernie, our rendezvous point a fashionable restaurant in a Beverly Hills hotel. The hostess seated me, and I checked my watch: plenty of time to get nervous. A business meeting over dinner has its own challenges. Does ordering a cocktail signal a lack of seriousness? By not ordering a drink, are you advertising yourself as uptight? How soon does one segue from small talk to business? Before or after ordering the meal? Often, I've made the mistake of plunging into my pitch too soon, and by the time the food arrives, I've completely run out of things to say. For the remainder of the meal, I circle back to points I've already made and repeat them less effectively.

Unlike an interview where a desk sits between you and your prospective boss, a dinner meeting demands social graces (e.g., not forgetting to put the napkin on your lap) and interpersonal skills (e.g., the ability to share a personal story, hopefully one that's germane to the business at hand). I don't fancy myself a natural raconteur. I have a repertoire of approximately six anecdotes designed to create the impression that: 1) I have something resembling a sense of humor; 2) I'm a confident director but also a good colleague; 3) I won't suck the air out of the room. This last point is particularly crucial when meeting the star. It's the star's prerogative to suck the air out of the room, and your job to let them.

A wave of doubt came over me. What did I possibly have in common with Bernie Mac? Well, we were both born in Illinois. In 1957. Apart from that, our backgrounds could not be more dissimilar, our cultural coordinates poles apart. Bernie gained prominence the hard way. He did stand-up for spare change in the Chicago subways. While honing his craft, he worked as a janitor in a dentist's office and as a Wonder Bread deliveryman. I went to a high-priced college and waltzed into a directing job the moment I left school. I could be the poster child for white privilege.

Now officially tense, I recalled once meeting a crass producer who asked me if I had any "urban cred." I didn't have a clue how to answer. Putting a finer point on it, he queried, "What kind of music do you listen to in your car?" Okay, the radio in my Volvo was set to a classical station featuring white guys who've been dead for a couple of hundred years. (As a tangent to this tangent, I once lost the chance to direct a zombie show pilot because, I was told, I lacked "zombie cred.")

Thankfully, Bernie made his entrance before I could go further down this rabbit hole. He was flanked by an entourage of two ("My boys," he called them). Saying Bernie cut an imposing figure is an understatement. More accurate is that he exerted a gravitational pull. For all his famous gruffness, his smile was gentle and beckoning. As I quickly discovered, what made Bernie unique was that he was as tender as he was tough.

To my surprise, Bernie was genuinely curious about me. I rarely meet stars who aim the spotlight away from themselves, but that's what Bernie did. He asked about my childhood in southern Illinois and about my children. I mentioned that my two young boys were going through an intense sibling rivalry, each resentful of the other's abilities, each determined to undercut the other in cruel if cunning ways.

Regaling Bernie with tales of my kids torturing each other, it suddenly occurred to me that my sons were the same age as Bernie's young charges in the script. Maybe I had some cred after all. Dad cred. Bernie and I compared notes on the many mistakes we'd made as fathers (his daughter was twenty-three at the time). The patented anecdotes I'd prepared, designed to impress the star, no longer applied. Bernie steered the conversation straight to the essential matter—namely, what is the right way to raise a child? In the script, Bernie's point of view on parenting is often wrongheaded, but his commitment to that point of view is unshakable. Bernie told me he simply says out loud what other parents feel but are afraid to say. In that moment, he handed me the key to the show.

After Bernie graciously picked up the tab, we walked to the valet stand. As we crossed the palatial lobby, everyone we passed seemed to know Bernie. Some stars have an aura about them that positively screams, "Keep your distance!" Other luminaries parade in public like monarchs greeting their subjects. Walking with Bernie was another story altogether. Everyone greeted him with great familiarity, as if he were a beloved friend. If there was some protocol against giving a shout-out to celebrity guests, you wouldn't know it from the bellhop who exclaimed, "Bernie Mac in the house!" What struck me—again—was Bernie's gravitational force. As he moved through the lobby, it felt like he was pulling everyone into a mighty hug.

The word *fuck,* as of this writing, is still not something you can say on broadcast network television. Before the rise of cable networks like HBO, hearing that word in your living room, emanating from your television set, would have been truly head-spinning. (To this day, in the feature world, the

MPAA decrees that two uses of the F-word guarantees you an R rating, regardless of any other content in the film.) Bernie repeatedly used the F-word in his stand-up act—it was an indispensable tool. In the *GQ* article "The New Chitlin' Circuit," Devin Friedman wrote, "People who come to [Bernie's] shows expect him to keep it real the way they've come to *think* is real: Anytime he wavers from his supercharged persona or rapid-fire profanity, the audience expresses its disapproval." When we began *The Bernie Mac Show*, there were rumblings in the snark-o-sphere that Bernie had sold out, that a broadcast network would filter him, neuter the power of his delivery. Bernie was on a slippery slope, naysayers noted, no doubt destined for garden-variety TV fatherhood. Without the F-bomb in his arsenal, what would Bernie do?

On the fourth day of shooting, we got the answer. Early in the pilot, Bernie lays down the ground rules for the new occupants of his house:

BERNIE

You don't touch my TV. You don't touch my TiVo. You don't touch my DVD player. You don't touch my dual-deck VCR. And you don't touch this remote control that works my TV, my TiVo, my DVD player, and my dual-deck VCR. Any questions so far?

Later, his fourteen-year-old niece, Vanessa (Camille Winbush), has the gall to touch . . . the telephone. When she coolly reminds Bernie that the phone was not on his Do Not Touch list, he demands she show more respect. Under her breath, Vanessa smirks, "You're not my daddy," and marches down the long front hallway of the Mac mansion, with a now utterly enraged Bernie on her tail. She retreats into the bathroom and locks the door, prompting the following exchange:

> BERNIE
> Keep going with that attitude, little girl. I may not be your daddy, but I will sure whup your ass like I'm your daddy.

> VANESSA
> And you'll go to jail like you're my daddy, too.

The scene description then reads, "Bernie doesn't respond to this. He stands there frozen, not knowing what to say. After a beat, he walks back down the hall." Needless to say, there was absolutely no chance of Bernie Mac slinking away without some parting shot. Stomping down the hall, he exclaims, "I'm going to bust your head 'til the white meat shows!"

I called, "Cut," and turned to the operator. "Did Bernie just say, 'I'm going to bust your head 'til the white meat shows'?" I asked. Nearby, the script supervisor double-checked the dialogue. Nope, there was no line in the scene about smashing a girl's head. I looked over my shoulder at Larry, who was simply delighted at what, to my ears, sounded like a call to inflict grave injury upon a child.

Larry saw a great opportunity. He quickly rewrote the following scenes (one of which had already been shot), to incorporate Bernie's off-the-cuff comment.

Addressing the audience, Bernie doubles down on the remark: "That's right. I said it." The unrepentant Bernie is then visited by a social worker (Matt Besser), who repeats, word for word, Bernie's violent threat back to him.

BERNIE
Who told you that?

SOCIAL WORKER
The littlest one.

BERNIE
(under his breath)
Stool pigeon.

The network gave its blessing, proof that Bernie didn't need the F-word to be real, raw, and incendiary. I want to focus on the "white meat" moment a little longer, for a reason unrelated to Bernie's triumph over Standards and Practices. Television shooting schedules are so tight that stopping to reconceive anything—in this case, taking a happy accident and spinning it into comic gold—almost never occurs. Making the day requires you to keep your blinders on; in the rush to complete the work, you're not inclined to stop everything and ask, "What if . . . ?" There's a pertinent anecdote about Buster Keaton's 1925 feature *Seven Chances*. A happy

accident occurred on location when Buster's character, fleeing an army of women hell-bent on marrying him, races
down a hill so rapidly that he dislodges several rocks. The
loose rocks on Buster's tail were unexpectedly funny, and he
seized the opportunity to reconceive the scene, transforming
a minor rockfall into a comic avalanche. Likewise, Larry took
a throwaway line—a rather inflammatory one—and built a
comic set piece around it.

We concluded the pilot by shooting all of Bernie's mono-
logues back-to-back. Sitting beside the camera, my only direction to Bernie was, "Let's talk. Just you and me." Before
each monologue, I offered a prompt ("What's on your mind,
Bernie?" "Wow, you must be pissed off about that . . ."), and
the speeches that followed felt like a conversation. After the
final take, Bernie offered me a bona fide token of his appreciation: a very fine cigar. Choking on my first puff, I managed
to thank him for inviting me to be on the team.

Wayward director that I was, I soon left for other adventures, but 103 episodes after the pilot, Bernie invited me
back to bring down the curtain. Directing the series finale
was the last time I saw Bernie. In front of the company, he
welcomed me like the prodigal son, teasing me mercilessly
for having the temerity to do anything other than direct *The
Bernie Mac Show*. He was still the arresting figure I'd met
that night in Beverly Hills, but he was engaged in the fight of
his life, battling sarcoidosis, a mysterious disease that attacks
the tissue surrounding the air sacs of the lungs. When I arrived on the set, I was alarmed to see Bernie toting a porta-
ble oxygen tank. It was imponderable that such an awesome
man needed oxygen from a puny metal cylinder. He was in

good spirits, proud that the series had recently hit the one-hundred-episode milestone. He invited me into his dressing room, where he draped a nasal cannula over his ears, inserted the breathing tube, sat back, and reminisced about the early days of the show. My presence seemed to bring him full circle, back to his original impulses for the series, and he spoke fondly about the adventure of bringing the pilot to life.

The series finale, "Bernie's Angels," was eerily prophetic; in the story, Bernie suffers a near-death experience (an electrical shock) and fantasizes about his own funeral. In his imagination, the children—Jordan, Vanessa, Bryana—stand over Bernie's open casket and make wisecracks about him. Studying Bernie's inanimate face, Jordan (Jeremy Suarez) quips, "They did a good job. He looks so lifelike." Vanessa adds, "Yeah, except his gums aren't flapping. This is the first time I've ever seen him quiet. It's nice." She rifles through Bernie's suit pocket and finds his car keys. "Thanks for the Escalade," she says and quickly exits. Not to be outdone, Jordan goes for Bernie's diamond ring and gold medallion. "He won't be needing these where he's going. They'd probably melt," he surmises.

It's a strong scene, and I was excited to shoot it, but at the last moment Bernie refused to climb into the casket. He was up-front with me: he was just too superstitious to lie down in a casket, even for a laugh. I managed to shoot one rather oblique angle using Bernie's stand-in, but it was a poor substitute for seeing the star in repose. I wasn't going to push him. I'd be leery about getting into a casket, too. Bernie knew how important the scene was for his character arc; his near-death moment inspires him to be a kinder parent, at least until the final scene, when he realizes that the children—Jordan, in particular—have taken full advantage of the new, "nice" Bernie. At that point, he reverts to his wonderfully belligerent self. Bernie finally agreed to do the shot, insisting he would only lie in the casket for ten seconds. With the camera rolling, he climbed in and shut his eyes. I stood next to him and counted to ten. After that, he opened his eyes and said, "You got it." It wasn't a question. And it wasn't hard to imagine that Bernie saw this bit as a portent of what was to come.

On the last day of the shoot—the final day of the series—the cast and crew gathered for a group photo. Bernie thanked everyone and used the occasion to, once again, roast me for my waywardness. He then pulled me into a hug and told me he loved me. It was like being hugged by a planet. Indeed, in that moment, he seemed like some natural wonder, utterly indomitable.

THE OBJECTIVE CORRELATIVE,
OR WHAT WOULD LUBITSCH DO?

In Cameron Crowe's book-length interview with writer-director Billy Wilder, Wilder recounts a breakthrough during the writing of Ernst Lubitsch's *Ninotchka*. His story perfectly illustrates that oft-used but little-understood phrase *the Lubitsch touch*. The title character, played by Greta Garbo, has a clearly defined emotional arc. At the start of the story, she's a coldhearted Stalinist apparatchik, in Paris to pawn off imperial jewelry seized during the 1917 revolution. By the end, she has fallen in love with an aristocrat (Melvyn Douglas) and been seduced by the allure of Western capitalism. Lubitsch felt the romantic story line with the aristocrat was working well, but he was eager to find a way to visually represent Ninotchka falling in love with capitalism. As Wilder put it, "We needed a *thing* [my emphasis] to prove . . . that she fell under the spell of capitalism." Wilder and Charles Brackett, his writing partner, pitched umpteen ideas to Lubitsch, all of which he rejected. They kept racking their brains until Lubitsch came bounding into their office one morning. Beaming, Lubitsch exclaimed, "It's the hat!"

Wilder continues the story:

And we said, "What hat?" He said, "We build the hat into the beginning!" Brackett and I looked at each other—this is Lubitsch. The story of the hat has three acts. Ninotchka first sees it in a shop window as she enters the Ritz Hotel with her three Bolshevik accomplices. This absolutely crazy hat is the symbol of capitalism to her. She gives it a disgusted look and says, "How can a civilization survive which allows women to wear this on their heads?" Then the second time she goes by the hat and makes a noise—*tch-tch-tch*. The third time, she is finally alone, she has gotten rid of her Bolshevik accomplices, opens a drawer and pulls it out. And now she wears it. Working with Lubitsch, ideas like this were in the air.

A frothy grace note, you say. That's the celebrated Lubitsch touch? I would argue that Ninotchka's "crazy," haute couture hat is a perfect example of the *objective correlative,* a term from the world of literary criticism first made popular by T. S. Eliot in his 1919 essay "Hamlet and His Problems." Here is Eliot's definition: "The only way of expressing emotion in the form of art is by finding an 'objective correlative'; in other words, a set of objects, a situation, a chain of events which shall be the formula of that *particular* emotion; such that when the external facts . . . are given, the emotion is immediately invoked." Eliot imagines a truly alchemical process in which various elements, combined in the correct amounts and appearing at the right moment, elicit the proper emotion from the reader. He adds, "The artistic 'inevitability' lies in this complete adequacy of the external to the emotion," which—for my money—is a precise, if somewhat highfalutin definition of the word *craft*.

Literary critics continue to debate Eliot's concept of the objective correlative, and I don't have quite the bandwidth to tangle with a trained aesthetician. But I do want to cite one dissenter, Eliseo Vivas, who in an otherwise scholarly essay offers the cutting quip: "You just do not work up emotion into poetry the way a cabinet maker works up a few boards into a table." I completely disagree. Clearly, Vivas has no appreciation of the many choices involved in making a great piece of furniture. But I leave it to Tom Stoppard for the final word on the relationship between woodworking and literary expression. In Stoppard's *The Real Thing,* the acerbic Henry (a probable stand-in for the author) and his wife, Annie, argue about the nature of good writing. Frustrated, Henry leaves the stage for a moment, only to reappear wielding a cricket bat. Waving it about, he launches into the following:

> This thing here, which looks like a wooden club, is actually several pieces of particular wood cunningly put together in a certain way so that the whole thing is sprung, like a dance floor. It's for hitting cricket balls with. If you get it right, the cricket ball will travel two hundred yards in four seconds, and all you've done is give it a knock like knocking the top off a bottle of stout, and it makes a noise like a trout taking a

fly . . . (He clucks his tongue to make the noise.) What we're trying to do is write cricket bats, so that when we throw up an idea and give it a little knock, it might . . . travel.

Back to Ninotchka's hat. Granted, it's simply one object. It's not a formula, but Lubitsch has succeeded in giving his heroine's entire journey an objective correlative. I suggest adding this concept to your directorial toolbox, and be on the lookout for objects—*things*—that support and amplify the emotional subtext of your story. They can be common things—a hat, a pair of shoes, a doorway, a set of stairs, a sled (of course!), even a driveway, and what follows are examples of each that I find quite inspiring. And moving.

SHOES

There are plenty of hats in film and television history that function as objective correlatives for a character arc (Walter White's porkpie hat in *Breaking Bad* is one notable example). But I want to leave the millinery department and focus on footwear. In the World War II coming-of-age drama *Jojo Rabbit,* writer-director Taika Waititi channels his inner Lubitsch, using a pair of shoes to chart the fate of the title character's mother, Rosie (Scarlett Johansson). Secretly anti-Nazi, Rosie sports a chic pair of single lace-up red-and-white spectators that stamps her as artistic, brave, and full of life. In contrast to her son, who yearns to march in lockstep with the Nazis yet struggles to tie his own bootlaces, Rosie comports herself freely, answerable to no one, dancing her way through life. As with Ninotchka's hat, Rosie's shoes form a three-act play. In act 1, we find Jojo lying on his back after a painful stretching exercise. From Waititi's script: "His mother's OXFORDS enter frame, next to his head. They click-clack on the tiles in front of him and he watches as her shoes spin next to his head." In act 2, mother and son take a stroll by the river, and Waititi's staging directions are very specific: "She walks next to Jojo but on an elevated retaining wall so her feet are next to his head." Rosie extols the importance of dancing as a way to celebrate life, and the scene description reinforces her dialogue: "She does a small twirl next to him, her shoes spinning near his head." In the tragic final act, Rosie is hanged in the town square for her anti-Nazi activities, a fact Jojo discovers when he sees, dangling in front of him, her stylish shoes. Her uninhibited feet are now still, but Waititi gives Rosie's shoes a life-affirming postscript; in the final scene, after the Nazis are defeated, Jojo does something he claimed he would never, ever do: he dances.

GLASSES

Agnès Varda's penultimate feature *Faces Places,* codirected with photographer JR, follows the directing duo as they travel across France, creating mural-size portraits of the people they meet. JR sports a pair of sunglasses that lend him a remoteness, much like his directing hero Jean-Luc Godard, who seemed to spend most of the 1960s hidden behind a pair of dark glasses with tortoiseshell rectangular frames. In act 1 of the glasses, Varda pesters JR to remove them so she can see what he looks like, but he gently refuses. Clearly, the glasses stand for a barrier in their collaboration, with Varda pushing for intimacy while JR maintains a cool remove. Resigned to her partner affecting a Godard-like aloofness, Varda ups the ante by offering to introduce JR to the reclusive legend, someone she's known since the early days of the *nouvelle vague*. When they arrive at Godard's home in Switzerland, however, he completely snubs them, leaving a vaguely hurtful message for the teary Varda. In the denouement, JR consoles the crestfallen Varda by finally offering to remove his glasses, to fully present himself to his partner. In a wonderful twist, Varda's eyesight is so weak that her point of view of JR's naked face is out of focus. But the sunglasses have done their job; they neatly trace the arc of Varda and JR's relationship, and by film's end, each lowers their guard for the other.

DOORS

Unless your story takes place on the moon, it's a safe bet you'll be directing scenes with characters moving through doorways. Stepping into an elevator, slamming a bedroom door, climbing into an attic, crawling through a hatch—our stories are filled with portals, and it's easy for a director to take them for granted. In and of themselves, doors are not terribly interesting. In the right hands, however, a door can intensify the emotional content of a scene. At the end of Francis Ford Coppola's *The Godfather*, Michael Corleone's wife, Kay (Diane Keaton), stands in the anteroom outside her husband's study.

She watches as various henchmen pay obeisance to the newly ascendant godfather (Al Pacino). In the final moments, one of Michael's retainers moves to close the door, thereby blocking Kay's view. The closed door becomes a potent correlative for Michael and Kay's relationship. Their marriage cleaved in two by Michael assuming the mantle of mob boss, Kay is effectively barred from his world. From now on, what goes on behind that door is none of her business.

In Orson Welles's *The Magnificent Ambersons,* the front door of the Amberson mansion, like Ninotchka's hat, is a full story with several acts. Eugene Morgan (Joseph Cotten) is in love with Isabel Amberson (Dolores Costello), but his youthful attempt to serenade her one evening backfires when the inebriated Eugene falls face-first into his cello. Isabel has never forgiven him for this doltish episode; moreover, she's now a married woman, ensconced in the opulent Amberson home with her unexciting husband, Wilbur. Quietly persistent, Eugene pays a call on Isabel. The large front door opens, and the family butler (clearly on orders from the lady of the house) announces, "Miss Amberson's not home, Mr. Morgan." There's no reverse angle to highlight Eugene's reaction. The door itself is the subject of the shot. Eugene makes a second attempt, and this time the butler is more explicit: "Miss Amberson ain't home to you, Mr. Morgan." Again, we linger on the door, not Eugene's face. In the next act, we begin on the door and quickly notice a funeral wreath hanging from it. This time, the grim-faced butler opens the door as Eugene enters, the camera following behind him, whereupon we learn that Isabel's husband, Wilbur, is dead. For Eugene, the path to Isabel's heart, blocked by an ancient grievance (her embarrassment over his juvenile folly), not to mention conventional morality (her marriage), has been cleared. But Eugene's happiness is short-lived. The mansion door makes a final appearance when George, Isabel's insufferable son, prohibits Eugene from seeing the now ailing Isabel. For the first time, the camera focuses on Eugene, and as the door closes, his silhouette remains visible through translucent glass, as if shrouded in defeat. With four scenes staged at the front door, Welles graphs the entire arc of Eugene and Isabel's relationship. The expressive power of a door in this director's hands should come as no surprise; after all, Welles created the most memorable objective correlative in the history of cinema—namely, Charles Foster Kane's sled in *Citizen Kane*.

Another masterful example of a front door with its own narrative arc can be found in Bernardo Bertolucci's *The Last Emperor*, the story of puppet emperor Puyi, nominally in charge of China but basically a prisoner in his own home. In Bertolucci and co-screenwriter Mark Peploe's telling, the gate to the imperial city has the qualities of a fully developed character. It's the portal through which key characters (e.g., his mother) depart, abandoning the young emperor. It's the wall that separates Puyi from the outside world, keeping him ignorant of the very people over whom he rules. In one harrowing scene, Puyi is so frustrated by his entrapment that he hurls a pet mouse against the door, gruesomely killing it.

Time and again, Puyi intones, "Open the door!" But his pathetic pleas go unheard. Toward the story's sad conclusion, adult Puyi watches as his barely coherent wife, sedated after an emotional collapse, is driven away through the imperial gate. The doorway charts the arc of a character with absolutely no agency in his life. In a final irony, elderly Puyi, now a lowly gardener in communist China, must buy an admission ticket to pass through the gate of his former home, now a government-run tourist attraction.

A quick sidebar. Stories about princes and kings yearning to escape the confines of royal life are numerous. In the 1927 film *The Student Prince in Old Heidelberg*, there's a key moment in which the title character races after his departing nanny as she's chauffeured through the palace gates that quickly close on the boy. The moment is nearly duplicated in *The Last Emperor*, and it's hard to imagine that Peploe and Bertolucci weren't aware of, and inspired by, *The Student Prince*.

That film was directed by—who else?—Ernst Lubitsch.

STAIRS

Directors have long used stairways to create striking imagery (e.g., Jimmy Stewart's point of view of the clock tower stairwell in Alfred Hitchcock's *Vertigo*) and dynamic staging (e.g., Errol Flynn and Basil Rathbone's sword fight in Michael Curtiz's *The Adventures of Robin Hood*). Stairs also have the potential to act as an objective correlative for a story's subtext. In Frank Capra's *It's a Wonderful Life*, the stairway of the Bailey home—specifically, the busted newel post on the stairs' lower landing—gives us the hero's entire emotional journey in capsule form. George Bailey (Jimmy Stewart), realizing his business is on the verge of collapse, returns home in a state of deep depression. Climbing the stairs, he accidentally yanks the wooden finial off the newel post. It's as if the finial is taunting him: your dream of leaving this provincial town has failed; the bank you inherited from your father has failed; you are a failure. Soon thereafter, George finds himself on a bridge, contemplating suicide. At the conclusion of the story, having discovered how truly wonderful his life is, George returns home. He climbs the stairs and once again pulls off the finial. This time, he joyfully kisses the wooden ornament as his wife looks on, bewildered. Once the measure of his failure, it now represents his success—as a father, a husband, and a citizen. A wobbly object, the loose finial firmly underpins the emotional architecture of George Bailey's story.

Frank Capra is one of four credited screenwriters on *It's a Wonderful Life,* so it's a good bet that he came up with the idea for the knob on the bannister in the Bailey house. More often than not, you'll be handed a script, whether a feature or television episode, and those objective correlatives will simply not be on the page. It's your job is to mine the scenes for objects that have the potential to amplify the core of your story. Max Ophüls did just that in *Letter from an Unknown Woman,* written by Howard Koch, using a stairway to neatly trace the main character's trajectory.

The teenage heroine, Lisa, living in an apartment with her family in fin de siècle Vienna, becomes romantically obsessed with pianist Stefan (Louis Jourdan), who recently moved into the building. Desperate for his attention, nurturing a fantasy that he could love her, Lisa waits outside his apartment one night. Stefan returns, but he's not alone. Lisa scampers up the stairs and, hidden on the upper landing, watches as Stefan and his female companion disappear into the apartment. Later in the film, the now grown Lisa (Joan Fontaine), still carrying a torch for Stefan, crosses paths with the pianist—accidentally on purpose. A romantic evening ensues, which ends with Stefan inviting Lisa to his place—it's the same apartment. This is her dream come true, and Ophüls shoots them disappearing into his apartment from a high angle—indeed, from the same upper landing where teenage Lisa once witnessed Stefan's assignation with another woman. It's as if the ghost of young Lisa is watching herself, fulfilling a childish fantasy. The stairs are an objective correlative for her romantic fixation, one that proves to be doomed. The unexpected camera angle is not specified in Howard Koch's script; this is a purely directorial touch from someone who understands how the very space itself can enhance his character's subtext.

DRIVEWAYS

Visually, I can't imagine anything duller than a driveway. Or a garage. I've directed plenty of scenes in which characters exit the front door of a house, pile into a car, and head down the street. I try my best to come up with clever ways to photograph a car pulling into or backing out of a driveway. That short stretch of concrete between house and street is a bête noire for this director, which is why the garage of the family home in Alfonso Cuarón's *Roma* struck me as a revelation. It's a patio that functions as a driveway, and it's a major character—one of the most important characters—in *Roma*. Here's how Cuarón introduces the space in his screenplay: "The tile floor of a long and narrow patio stretching through the entire house: On one end, a black metal door gives onto the street. The door has frosted glass windows, two of which are broken, courtesy of some dejected goalie." The backstory of the windows is not something a viewer will grasp, but the broken glass personalizes the patio. It transforms space into character. Over the course of *Roma*, the patio becomes the objective correlative for many things: the dissolution of a marriage, the relationship between the family and the outside world, and the exploitative relationship between the family and their Mixtec maid, Cleo (Yalitza Aparicio). A mundane space, it's the gift that keeps on giving.

The patio is too narrow for the family's 1970 black Galaxie 500, and watching the car inch its way inside is excruciating. In the screenplay, Cuarón describes the process in grueling detail:

```
The front of the car is in, then it
brakes—

The left side is about to touch the door
frame.

The tires turn right accompanied by the
SCREECH of rubber against tile.

The Galaxie 500 moves farther in but then
brakes again—
```

```
The right side is about to touch.

The black power steering wheel turns and—
The wheels veer left, SCREECHING.
```

The car's driver, Señor Antonio (Fernando Grediaga), feels hemmed in as well, stuck in a stale, loveless marriage. The patio, too tight for the wide-bodied American vehicle, is the perfect correlative for the husband who feels his life is cramped. He yearns for a bigger garage, as it were, and soon he takes a decisive step, leaving his wife and children. In act 2 of the patio's story, the abandoned wife, Señora Sofia (Marina de Tavira), returns home after a night of drowning her sorrow in drink. She's in no condition to pull the Galaxie 500 into the patio. Again, Cuarón describes the process in agonizing detail. As the car rolls in:

```
Its left side scratches against the
door frame.

The car brakes and moves back a couple of
inches. Adjusts its trajectory and pulls
forward—

Now its right side hits the frame.
The car stops and veers its wheels left.
Moves forward.

The left molding catches the frame and
begins to bend. The car stops. Backs up.
```

Goes forward again and now the right side
molding is the one that's caught. The car
stops.Backs up.

It starts forward again and the right side
molding is ripped from the metal, but
now the car doesn't stop. It just heads
straight in, ripping the entire left side
molding, too.

Cuarón could have chosen any number of ways to dramatize Señora Sofia's anger and pain. She could've trashed mementos of their marriage or thrown her husband's clothes into the street. Instead, she sideswipes the patio wall, wrecking both garage and car.

For the family dog, Borras, the patio is basically a toilet. The tile floor is often decorated with his droppings, and it's Cleo's job to scoop up the shit and mop the tiles clean. The space is the correlative for Cleo's status in the household. She's on the bottom rung, performing the lowliest tasks, invisible to the children, often berated by Señora Sofia ("Goddammit! Clean up that dog shit!").

To leave the house, the family uses the patio door, which opens on Tepeji Street in the neighborhood that gives the film its title. For me, the patio also functions as a correlative for the bubble of privilege in which the family lives. Preoccupied with American pop culture and sports, the children are insulated from the turmoil in their own country, dramatized most spectacularly by the slaughter of student protesters in downtown Mexico City (based on a real event, the Corpus

THE OBJECTIVE CORRELATIVE, OR WHAT WOULD LUBITSCH DO? › 193

Christi Massacre of 1971). When the children do venture out-side, it's to catch a Hollywood movie, before returning to the bubble where they're safely ensconced. The patio is their pas-sageway into that comfort zone.

Cuarón takes the least likely location and suffuses it with meaning. It's amazing how the broad themes of the picture are reinforced by a narrow parking space. Whether you're a writer-director or a helmer for hire, the patio in *Roma* offers an inspiring lesson: the simplest objects have the power to convey the entire theme of a film or chart the emotional jour-ney of a character. In other words, don't take that garage for granted.

OPENING THE OFFICE

"They're going to kill you. The critics are going to kill you." That was the sobering reaction of a well-meaning friend when I reported that I'd been hired to direct an American version of the British comedy *The Office*. The BBC series, created by Ricky Gervais and Stephen Merchant, quickly established a place in the television comedy pantheon. Everything about the show was contrarian, from its politically incorrect, tone-deaf hero to its unique use of the mockumentary format. The premise: an unseen filmmaking team documents the day-to-day workings of a drab paper company in a drab London suburb; manager David Brent (Gervais) welcomes the crew with open arms—he's absolutely certain the documentary will catapult him to stardom. Meanwhile, the employees are unwilling participants in this cinema verité experiment; the last thing they want is their dreary lives on display for the world to see. The BBC series was short-lived, by design: two six-episode seasons followed by a feature-length finale. Needless to say, this was hardly American broadcast network fare, and the general feeling among my associates was that trying to replicate it was a fool's errand. There was no way that NBC would embrace such a trenchant and downbeat comedy. The network would no doubt sanitize the show, insist on a laugh track, a snappy underscore, an up-tempo pace, plenty of milquetoast jokes, and, of course, a life-affirming theme song. *The critics are going to kill you* was the refrain playing in my head as I reported for work to begin prepping what was tentatively titled *The Office: An American Workplace.*

Showrunner Greg Daniels knew what kind of minefield we were traipsing into, and all credit to him for convincing NBC that the American version of *The Office* would only succeed if it went against the grain of conventional half-hour comedies—tonally, visually, and particularly in the show's casting. The standard approach would be to stock *The Office* with faces familiar from other TV shows—or, short of that, pack the ensemble with sexy young people who, in reality, wouldn't be caught dead working at any paper company, let alone one in Scranton, Pennsylvania. Our job was to create the illusion that Dunder Mifflin was a real workplace. To do so meant casting people who looked like they didn't belong on network television, particularly in prime time.

Traditionally, the casting process for network comedies culminates in the onerous ritual of bringing your top choices to the network. The comedy executives file into a conference room, and one by one, the actors are ushered in to perform a scene or two. I should note that comedy executives are a notoriously humor-free bunch, and trying to generate mirth in a roomful of such dour and distracted faces would make any thespian suicidal. To raise even a titter, actors lean into the jokes, as opposed to breathing life into their characters.

This approach may be okay for a joke-laden show performed in front of a studio audience, but it could not have been more antithetical to the spirit and humor of *The Office*. Awkward pauses, embarrassing behavior, characters who are muted and miserable: none of this would have played well to a roomful of executives.

Instead, at Greg's insistence, we did an expansive series of screen tests, featuring many actors in different combinations. There was a lot of improvisation, and we actually filmed on the Dunder Mifflin set, giving me the unheard-of opportunity to try out staging ideas while conducting auditions. The layout of the bullpen was still in flux, and the screen tests gave me a chance to experiment with desk orientation. Not a small matter. Sorting out how characters relate spatially, you can create an objective correlative for their emotional relationships. For example, Jim's desk is perpendicular to Pam's. She always looks directly at Jim, while he sits at a right angle to her. For Jim's part, to look at Pam he must turn his head. He must make an effort, an active choice to look in her direction. The desk arrangement inspired their signature two-shot: Jim (John Krasinski), in profile, unaware (or pretending to be unaware) of Pam (Jenna Fischer), in the background, gazing at him. The arrangement of their desks perfectly underscores the romantic tension between them. By the way, this is a good example of how a pilot director sets the style of a series, by finding ways to visually reinforce the emotional subtext of the piece.

Casting the role of Michael Scott, the Dunder Mifflin manager, was particularly treacherous because Ricky Gervais's performance was so vividly etched in many viewers' minds. Gervais's creation, David Brent, was a pitiable man, and Ricky brought this often revolting character to life in a way that de-fied the audience to find anything likable about him. It's a fear-less performance, impossible to re-create. On paper, Michael Scott is just as contemptible. Here is Greg's original description of the character: "Horribly overconfident, Michael is a train wreck of bad leadership characteristics, only redeemed a bit by his childish enthusiasm. Despite continual proofs that he's an ass, he clings shamelessly to his deluded self-image like a shipwreck survivor clinging to a scrap of wood." Could such a character thrive in prime time? Was there any actor who could make viewers care about this obnoxious man? Steve Carell was among a handful of frontrunners for the role, and despite comic credentials as a *Daily Show* correspondent, not to men-tion winning performances in such features as *Anchorman,* NBC insisted Steve do a screen test.

When Steve and I met to rehearse the scenes for the test, he shyly confided that he'd never seen the original series. Well, that's not 100 percent true. According to Steve, after watching a couple of minutes of the UK version, he quickly turned off his TV. He feared that if he watched another minute, his au-dition would turn into an impersonation of Gervais's charac-ter. Not knowing how Ricky approached the role, Steve said he would simply channel all the boobs he'd worked for over the years. There were, he added, more than a few. The moment we began the screen test, Steve completely inhabited the role. The character was wholly his own: narcissistic, desperate for attention, utterly convinced he's a sensitive boss, and perfectly clueless. Even in the screen test, Steve accomplished something I didn't think possible: spouting the most derogatory and im-politic dialogue, he made Michael Scott likeable. I found myself rooting for him. By the way, the word *boob* is a key to understanding the difference between Michael Scott and David Brent. A boob is foolish, but not hateful. Well-meaning, but inept. Ricky Gervais played David Brent as a jerk—prickly, edgy, unlovable. Steve knew that even a small dose of David Brent would taint his audition. In this case, ignorance was the right tactic; it allowed the actor to find his inner boob.

On the day we held callbacks for the role of Pam the receptionist, half a dozen candidates waited in our outer office. All exuded a bubbly, eager-to-please quality, except for one woman who sat off to the side. She looked singularly out of place, as if she'd be much happier at home doing a crossword puzzle. Was this woman even an actor? Perhaps she's here by mistake, I thought. Maybe she's actually looking for a receptionist's job. Needless to say, that woman was Jenna Fischer, who artfully won the role of Pam by being *less interesting* than every other candidate. I once asked Jenna how she prepared for the audition. She told me that our casting director Allison Jones gave her firm advice: "Just go in there and bore them." It was a risky strategy, but the right one.

Several Dunder Mifflin employees had no speaking lines in the pilot; indeed, they didn't have defined characters at all. We had to fill out the bullpen with a few background players, and it was a thrill for me to watch these "extras" grow into indispensable members of the ensemble. I take particular pride in the casting of two of those background artists, Creed Bratton and Phyllis Smith.

I met Creed years earlier while directing the pilot of *The Bernie Mac Show*. Creed was a stand-in—that is, a surrogate for one of the actors during the lighting process. During one hectic afternoon, when I should've been focused on the task at hand, I was continually distracted by Creed chatting up a fellow stand-in. Walking past, I caught snatches of the conversation: "Oh, yeah, we opened for Janis in '67." Or "The scene backstage at the Whiskey was crazy." Who was this mystery man? My interest piqued, I glanced over my shoulder and caught him performing some wild air guitar.

Edging closer, I heard him say, "And that's the lick Hendrix taught me." Creed's audience of one shook his head in awe. "Excuse me," I interjected. "Did you say *Hendrix*? As in Jimi Hendrix?" At this point, the enigmatic stand-in introduced himself as Creed Bratton, the original lead guitarist of the Grass Roots, a popular band from the 1960s that opened for such luminaries as Hendrix, Janis Joplin, Cream, and The Doors. During Creed's two-year tenure with the Grass Roots, the band released the iconic Summer of Love anthem, "Let's Live for Today." Creed left the band on less than amicable terms and managed to survive the 1960s intact; now, thirty years later, he was making ends meet as a stand-in. It was the year 2000, and Creed had just turned fifty-seven. During the remainder of the *Bernie Mac* shoot, I would pull Creed aside and grill him about his glory days (he was particularly coy and circumspect when I asked about Janis Joplin, which only added to his mystique).

The shoot ended, and we parted company. Frankly, I didn't expect to cross paths with Creed again, but in January of 2004, he reached out to me. He'd heard I was prepping a new show entitled *The Office* and wondered if there was any stand-in work. I explained that the mockumentary style obviated the need for stand-ins, and the disappointment in his voice was obvious. "But," I quickly added, "there are several desks in the bullpen that need to be filled." Would he consider sitting at one of them? With no guarantee other than a week's worth of pay as an extra? Creed accepted my invitation, took a seat in the back of the room, and nine seasons later, he'd become one of the most beloved stars of the series. It was Greg's decision to name Creed's character Creed, and Greg actively drew upon Creed's history as a rock-and-roll survivor to develop his odd, inscrutable alter ego. For instance, in the episode "Gay Witch Hunt," written by Greg, here's Creed declaring that he's open-minded about homosexuality: "I'm not offended by homosexuality. In the sixties, I made love with many, many women, often outdoors and in mud and rain, and it's possible that a man slipped in. [There] would be no way of knowing."

Casting director Allison Jones employed an associate, a woman whose job was to read the off-camera dialogue during auditions. That woman, Phyllis Smith, sat next to me as one actor after another entered and gave it their all. Clearly, many of the aspirants didn't get the memo about the style of the show, for they were playing to the balcony in our tiny room. Meanwhile, Phyllis read her off-camera lines in a singular monotone tinged with a slight midwestern drawl. Her whole presentation was strikingly un-Hollywood; in fact, she reminded me of the matronly librarian at the Belleville Public Library of my childhood. There was a heart-of-the-heartland aura about Phyllis—I could imagine her ordering *pop* as opposed to *soda*. The poor auditionees must have been dismayed to look up and find me staring, not at them, but at the "reader." I was smitten with Phyllis, and during a break I said to Greg, "I can easily see our casting associate working for a paper company in Scranton, Pennsylvania." At first, Greg was puzzled by my enthusiasm for Phyllis, but after arguing that her lack of pretense and utter sincerity made her a perfect fit for Dunder Mifflin, he gave his blessing to invite her into the fold. "There's an empty desk behind Dwight Schrute," I said to Phyllis. "Would you be willing to sit there for six days?" Working with one of the industry's top casting directors is nothing to sneeze at. If the show got picked up, she would have to cut those ties. Phyllis didn't hesitate. She took the plunge. My barometer for all things midwestern was accurate; Phyllis was a native St. Louisan.

After welcoming her to the cast, Greg pulled me aside to ask, "Do you think Phyllis has any acting experience?" I shrugged. "I have no idea," I replied. "I'll find out." I caught up with Phyllis and delicately asked about her acting credentials. "Don't worry," I hastened to add, "you've got the role. I was just . . . curious." Phyllis then revealed that, twenty years earlier, she performed in a burlesque show in Branson, Missouri. While I tried to wrap my small brain around the image of Phyllis as a latter-day Sally Rand, she added, "I didn't take off my clothes. In case you were wondering." On the first day of rehearsals, Phyllis delivered the proof: a weathered photo from the early 1980s featuring a thirtysomething Phyllis backstage in Branson, decked out in a feathery burlesque costume. "No stripping," she reminded me. Naturally, Greg dubbed Phyllis's character . . . Phyllis.

At the big production meeting, held two days before shooting commenced, Greg and I instructed our department heads (camera, sound, makeup, hair) to toss the rules out the window. I announced that certain kinds of mistakes, ones that would get a person fired under normal circumstances, were welcome on this show. Encouraged, even. If the camera operator failed to pull focus smoothly, no worries. In fact, to create the illusion of a documentary, these technical flubs would be planned. To reinforce the sense that we were capturing things on the fly—that we weren't privy to what was about to happen at any given moment—the camera might be looking in the "wrong" direction, forcing the operator to hastily pan and find the action unfolding. Likewise, if the boom operator "missed" a line of dialogue, that was okay. Our job was to conceive and choreograph credible mistakes.

As for production design, most film and television sets are built with modular sections. Certain walls are designated as "wild"—that is, they can be removed to afford better camera angles. On *The Office,* Greg and I insisted that the physical limitations of the set be respected. For the record, the pilot was shot on location; Dunder Mifflin occupied an empty office suite in a building in Culver City. When NBC ordered the series, we re-created that office suite in a warehouse in a scrubby, industrial neighborhood in the San Fernando Valley. Greg and I agreed that the set should be built with no removable walls, forcing all future directors to wrestle with the physical constraints of the space. If your view of the action is obstructed by a column or file cabinet, so be it. Often, I staged scenes in which the sight line was deliberately compromised, to remind viewers they were watching something caught by chance, not staged for their benefit.

For the pilot, we enlisted a director of photography with sterling mockumentary credentials. Peter Smokler was the cinematographer on Rob Reiner's debut feature *This Is Spinal Tap.* I had worked with Peter extensively on *The Larry Sanders Show,* which was not a mockumentary but boasted an observational camera style (I'll call it *cinema verité adjacent*). Peter and I discussed all the strategies of cinema verité filmmaking. For example, a camera operator might use a "whip zoom" to obtain multiple image sizes of the same event. If the operator changes the focal length quickly enough, you can eliminate the "whip" in the cutting room and effectively have traditional coverage of action over which you had no directorial control. I argued that it was vital to keep the "whip" to signal to viewers that we were covering things on the fly. The erratic zoom quickly became a hallmark of the series, for better or worse. At times, it gave the impression less of a documentarian gathering coverage and more of a camera operator with a nervous tic.

To the befuddlement of some department heads, Greg and I laid down outlandish ground rules for the pilot, among them that hair and makeup people were not allowed on the set at all. It was a cockamamie idea, but we wanted to do everything possible to make the cast feel they weren't on the set of a television show. Of course, the actors began each day with a trip to the makeup and hair trailer, but on set they made do with compact mirrors and makeup kits tucked into their desks. We urged them to do their own touch-ups. We also insisted that once filming began, the only crew members allowed on the set were the "documentary team"—namely, the camera operator, boom operator, Greg, and me.

We shot the pilot in six days. I asked the cast to report

to work each morning as if they were employees at Dunder Mifflin, not actors on a show. Each shooting day began with thirty minutes devoted to "general views." The cast sat at their desks and I roamed the bullpen with Peter Smokler, getting shots of the characters engaged in such thrilling activities as stapling or going to the watercooler. It wasn't just mundane. It was perfectly mundane. Each desk had a dummy phone, and I directed the actors, especially those with no scripted dialogue, to improvise sales calls. At her reception desk, a weary-looking Pam answered the phone ("Dunder Mifflin, can I help you?"). In the accountants' corner, Angela doodled a portrait of her cat Sprinkles. At his desk, Creed stared off at nothing in particular. In his private office, Michael meticulously arranged tchotchkes on his desk. Boredom, apathy, a permanent case of the blahs. "The mass of men lead lives of quiet desperation," wrote Thoreau. Indeed, our morning ritual was the ensemble acting out quiet desperation. My job was to observe at a discreet distance, like Jane Goodall crouching in the Tanzanian bush. Over the course of six days, we shot an enormous number of "general views." Reviewing the footage, the executives at NBC probably thought we'd all gone insane. *Why is there a ten-minute shot of Rainn Wilson sharpening pencils? Why are there close-ups of bubbles in the watercooler? What the hell are you people doing?*

What we were doing was creating an atmosphere that let the actors feel at home in their new workplace. Almost none of the "general views" made it into the final cut of the pilot, but the exercise was invaluable. It gave the office and *The Office* a "lived-in" quality. And it was a daily reminder to the cast that we—the "documentary team"—were simply there to eavesdrop on their lives. As we segued into a scripted scene, the actors maintained that sense of being subjects under observation. The morning ritual informed the performance style for the whole day. Conceptually, there's no difference between a shot of Dwight sharpening pencils and a comic argument between Dwight and Jim. Whether quotidian drudgery or high drama, it's all grist for the mill, all material for the docuseries *The Office: An American Workplace*. Michael Scott, of course, is excited for the documentary team to capture his comic genius. He hams it up for the camera, but he's completely unprepared for that camera to catch his many flaws (e.g., his gross insensitivity in subjecting Pam to a humiliating prank).

Like everyone else at Dunder Mifflin, Michael is under observation.

In the pilot, most of the action takes place in the bullpen. There are full-ensemble scenes in which the employees react to Michael's cringe-inducing antics, and I told everyone the camera would seek out their reactions randomly. As a scene unfolded, I'd stand behind Peter and whisper, "Find Stanley!" or "Pan to Oscar!" Peter had to fight the urge to execute crisp, precise pans; for this show, it was better to be inelegant, to pan past the subject, then clumsily double back. The cast understood they were all fair game. At any moment, they might be caught in close-up. In other words, it was critical for everyone to be "on" all the time. Plus, each actor needed to determine his or her character's "camera awareness." A few employees—Jim, for one—warm up to the camera quickly. Others are wary, finding the presence of the camera unsettling. Pam seems to loathe the lens; at times, it feels like she's about to crawl under her desk. Dwight, intense and conspiracy-minded, is suspicious of the camera crew. Here's a short scene from the pilot script that didn't make the final cut, but it displays Dwight's paranoia about being surveilled, as well as the show's general goal to document the interstitial, throwaway moments in the lives of its characters:

```
INT. DESK AREA-DAY

Dwight is sitting at his desk, playing with
some chewing gum in his mouth. He notices
the camera and puts the gum in the garbage
as discreetly as possible. He goes back to
work.
```

After wrapping the pilot, I was plagued with doubt, convinced it had been all for naught. A comedy this unconventional—no laugh track, no musical prompts (apart from the ditty by Jay Ferguson under the opening titles, there was no underscore), an unsteady camera style, a decidedly unsexy cast, a dearth of traditional jokes, an ensemble of vaguely depressed characters, not to mention a self-deluded hero—would never pass muster with American viewers.

Two hundred episodes later, I'm still shaking my head. Over time, some of the unorthodox choices (e.g., keeping hair and makeup people off the set) gave way to more traditional ones. But the show never lost its original off-center instincts, born during a golden moment when a major broadcast network gave us the green light to throw caution to the winds. And, happily, we didn't hesitate.

ESCAPE FROM VIDEO VILLAGE

The quintessential image of a director at work, at least in the classical Hollywood era, is a man standing beside the camera, looking on as the scene unfolds before him. The typical image of a contemporary director at work is a man or woman, sitting in a chair at a video monitor, surrounded by other people in chairs.

This assemblage has a name: *video village*. Its inhabitants include the script supervisor, who you can easily identify because he or she looks like they have a real job to do. Seated behind the director are men and women suspiciously over-dressed for a film set. These would be executives, dispatched by their respective studios and/or networks to oversee (read: second-guess) the director. When not texting or reading the trades, executives offer "comments" after each take, sometimes for the director's benefit. Sometimes not. Of course, not saying anything qualifies as a comment in itself.

In the case of series television, next to the director you'll probably find the showrunner. There may be staff writers, lower on the food chain, hovering near the showrunner.

More likely than not, these writers are on their feet; after all, there are only so many chairs a set can accommodate. Actually, I take that back; it's remarkable how many chairs any set can handle. Between takes, staff writers quietly confer with the showrunner, who then turns to the director and delivers notes. Personally, I distinguish between notes and comments. The former have a certain force of authority, while the latter can be maddeningly tentative and inchoate.

On a feature film set, the screenwriter, in all likelihood, will not be present at all, his or her script having been rewritten over time by various specialists (e.g., someone to "punch up" a script with jokes). In place of the screenwriter's chair, you may find one occupied by the film's producer. An industrious producer no doubt has a full slate of projects, all of which need constant nurturing. What this means is the producer's phone will regularly vibrate during a take, and he or she will leap from the chair with great urgency (in show business, everything is urgent) and march off to some corner to take a "very important call."

In the village, a third row of chairs may be filled by, variously: 1) actors who are not in the scene; 2) makeup and hair people; 3) guests. This final category could include: a) someone's spouse; b) someone's parents; c) someone's entire extended family, visiting from out of town. Invariably, a gregarious guest will corner the director and ask questions. A budding cinephile might ask, "How did you get started in the business?" Or "Do you have a favorite Tarantino film?" At the end of the day, I'd be happy to parse the particulars of Tarantino's résumé, but not while I'm busy trying to beef up my own. And, unfailingly, a visitor will ask me where they can find the bathroom. I suppose I just look like the kind of person who knows.

Video village is a fairly recent development in film and television production. Once upon a time, the only person who could see what the camera sees was the camera operator. Directors framed the shot, then left it to the operator to execute properly. Enter Jerry Lewis, who made the transition from performer to director in 1960 with *The Bellboy*. Eager to monitor his own performance, Lewis essentially attached a video camera to the film camera. Each take was simultaneously captured on celluloid and videotape. Many have questioned Lewis's claim to having invented "video assist," but there's no doubt that he fine-tuned and popularized the nascent technology.

When I began directing in the early 1980s, video assist was still a bit of a luxury. "Ken, do you really need it?" I was routinely asked by the people holding the purse strings. Producers rightfully worried that replaying take after take on videotape would slow down the shooting day. Directors rightfully worried that giving so many people access to the image would create a deluge of unwanted opinions. The video image, however, proved far too addictive, and over the succeeding decades, video monitors became ubiquitous on sets, as did the attendant cluster of onlookers.

Today, when a director considers a particular location, a conscientious location scout will ask, "Where do we put the village?" Indeed, where to corral the many executives, producers, writers, and guests is no small undertaking. Arranging no fewer than a dozen director chairs so that a hierarchy is maintained while affording everyone a fighting chance to see the monitor, making sure each occupant has a pair of headphones to hear the dialogue, and being able to quickly decamp from one location to the next as the shooting day proceeds—video village is truly a production within a production.

Here's the dirty secret of video village, one that many directors fail to apprehend. If you, the director, are sitting at a monitor, the power center of the set is, effectively, at video village. Directorial decisions will be made at the monitor, too often by consensus. Executives who need to justify their presence on the set will no doubt speak up. Whether you agree with them or not, you're trapped by their babble. Showrunners may give line readings for you to deliver to actors. The script supervisor will remind you that so-and-so shouldn't do such-and-such until they say this or that line. Pretty soon, you feel less like a director than an errand boy. Meanwhile, the poor actors are stranded, sitting on their hands, desperate for a little direction. Perhaps you resort to a megaphone and broadcast notes from your comfy chair. I've actually watched directors give line readings via bullhorn. If the committee at the village gets into a heated discussion, everyone on the set loses their focus. Crew members wander off to the snack table, and actors check their phones. Whatever esprit de corps you instilled in the company has quickly gone down the drain.

Sadly, there are more than a few directors who are perfectly content to be engulfed by such a gabfest or too insecure to disentangle themselves from the morass that is, essentially, "directing by committee."

But it is possible for you to escape from video village. All you need to do is get off your butt . . . and stand next to the camera.

If you're stationed at the camera, the entire dynamic on the set shifts for the better. You're now part of the crew. You're not relaxing in the executive suite. Most important, you're in physical proximity to the cast. The actors will feel your presence and be nourished by it. The moment you call, "Cut," they'll look up and yours will be the first face they see. They're not on pins and needles while you're half a mile away, trapped in a groupthink quagmire. I can't tell you how many actors, eager for some affirmation, turn to the camera operators to ask, "How did I do?" Your relationship to the actors should be up close and personal. Your notes should be direct and imme-diate, not bellowed across the set after a lengthy silence. So, let the denizens of video village debate the merits of the take. The power center of the set is now at the camera, and if a note does emerge from the village, it needs to be pertinent enough for some designee to actually stand up and deliver that note to you. I guarantee that standing by the camera will cut down the number of needless notes by 90 percent. In many cases, certain video village habitués, deprived of the pleasure of continually bending the director's ear, will simply get bored and leave the set.

As the director, think of yourself as the person with the best seat in the house. Right next to the lens. Of course, it's possible for you to keep tabs on the shot via a small monitor, either attached to the camera (an onboard monitor) or placed on a stand. But my suggestion is to wean yourself from the need to consult any monitor, big or small, and keep your eye trained on the action itself. Your actors will feel the difference between you watching them and you watching an image. Plus, by paying attention to the cast instead of the monitor, you end up seeing things the camera doesn't. A facial gesture from an off-camera actor might open up a whole new avenue for playing a moment, something you wouldn't have noticed if you were staring at a screen or sequestered at the village. On a subtler level, the less you're hooked to the monitor, the more you strengthen your ability to—perish the thought—*imagine* the composition.

The camera crew will feel the difference as well. If you're not micromanaging every image, your operators will feel more empowered to do their best job. The operator will bring an increased sense of ownership to the work. Many filmmakers will argue that it's critical to concentrate on the image. Isn't that what directors do? Create images? I suppose if your visual style is highly manicured, you'll be anxious to make sure each composition is pristine. And, yes, if a shot is technically complicated, with an elaborate camera move, who wouldn't want to oversee it with precision and care? But is there any reason to ride herd over the most basic shots? Trust your operator's eye.

Lest the sound department feel left out of this jeremiad, I would argue that the proliferation of headphones at video village undercuts the authority of the director. Among the perils of passing out headphones to the villagers is that anyone can hear your direction to the actors between takes. That conversation should be completely private; instead, it's now possible for studio executives, writers, producers, and hangers-on to effectively surveil the director. Indeed, I often feel like I'm simultaneously directing the cast and performing for the gallery. Giving notes is a delicate business. It's not only important to give effective notes, it's also important to know when to give them. Often, I choose not to deliver certain notes too quickly, preferring to let the cast find the rhythm of the scene and uncover its layers. Frustrating to me is that even while guiding the scene I'm painfully aware of what's being said back at the village. It's an absolute given that after the first take of any scene, some member of the gallery will grumble, "Oh, God, they have to pick up the pace." Comments about pace are the default position of any villager with nothing more insightful to say. Once, out of sheer perversity, I planted a spy in the village to confirm my suspicion that someone would whine about pace after the first take. My instincts were spot-on. As we've already discussed, once the actors "find" the scene, they will naturally pick up the pace.

Finally, one simple reason to steer clear of video village is that it improves what I call the *signal-to-noise ratio* in your head. Keeping your thoughts focused on the scene—that's the "signal." Examples of "noise" are, unfortunately, far too numerous. Inevitably, you overhear somebody at the village trash-talking the scene. Executives trade scuttlebutt about the business. Crew members loitering at the monitors compare notes about other job prospects. A showrunner and his or her staff noisily rewrite an upcoming episode. Indeed, I've seen showrunners turn video village into a veritable writers' room. There's benign babble. People complaining about their commute time. Planning their weekends. Dissecting the box office report. Sharing posts. There's no grand conspiracy to derail your thoughts, but the culture of video village is inherently chatty, and you need to remain connected to the story you're telling. At the end of each day's shoot, when the assistant director announces, "That's a wrap," nothing makes me happier than knowing that my chair—the one marked *Director*—has remained empty all day.

(left) The author at age 10. "The year I broke my first camera." (courtesy of the author)

Directing the *CBS Afternoon Playhouse* in 1983. (courtesy of the author)

With Jim Henson on the set of *Sesame Street Presents: Follow That Bird*. (courtesy of the author)

(below) Big Bird (Caroll Spinney) in *Sesame Street Presents: Follow That Bird*. (courtesy of the author)

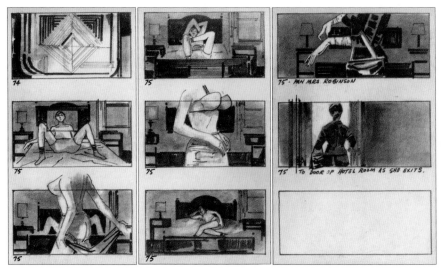

Using off-screen space: Harold Michelson's storyboards for
The Graduate. (courtesy of Lillian Michelson)

The Sisterhood of the Traveling Pants: Carmen (America Ferrera) confronts her father, Al
(Bradley Whitford), who hides his shame from the audience. (frame enlargements)

He Said, She Said: the codirecting team of Ken Kwapis and Marisa Silver . . . and their movie alter-egos, Dan (Kevin Bacon) and Lorie (Elizabeth Perkins). (Paramount Pictures)

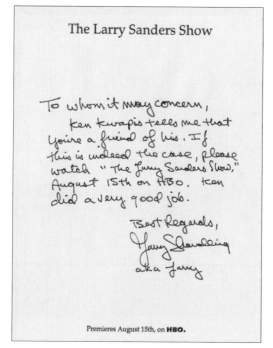

The Larry Sanders Show

To whom it may concern,
Ken Kwapis tells me that you're a friend of his. If this is indeed the case, please watch "The Larry Sanders Show," August 15th on HBO. Ken did a very good job.

Best Regards,
Garry Shandling
aka Larry

Premieres August 15th, on **HBO.**

Garry Shandling penned this note to promote the premiere of *The Larry Sanders Show.* (courtesy of the author)

Dunston Checks In: Dunston (Sammy) prepares to leap from a chandelier . . . onto Mrs. Dubrow (Faye Dunaway), with Kyle (Eric Lloyd) in her clutches. (Twentieth Century Fox)

With Bernie Mac on the set of *The Bernie Mac Show*. (Getty Images)

The Objective Correlative: Ninotchka's hat. (from the collections of the Margaret Herrick Library, Academy of Motion Picture Arts and Sciences)

It's a Wonderful Life: the newel post in George Bailey's home. (frame enlargement)

Roma: Señor Antonio's driveway. (Participant Media)

(above) Shooting the pilot of *The Office.* (NBCUniversal)

With Jenna Fischer and Greg Daniels on the series finale of *The Office.* (NBCUniversal)

The stateroom scene in *A Night at the Opera*: a workplace comedy in miniature. (from the collections of the Margaret Herrick Library, AMPAS)

Justin Long and Ginnifer Goodwin in *He's Just Not That Into You*. (Licensed by Warner Bros. Entertainment Inc. All Rights Reserved)

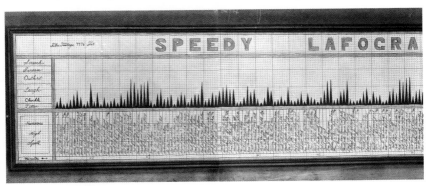

Harold Lloyd's Lafograph for the film *Speedy*. (courtesy of Suzanne Lloyd)

The Sisterhood of the Traveling Pants: the "Fate" theme by Cliff Eidelman. (courtesy of Cliff Eidelman)

With Drew Barrymore in Alaska on the set of *Big Miracle*. (Universal)

A Walk in the Woods: on the Appalachian Trail with Robert Redford and Nick Nolte. (Broad Green Pictures)

WHO ARE YOU?

The best landscape a director can photograph is the face of a character in turmoil. I wish I could take credit for that line, but it's not mine. And I have no clue who coined it. There's one particular close-up of a man in duress I want to explore. A powerful, haunting shot, it's also enigmatic; it poses a question that, depending on your point of view, may or may not get answered by the end of the story. This close-up occupies a privileged position in my pantheon of favorite shots, but to get there, we need to take a circuitous route by way of the Skyview Drive-In in Belleville, Illinois, the site of many formative moviegoing experiences.

The Skyview was an open-air temple of the cinema. It boasted a marquee with a neon rocket ship that offered the promise that a movie could transport you to another realm. The Skyview opened in 1949, and a tornado destroyed the screen in 1955, lending the drive-in a mythic aura in my young mind. The first film I saw there was *King Kong vs. Godzilla*, directed by Ishirō Honda. The final bout between the titular monsters takes place atop Mount Fuji. At first, Godzilla seems to have the upper hand (or claw, I suppose), but Kong manages to rally, and the brawling duo tumbles off a cliff into the Pacific. At this point, the rumble resumes underwater. Only Kong emerges, but a Japanese military spokesman suspects that Godzilla survived the ape's pummeling and will return. To be honest, I don't recall any of this, not because it's been half a century since I saw the film—rather, because I spent most of *King Kong vs. Godzilla*'s ninety-seven-minute running time hiding under the dashboard of my father's Thunderbird in a state of abject terror. What can I say? I was an impressionable viewer.

Two years later, my father took me to the Skyview for what turned out to be a pivotal movie night. This time, I didn't take refuge under the glove box. Indeed, I couldn't take my eyes off the screen for a moment and thereafter became obsessed with the story's hero, Thomas Edward Lawrence. The film was *Lawrence of Arabia*. The Skyview was not the ideal venue for appreciating David Lean's epic. For starters, it was midsummer, and the sky was still bright when the film began. To entertain youngsters before showtime, the Skyview offered a playground with pony rides, a miniature train, and a small Ferris wheel. There was also a hayride that circled the perimeter of the grounds. Because of the long twilight, the playground was still packed when the Columbia Pictures logo appeared. On top of that, Maurice Jarre's sumptuous score sounded pretty thin coming through those unwieldy metal speakers. You had to crack your window a tad to hang the speaker, which meant you got an earful of those noisy kids, squeaky swings, and that belching tractor pulling the hay wagon. In the car next door was a teenage couple with absolutely no interest in the Arab revolt against the Ottoman Empire. To make matters worse, the Skyview's screen could not quite accommodate the film's 2.20:1 aspect ratio. I distinctly recall shots in which there was nothing on-screen but desert and two noses poking into either side of the frame.

Yet with all these impediments, I didn't stir for nearly two hundred minutes. I didn't feel like I was watching a movie. I was simply there, in the Arabian desert, alongside this compelling—if curious—hero, and for days after seeing the film, I strutted about emulating his peculiar swagger.

My childhood home abutted a thick woods. A short hike led to a clearing, a couple of acres stripped of trees, the future site of a new subdivision. Bulldozers were haphazardly parked, poised to excavate a basement or two. Huge mounds of dirt were everywhere. This was my Arabian desert, the perfect location to reenact scenes from *Lawrence*. Absconding with a white sheet from the family linen closet, I fought through the thicket and emerged on the dusty tract. Selecting a stick approximately the length of the scimitar gifted to Lawrence (Peter O'Toole) by Sherif Ali (Omar Sharif), I tied the sheet around my neck and pranced through the dirt, mangling whatever dialogue from the film I could recall. "Nothing is written!" I announced to no one in particular. Running to the top of a mound, I yelled, "I shall be at Aqaba!" Then, running down, I gave a war whoop and screamed, "No prisoners! No prisoners!" After an hour or so of skewering imaginary Turks, I trundled home, desperately in need of a Mountain Dew. Routing those Ottomans could really build up a thirst.

Little did I realize at the time, but what I was doing with a stick and a sheet was essentially the same thing T. E.

Lawrence did during his tenure with the Bedouin—namely, play dress-up and pretend to be someone he wasn't. This radical idea, that the hero of *Lawrence of Arabia* was basically a poseur, didn't occur to me at the time. What I did sense was that Lawrence was a curious man, a character I couldn't quite grasp. My view of the film was mainly shaped by my father, a military history buff who stocked our living room shelves with books about every bloody battle from time immemorial. Nestled among these tomes was T. E. Lawrence's memoir *Seven Pillars of Wisdom,* a book decried by many for Lawrence's loose handling of the facts. The thought that a celebrated soldier might embroider his exploits would have been anathema to my father. Accuracy was everything; it was how he measured the worth of a war movie as well.

He was a veteran himself, an oral surgeon who rebuilt bullet-ridden jaws in a MASH unit at the height of the Korean War. I remember how much he anticipated seeing the film *M*A*S*H* when it opened in 1970. Finally, he said, "the forgotten war" would get its proper treatment on the big screen. As a thirteen-year-old with a finely tuned cultural antenna, I knew good and well what kind of treatment the Korean War would get from *M*A*S*H*. He went expecting *Sands of Iwo Jima.* He got *Duck Soup* instead and returned from the theater quite dispirited. *M*A*S*H* turned his wartime service into a joke.

For my dad, *Lawrence* was as a window into history. The Arab revolt against the backdrop of World War I; the secret agreement between France and England to carve up the Middle East after the war; the fact that pretty much every conflict in the region today can be traced back to events depicted in the film—this was the stuff that mattered. Most of the history went right over my head, but with repeated viewings, one thing became clear: at the center of this sprawling film was a puzzle, and that puzzle was Lawrence himself. More than just an Englishman impersonating an Arab, he seemed to be a kind of shape-shifter, continually donning different masks. To quote Kris Kristofferson's famous lyric, "He's a walkin' contradiction, partly truth and partly fiction."

All of which brings us to the close-up in question. The shot occurs two hours and three minutes into the film. It's a silent reaction shot in a nearly wordless scene. Here's the setup. Galvanized by Lawrence's belief that the Arabs deserve a nation of their own, the Harif tribesmen (along with warriors from the Howeitat tribe) overtake the Turkish garrison at the strategically vital Red Sea port of Aqaba. Lawrence is eager to announce the successful raid to his English superiors, and accompanied by his teenage charges Daud and Farraj, he embarks across the punishing Sinai Desert to Cairo. Along the way, young Daud dies after stumbling into quicksand. His death casts a pall over the rest of the journey, as Lawrence descends into a guilt-ridden funk. Lawrence and Farraj, sharing a camel, trudge into an abandoned military outpost. Farraj dismounts, but Lawrence, looking comatose, remains on the camel. Farraj makes his way through the dilapidated barracks, spots something, and excitedly returns. Dragging Lawrence by the hand, Farraj leads him to a berm, beyond which Lawrence is startled to see the smokestack of a huge steamship, gliding past like a ghost. It's a surreal moment and, given Lawrence's narcotic stare, you might guess he's actually hallucinating. When Lawrence and Farraj overtake the berm, they discover they've reached the Suez Canal.

Across the canal, an English soldier approaches on a motorcycle. Stopping directly across from Lawrence and Farraj, the soldier yells, "Who are you?" At this point, David Lean cuts to a close-up of Lawrence, his face caked in sand, staring dead-eyed at his interlocutor. After a beat, the patrolman repeats his question. "Who are you?" he shouts. Another beat. Lawrence says nothing. End of scene.

Who are you, indeed. Lawrence doesn't answer the question, and neither does Lean. The sand plastered on Lawrence's face gives him a deathly pallor, but mostly it looks like pancake makeup. It's another mask, part of Lawrence's Bedouin getup. This visage certainly reinforces the sense that Lawrence is not himself—moreover, that he has no idea who he is. In a film notable for hypnotic landscapes, Lawrence's sand-encrusted face may be the most mysterious one of all.

Lawrence is the story of a penumbra. The hero is an outline—never filled in, never conventionally fleshed out. As a child, I looked to film heroes to create my own sense of identity. I'm hardly alone in this regard. We all measure ourselves against film icons. At age seven, I was very much puzzling out who I was. How do I carry myself on the playground? Am I a leader or a follower? T. E. Lawrence, as portrayed by O'Toole, is a frustrating role model. Bookish, retiring, at times a bit pixieish, he's alternately audacious, egotistical—messianic, even. During Lawrence's first encounter with Sherif Ali, after the latter murders the Englishman's Bedouin guide, Lawrence offers a bold challenge:

"Sherif Ali, so long as the Arabs fight tribe against tribe, so long will they be a little people, a silly people, greedy, barbarous, and cruel, as you are." By all rights, Ali should have put a bullet in Lawrence's head there and then. Instead, he's impressed by Lawrence's bravura. For the audience, Lawrence's gall is kind of baffling.

Who is this guy? Intellectual misfit or crazy maverick?

A quick dive into the T. E. Lawrence literature confirms that this man was, to borrow Winston Churchill's phrase, a riddle wrapped in an enigma. Terence Rattigan's 1960 play about Lawrence, *Ross,* covers much of the same territory as Robert Bolt and Michael Wilson's screenplay for David Lean's film. From the play, here's an astonishing exchange between General Allenby (played by Jack Hawkins in the film) and Ronald Storrs, an English compatriot of Lawrence's in Arabia. At issue is the nature of Lawrence's character:

ALLENBY: I want you to tell me what you think of [Lawrence] as a potential leader. Storrs?

STORRS: Lawrence as a leader? (*Thoughtfully.*) He's pure intellectual, and not by nature a man of action at all. He's strongly introverted, withdrawn and self-conscious, and will never allow anyone to see his true nature. He hides everything behind a manner that's either over-meek, over-arrogant, or over-flippant, whichever is going to disconcert the most. He thinks far too much for the good of his soul and feels far too much for the good of his mind. Consequently he's a highly unstable personality. Finally, he has a sublime contempt for authority—in any form, but chiefly military.

ALLENBY: I see. Not very promising—

STORRS: On the contrary, sir. I think he'd make a military leader of the highest class.

I was still several years away from adolescence when I first saw *Lawrence,* but I knew there was a sexual layer to this character, one that frustrated me in its vagueness. Growing older, I was vexed by conflicting messages about sexuality. Riffling through my father's briefcase, I discovered an issue of *Playboy.* I was afraid to touch it, lest I leave fingerprints. As a Catholic boy in the Vatican II era, I was titillated when school nuns began wearing coifs that revealed a glimpse of their bangs. At the same time, I was instructed that entertaining sexual thoughts was tantamount to turning one's back on God. Needless to say, I was aswirl in mixed signals.

Add to this confusion a hero with a penchant for physical pain. The film did not explore Lawrence's sexuality in any explicit way, but the suggestions it offered were unnerving to me. Sadomasochism was not a dinner table topic in the Kwapis household, so I had to decipher the clues on my own. First, Lawrence is obviously a sadist. He confides to General Allenby that he enjoyed executing one of Ali's men. He took pleasure in it. Later, when Lawrence single-handedly butchers a slew of Turks, he luxuriates in this orgy of blood. Only when catching his reflection in the blade of his bloody scimitar does Lawrence feel any remorse.

Second, he's clearly a masochist. When we first meet Lawrence, he deliberately burns his fingers with a lit match. Most telling is the scene in which Lawrence is tortured at the hands of the Bey, the Turkish chieftain (José Ferrer). Not pictured but certainly implied is the fact that Lawrence's flogging was mere foreplay. A sexual assault by the Bey and his henchmen was no doubt the main event.

This action is directly inspired by Lawrence's account of his torture and rape in *Seven Pillars of Wisdom,* a controversial passage he continually tweaked before publication. What didn't make it into his memoir, something Lawrence later confided in a letter to his friend Charlotte Shaw, was that he found the torture quite gratifying. Lawrence wrote of feeling "a delicious warmth, probably sexual . . . flooding through me . . . a fascination and terror and morbid desire, lascivious and vicious perhaps, but like the striving of a moth towards its flame."

The Lawrence literature is rife with accounts of him submitting to physical pain. Lawrence's brother Arnold, interviewed for a 1986 documentary entitled *Lawrence and Arabia,* offered this theory of his sibling's proclivities: "He hated the thought of sex. He had read any amount of medieval literature about characters, some of them saints, some of them not—who had quelled sexual longings by beatings. And that's what he did." Regardless of Lawrence's sexual orientation, the operative word here is *quelled.* The great project of his life, it seems, was to repress himself.

One moment brash and swaggering, the next self-loathing and guilt-ridden, Lawrence, as portrayed by Peter O'Toole, is messed up and mystifying. Pinning him down is like keeping sand from slipping through your fingers. There may be legendary exploits on his résumé, but as a man, he's completely disconnected from himself, vaporous, unknowable. What's amazing is that Lean mounted a massive epic centered around such a cryptic character.

As storytellers, we're taught to strive for clarity. We want the audience to understand our characters. We want to represent their motivations precisely. An audience may shift its feelings about a character; indeed, viewers may decide that a villain actually has a heart of gold. But they make that shift because we, as storytellers, give them a new understanding. Developing scripts for studios and networks, we're constantly tasked with making things clearer. Imagine a development executive at a major company asking, "Could you make the hero's motivation more nebulous? We'd love it if the audience was fuzzy about why he behaves this way." Midway through *Lawrence of Arabia*, the hero faces us as a blank slate. We've crossed the desert with this man and we are no closer to understanding what makes him tick. At two hours and three minutes, I have more questions than answers, but I trust all will be revealed by the final fade-out.

In fact, nothing is revealed.

As a director, how do you visualize an enigma? In the Suez Canal scene, David Lean gives the hero a mask of sand, but he saves his masterstroke for the final shot of the film. The climactic scene of *Lawrence of Arabia*—it's an anticlimax, really—depicts the Arab forces, under Lawrence's command, taking the city of Damascus. Lawrence's dream of Arab self-rule collapses, though, when the Bedouin prove incapable of administering a provisional government; moreover, his

British overseers arrive and order Lawrence back to England, giving him a token promotion to colonel in the bargain. In the final scene, Lawrence, deflated, clad once more in his army fatigues, is ferried out of Damascus in a jeep. Along the way, the jeep passes a line of camel-riding Bedouin, Lawrence's "people." Then, a motorcycle zooms past the jeep, foreshadowing Lawrence's own cycling calamity at age forty-six, but more immediately kicking up dust on the jeep's windshield. The last image in the film is a medium shot of Lawrence as seen through this sand-blotted windshield. Maurice Jarre's score concludes on a noticeable decrescendo, rare for any film of such epic proportions. Truly, *Lawrence* ends not with a bang but a whimper. As the shot fades, we cannot discern Lawrence's expression at all. Buried behind a dusty scrim, he remains as inscrutable as ever.

THE NOTE BEHIND THE NOTE

"Stand up straight, Ken. You walk like a duck," said my eighth-grade teacher. Let's call her Mrs. Johnson, which may or may not be her real name. I stood with forty other eighth graders on the school playground, engaged in some tedious physical exercise, probably walking in a circle (Van Gogh's 1890 painting *Prisoners Exercising* comes to mind). As you might imagine, my peers found Mrs. Johnson's put-down of my posture quite amusing, and there were no doubt a few quacks (so clever!) amid the general snickering. Already painfully self-conscious about my looks, I was mortified by my teacher's ridicule. Trust me, during the ensuing decades, I've bounced back from far more blistering criticism, but what intrigues me is the way Mrs. Johnson's casually cruel remark, instantly forgettable to her, has permanently lodged itself in my brain. Indeed, it's the most potent memory of eighth grade I have.

I thought about Mrs. Johnson on my first day of graduate school. A gray-haired professor greeted our class of forty or so would-be directors. Let's call him Mr. Johnson, which may or may not be his real name. By way of welcome, Mr. Johnson informed us that becoming a professional film director was a statistical improbability, that we were essentially wasting our parents' money on a useless degree. Mr. Johnson, like many on the faculty, felt it was his job to toughen us up, prepare us for the real world. In practice, that meant delivering incredibly cutting critiques of our work. It's clear to me now that these pitiless put-downs were simply an index of the instructor's own deep insecurity. "Tough love" teachers are a dime a dozen. What fascinated me was how quickly the students internalized this "take no prisoners" attitude and aimed it at their fellows. Showing your rough cut to the class was akin to being a contestant in some blood sport. One insensitive jab begat the next. Rather than moderate this cascade of negativity, our superiors enjoyed watching the class devolve into a mob. A quick sidebar: in Arthur Penn's *Night Moves*, Gene Hackman says, "I saw a Rohmer film once. It was kind of like watching paint dry." My film school cronies quickly adopted this line, with many variations, as a pointed way to inform someone that his or her film (or screenplay) was really dull. "Watching your film was like picking grass" was one memorable variant. The student at the business end of such a barb would just wilt, some never to recover. It's bad enough to be savaged by your teachers. What was new to me, what I was not prepared for, was the eagerness with which students flung destructive feedback at each other. Even after your film was finished—locked, color corrected, answer-printed—some students persisted in reminding you of its shortcomings. Excuse me, *perceived* shortcomings.

I've developed my own code of etiquette about feedback, the major point being that if a work is in progress, if a director invites you into the cutting room or a writer shares a first draft, you should roll up your sleeves and dig in. When a film is completed, on the other hand, you should put away any misgivings and celebrate the achievement. You may still have valid points or astute suggestions, but unless the director has the wherewithal to recall a thousand prints or stop the network from airing a pilot, your comments are irrelevant, so shut up and offer heartfelt congratulations. There's nothing hypocritical or disingenuous about congratulating a director even if you have aesthetic reservations about the final product. As you know, it's well-nigh impossible to get anything made. Crossing that finish line should be cause for praise only. Nobody needs your two cents' worth now, and nothing irks me more than colleagues who are reluctant to embrace your accomplishment because they're clinging to their suggestions. At your big premiere, if a friend pats you on the back and says, "I still think you could've tightened the second act," well, they're probably not your friend.

Having said this, if you're asked to be part of the process, it's a whole different ball game. Now, giving honest feedback requires a bit of delicacy. There are plenty of people in show business who pride themselves on brutal honesty, but what usually lies behind that brutishness is just an insecure need to outrank or overpower someone. I try to keep the human component of feedback in mind. Whether a first draft or a rough cut, somebody birthed this baby; in other words, it couldn't be more personal. But it is possible to represent yourself honestly and take care of someone at the same time.

Here's my ground rule for constructive criticism. The only way to support someone's vision is to understand his or her intentions. Be it a writer or director, somebody made the choice to tell a particular story in a particular way.

Appreciate and honor those intentions. If a director wants to tell a story from a child's point of view, don't advise her to tell it from an adult's point of view. If a writer names his characters the Kid, the Woman, or the Man (this is the case in films as diverse as *Purple Rain* and *The Road*), clearly his intention is to strip away particularities. The vagueness is purposeful. It may not suit you, but don't pull the rug out from under the writer by saying, "These characters are vague."

You may be invited into the process at various points. Let's start with script development. A friend or colleague may want your feedback on a draft, or you may be working with a writer on your own project. Either way, your challenge is to say something precise and useful.

Often the hardest thing to do is actually identify a problem in the script. Many people are quick to offer writers solutions to things that don't need fixing. Plus, it's not necessarily your job to fix anything. Your feedback should inspire writers to come up with their own solutions. Don't do the job for them. "Here's what you should do—" is a dispiriting way to launch a note. Stop pretending you're the savior and vest that power in the writer.

"This dialogue doesn't work for me." If a line in a script sounds clunky, you may be inclined to pitch an alternate, but I urge you to avoid that temptation. Rewriting someone's words is not remotely the same as giving constructive feedback. I don't care if you have a good line up your sleeve. It's more important to specify why you feel the current dialogue isn't working. That usually means shining a light on something other than the dialogue itself. If a line feels inappropriate for a certain character, punching it up may not solve the real problem—namely, that the character is unfocused. "This line is flat" is a common critique, but it's of no use. "I don't understand what's driving this character," on the other hand, directs your writer to confront something more fundamental. And, again, it empowers the writer to come up with the answer.

"It's too expositional." If a piece of dialogue seems top-heavy with information, don't ask your screenwriter to simply massage the line and disguise the information. Pointing out that a line feels overly expositional is less helpful than asking, "Do we need this information?" This shifts the conversation to the larger issue of how to best tell the story. It's possible the audience does need to learn certain facts, but not at that moment in the story. At what point will these details be most impactful? During what scene will the audience be grateful to get the information?

"Your lead character is passive." This is the Molotov cocktail of notes. You're basically telling a writer the story's protagonist is boring. By the way, it's a pretty common problem. Many stories trace the arc of characters who find their voice, who take the reins of their life. In reverse engineering that arc, however, the writer manages to introduce a lifeless character.

Handle this note with care. I've seen more than a few writers freeze at what sounds like a wholesale dismissal of their creation. Your suggestions should be additive: urge the writer to invest the protagonist with a particular set of behaviors. Just because the hero has yet to make a big breakthrough doesn't mean he or she isn't a fully developed person with specific personality traits, drives, and dreams.

"This line isn't funny." Another potential minefield. On more than a few occasions, I've had to persuade a writer that another joke about the male anatomy is not what our story needs. Of course, what's unpalatable to me may be agreeable (and hilarious) to you.

Developing a comic script, there are two challenges you routinely face. The first: urging your screenwriter not to "write to the joke." A well-constructed scene with one joke will be funnier than a humdrum scene with ten. I'm not brushing aside the importance of laughs; I'm just suggesting that the top priority is to shore up the emotional underpinning of the scene. Better for the audience to laugh because they're emotionally involved than chuckle at a snappy one-liner. The second challenge: how to control the comic tone of the script. Sharing a comic sensibility with your writer is like having a secret handshake. Neither of you should have to explain to the other what makes something funny. Invariably, though, a scene or character may feel too farcical or outrageous. "I think this scene is too broad," I once told a writer, who immediately shot back, "You mean, it's too funny?" It was as if I'd breached a sacred trust, and I failed to regain my footing with that writer. If you're convinced the tone isn't *landing,* better to suggest that it's not landing the way the author intended it. Avoid the pitfall of judging someone's sensibility (i.e., I'm sophisticated, you're not). Better still, lean into your writer's strengths. Don't ask Anton Chekhov to write Mel Brooks. Or vice versa. If your writer's instinct is to add a pratfall to the scene, make sure it's a thoroughly organic and character-specific pratfall.

Thinking versus feeling. As discussed in our chapter about being proactive on the set, couch your feedback in "feeling" terms. In the aforementioned example, I said, "I think this scene is too broad." By using the word *think,* I shifted the dialogue to an intellectual plane. Relying on the head rather than the heart, I'm now arguing from a logical point of view. The writer and I are sparring on a left-brain basis. Maybe I should have reframed the comment: "I have a gut feeling this scene is too broad." From a rhetorical stand-point, I'm on much more solid ground. Remember, no one can argue with a feeling. No one can counter, "You don't feel that way."

The sarcasm trap. Here's one more thought about being effective with comic writers, especially those who excel in biting or irreverent humor. As we all know, purveyors of comedy are among the most fragile people in show business. When critiquing a scene, don't forget that even the snarkiest writer doesn't respond well to sarcasm. Often, directors make the mistake of using sarcasm as a crutch to deliver a note to a comedy writer. Don't try to out-snark the writer; let that be his or her domain. Just mindfully communicate. Let the writer translate your idea into suitably caustic form.

Now let's move on to postproduction. After a film wraps, you may be invited to watch a rough cut in the editing room or attend an informal "family and friends" screening. Certain parameters are now set in stone. The film is no longer hypothetical. It exists, even if it does as a work in progress.

"This scene is slow." If a scene or an entire section of the film sags, the easiest and laziest thing to do is suggest trimming or deleting. Another trifling suggestion is to add music to energize a scene. You may feel you're saving the picture, but if you dig below the surface, you'll find the problem lies elsewhere. For instance, what strikes you as a pace problem in the middle of the picture is, in all likelihood, an act 1 problem. If a character or plot element hasn't been properly set up at the beginning, the audience may grow impatient during the middle of the film. Tightening a scene midway through act 2 could turn out to be a useless Band-Aid. The solution to the problem lies in laying the groundwork better at the outset.

"I don't like his performance." In the cutting room, nothing is more counterproductive than complaining about a casting choice. If an actor bungles a line, if his or her performance is ham-handed, don't graciously offer, "You shouldn't have cast so-and-so." Obviously, that ship has sailed. More beneficial is to ask the director to clarify the character's motivation. It's never too late to revisit the basics. The actor in question may have been so taxing that the director lost sight of his or her original intentions for the character. Once reminded, the director can hunt for alternate takes to reinforce that intention. The goal is to inspire your fellow director to excavate the footage for hidden performance moments. Turning one bad line reading into a referendum about an actor's skill is pointless and discouraging.

"If you could only . . ." If a film is in trouble (i.e., audiences don't care for it), unless the financier is eager to shoot more material, it's fruitless to pitch new ideas. Focus your suggestions on what's at hand. You may have a wonderful notion for a scene in your back pocket, but keep it there unless the studio or network opens the floodgates to additional photography. If reshoots are a possibility, one danger is that the director will be deluged with ideas from all corners. It can become quite a free-for-all. If you're part of this process, it behooves you to be laser-specific about what might shift the audience's perception of the story.

Finally, let's switch roles. Now you're in the hot seat. It's the script you wrote or developed with a writer. It's your rough-cut screening. First of all, pat yourself on the back for having the courage to expose yourself to criticism. Whether you directed an infomercial for a hair loss remedy or a searing, autobiographical story, everyone wants to hear their work is flawless. The key is to develop an ability to use feedback—even thoughtless, negative feedback—in a productive way. Needless to say, you should be very discerning about who you invite into the process. It should not come as a shock to learn there are people who actually don't want you to succeed, colleagues who seem well intentioned but would really enjoy watching you fall on your face.

Cast your feedback crew with care. If you ask another director to view your rough cut, you'll presumably have a sympathetic ear, someone who's been in your shoes. At the same time, the critiques you get from other directors may be overdetermined by bad experiences they've had sharing their work. They may unwittingly bring a lot of baggage into the cutting room. The other danger is that a fellow helmer will simply start directing your film for you. "What I would do . . ." is an unmistakable red flag, no matter how reassuring the tone.

If you invite civilians into the cutting room, the upside is their feedback will be untainted by any connection to the business. The downside is they may not be able to articulate what's bothering them about any given moment in the story. Without spelling out your intentions, it's up to you to probe their reactions.

Whether your audience is a seasoned professional or a supportive spouse, an anxious agent or a complete stranger, you need to look for *the note behind the note*. "I didn't like this scene . . ." or "You should cut here . . ." or "Feels a little long . . ." or "The temp music isn't working . . ." are symptoms of problems your viewers aren't able to identify. And as we've seen, you will get many solutions to nonproblems. "Something's bugging me but I can't tell you what it is" may be the most helpful critique a director can receive. By asking the right questions, you can use that gut reaction as a signpost, one that will lead you to the heart of the matter.

TRAPPED AT WORK

More than a few pundits opined that *The Office* took a while to find its footing, but I would argue that the second episode of the series, "Diversity Day," written by B. J. Novak, marked a rare moment in which all the elements—writing, performance, comic tone, shooting style—were in perfect alignment. I want to single out one directorial choice that I feel was critical to the episode. It was a simple blocking idea, and you may wonder whether it's worth all the scrutiny I want to give it. Basic as it was, though, the decision not only fortified the comedy but proved to be a signature bit of staging for the series as a whole. And this blocking choice also speaks to bigger questions about what makes a workplace comedy tick. Before examining that choice, however, here's a quick rundown of "Diversity Day."

An unnamed Dunder Mifflin employee files a complaint with Human Resources after Michael Scott tells a racially insensitive joke. The corporate office assigns Mr. Brown (Larry Wilmore) to hold a diversity seminar at the Scranton branch, which gets out of hand when a frustrated Michael blurts out the joke again, much of which is bleeped out (by design, of course). When Mr. Brown privately informs Michael that he was the sole reason for the sensitivity seminar in the first place, Michael retaliates by holding his own diversity seminar, which is by turns appalling and utterly birdbrained. As part of Michael's "training" session, each staff member must wear an index card Scotch-taped to his or her forehead.

Unseen by the wearer, each card is labeled with the name of a racial or ethnic group, and Michael urges staffers to pair off and interrogate each other using the broadest stereotypes possible: "You're going to treat people like the race on their forehead. Sounds like fun, huh?" Michael thoughtfully excludes a few ethnic groups. As he tells us in an aside, "You'll notice I didn't have anybody be an Arab. I thought that would be too explosive. No pun intended. But I just thought too soon for Arabs. Maybe next year. You know, the ball's in their court."

Michael's daft seminar covers the latter half of "Diversity Day," and there was discussion about how and where to stage it. With all the characters milling about, it was akin to a cocktail party. Wouldn't it be prudent to set the action in the Dunder Mifflin bullpen? We could position characters throughout the space and let Michael careen from desk to desk, overseeing his experiment. From a practical standpoint, this was certainly advantageous. It would enable us to isolate and fine-tune individual vignettes. And it would give the set piece a real sense of scope.

My gut, however, told me the sequence would actually lose its punch in an open space, that its energy needed to be contained. I argued for staging Michael's entire seminar in the small Dunder Mifflin conference room. There were many good reasons not to do this. In the first act, Mr. Brown conducts his seminar in the conference room, with the staff seated as if in a classroom. That sequence alone spans nearly ten pages. Would the episode feel stifling if most of the action took place in one room, and a crowded room at that? Plus, as a director, shouldn't I create variety in my staging? With the cast arrayed across the bullpen, I could feature all corners of the set, adding production value to the story. There were other considerations. This was our second episode out of the gate, and given the enormous shadow cast by the British original, the stakes felt particularly high for me. Cramming the whole ensemble into a tight space would no doubt make everyone irritable. Working in confined quarters was bound to be a headache for the crew as well. Still, my hunch was the comedy would be stronger if the employees were essentially trapped in one room. I racked my brain for some movie antecedent, partly to assure Greg Daniels and partly to convince myself that this was a good plan, when I suddenly recalled one of the most celebrated comic scenes set in an absurdly cramped space: the stateroom scene in the Marx Brothers' *A Night at the Opera*, directed by Sam Wood.

Here's how the stateroom scene unfolds. Boarding an ocean liner bound for New York, Otis B. Driftwood (Groucho Marx) invites well-to-do Mrs. Claypool (Margaret Dumont) to his cabin for a tryst. Upon arrival, Driftwood discovers that his cabin is basically the size of a closet, with barely enough room for his steamer trunk. He's doubly dismayed to find Fiorello (Chico Marx), Tomasso (Harpo Marx), and Ricardo (Allan Jones) hiding in said steamer trunk. The stowaways refuse to leave without food, forcing Driftwood to summon a steward. After taking Driftwood's order, the steward departs, whereupon a succession of no less than a dozen people make their way into the tiny room, some by mistake ("Is my aunt Minnie in here?"), many to perform a job ("I've come to mop up").

The scene is a veritable ballet of comic claustrophobia, and watching it again for the first time in years made me confident that trapping the Dunder Mifflin staff in the conference room for the second half of "Diversity Day" was the right move.

The gambit paid off. The spectacle of discomfited employees milling about with labels Scotch-taped to their foreheads (e.g., *Black, Asian, Jewish*), all chagrined by the presence of a "documentary crew," not to mention Michael Scott gleefully encouraging everyone to "stir the melting pot!"—worked perfectly in the oppressive space. Steve Carell's unflinching commitment to Michael Scott's harebrained ideas about race is what drives the scene, but it doesn't hurt that Michael's tutorial takes place in a human petri dish.

Michael grows frustrated that his employees aren't making a "breakthrough," though it's hardly obvious what constitutes a breakthrough in this preposterous exercise. When Kelly Kapoor (Mindy Kaling) returns from a phone meeting, Michael decides to push her buttons by adopting an offensive Indian accent.

Kelly slaps him in the face, bringing the entire charade to a crashing halt. As if the staff hasn't been stuck there long enough, Michael insists on everyone staying put to hear his postmortem on the day's events, which quickly turns into a total pity party. The ordeal is so wearying that Pam falls asleep on Jim's shoulder, a singular moment for Jim that re-deems this otherwise disheartening day.

There are visual cues that add to the sense of entrapment. As I mentioned before, the Dunder Mifflin set was designed with no "wild walls." Nothing can be removed to give the crew any elbow room. The stateroom scene in *A Night at the Opera* is shot with a camera clearly positioned outside the state-room, but in "Diversity Day," the documentary crew feels just as trapped in the conference room as the employees. The camera swings from character to character, suggesting there's only room for one operator. The crowded quarters force us to use wide-angle lenses; as a result, the camera feels just as intrusive as Michael Scott as he monitors his workers.

"Diversity Day" paved the way for many episodes in which Michael orders the staff into the conference room for what turns out to be a mortifying spectacle. Greg once referred to the room as Dunder Mifflin's "crucible," the container in which employees are forced to endure Michael's boneheaded bromides. His showboating invariably results in someone be-ing humiliated. The episode "Gay Witch Hunt" ends with a lengthy conference room scene during which Michael "outs" Oscar (Oscar Nunez) in front of his cohorts—he effectively turns the conference room into an inquisition court straight out of Arthur Miller. Determined to prove he's a forward-thinking, open-minded boss, Michael unwittingly puts Oscar on trial:

MICHAEL

Gays today are not who some of you
think. Anybody can be gay these days.

```
Great athletes, like female weight
lifters; businessmen, like antique
dealers or hairdressers or even
paper salesmen. There's even a gay
mafia. Oscar, why don't you take this
opportunity to officially come out to
everyone however you would like?
```

Michael's henchman Dwight Schrute (Rainn Wilson) insists on rooting out the entire gay contingent of the Dunder Mifflin staff: "I think the other office gays should identify themselves, or I will do it for them." Dwight proceeds to "expose" various employees, Pam among them:

```
                DWIGHT
How about Pam?


                PAM
I'm sorry?


                DWIGHT
She canceled her wedding to Roy, who is
quite a catch, without giving any good
reasons.
```

Like the botched diversity seminar, Michael's attempt to establish his gay-sensitive bona fides only succeeds in offending everyone. Yet, objectionable as it is, no one leaves in protest. Not wanting to lose their jobs, everyone quietly suffers through the ordeal of Michael spouting every gay stereotype in the book. Oscar finally declares, "I don't know if I can work here any longer. This was one of the worst backward experiences of my life." Oscar makes a move to leave, but his escape is thwarted by Michael, who insists on publicly kissing him to make a statement: "You're my friend, and I don't care who knows it." There is no good reason for Oscar to remain in the room, but he does, suffering through the most uncomfortable, hard-to-watch kiss on record. Why does he stay? Oscar's immobility, his not leaving, feels completely relatable. His paralysis is just an acute version of what all the employees feel in that moment. It's as if the room has everyone in its clutches.

What is it about being trapped at work that's so conducive to humor? Is the conference room an emblem of some existential rut we're all stuck in? Let's return to Otis B. Driftwood's cabin in *A Night at the Opera* for a moment. I'm fascinated by the manner in which the ocean liner workers diligently go about their business. No one acknowledges the impossibility of getting anything done in such a densely packed space. To leave the room, on the other hand, seems unthinkable.

Everyone quietly tends to his or her task—it's a somnambulist chorus of worker bees. There are two maids ("We've come to make up your room"), an engineer ("I'm here to turn off the heat"), a manicurist ("Did you want your nails long or short?"), the engineer's assistant, a cleaning woman, and, finally, four waiters carrying large trays of food. Visually, this mad tableau is like a parody of a Depression-era WPA mural, with industrious men and women jammed elbow to elbow in a frieze celebrating the value of hard work and the importance of operating as a team. In the Marx Brothers' version, everyone has their nose to the grindstone, but absolutely nothing gets accomplished.

The stateroom scene is a workplace comedy in miniature. I've helped launch several TV workplace comedies, *The Office*, *The Larry Sanders Show*, and *Outsourced* among them. One ground rule, it seems, is that the workplace is populated by people who wouldn't otherwise socialize with one another, who are bound together by economic necessity. Everyone needs to make ends meet, so a motley family forms. Second, characters usually work together in one space, be it a bullpen or a tavern. They are effectively stuck together. Critic James Wolcott, in *The New Yorker*, described the workplace in *The Larry Sanders Show* as an "ant farm," adding, "The studio maze where 'Larry Sanders' is taped fosters a bunker-like mentality." Often, the work itself is uninspiring (selling paper products) or, in the case of *Outsourced*, ludicrous. The employees of the Mumbai call center in *Outsourced* are tasked with selling American novelty items, goofy trinkets for which the employees have no cultural coordinates. Some novelties are unfathomable (a cheese-head hat); most are simply childish (a toilet-bowl coffee mug). To do their jobs well, the Indian characters must embrace idiotic notions of what Americans consider funny.

Often the workers share a common enemy that's abstract and remains at arm's length. In *Outsourced*, the enemy over the horizon is American cultural hegemony, or, more broadly speaking, late capitalism in all its excesses. In *M*A*S*H*—yes, this is a workplace comedy—the real enemy is the American government that persists in prolonging the war. In *The Larry Sanders Show*, the enemy is the network, with its bean-counter mentality, its insistence that the talk show cater to the lowest common denominator. Against this soul-sucking apparatus, as James Wolcott noted, "*The Larry Sanders Show* is a small-unit guerrilla campaign to retain one's artistry and remain a reasonable facsimile of a human being."

Like Dunder Mifflin, many fictional workplaces are overseen by a narcissistic and, naturally, thin-skinned boss. For me, *Hogan's Heroes* is an exemplary workplace comedy. Like *M*A*S*H, Hogan's Heroes* lasted longer than the war it portrayed.

The prisoner of war camp is managed by the nincompoop Colonel Klink (Werner Klemperer) and sycophantic Sergeant Schultz (John Banner), perfect predecessors of Michael Scott and Dwight Schrute. In the series, the workplace is literally a prison, and the twist is that the POWs routinely escape to conduct espionage on behalf of the Allied forces. If Hogan's men had any sense, of course, they'd flee to freedom. Instead, as in all workplace comedies, the "employees" of Stalag 13 dutifully return to prison. Yes, there's a bit of logic here; Stalag 13 is the base of operations from which the men conduct underground missions. Emotionally, however, one gets the feeling these POWs prefer confinement to freedom. Or, to put it another way, they prefer their workplace family to a real one.

Indeed, one challenge of directing a workplace comedy is generating interest in the characters' lives outside of work. I am a fan of the genre, and I get impatient when a workplace story follows a character home. I'm eager to return to the interpersonal dynamic at the office. The characters seem to derive more sustenance from their ersatz families than their real ones. In *The Shop Around the Corner,* for my money the workplace comedy par excellence, director Ernst Lubitsch and screenwriter Samson Raphaelson solve the problem by simply keeping the employees' families off-screen. We hear about various relations but never meet them. The workers' off-camera lives may be compelling, but our interest lies with the dysfunctional unit that clocks in each morning at Matuschek & Company.

Greg Daniels brought these two worlds together in an episode of *The Office* entitled "Dinner Party," directed by Paul Feig and written by Lee Eisenberg and Gene Stupnitsky. In the story, Michael Scott has moved in with former Dunder Mifflin executive Jan Levinson (Melora Hardin), and the two host a dinner party for a handful of Dunder Mifflin employees. The dynamic of the office is transported intact to Michael and Jan's condominium, and the result is that the guests feel as trapped in the dining room as they would in the Dunder Mifflin conference room.

Speaking of being stuck at dinner, it would be criminal not to mention one of the singular comedies of entrapment, Luis Buñuel's *The Exterminating Angel.* In the story, written by Buñuel and Luis Alcoriza, a black-tie dinner party is held at the posh residence of an upper-crust Mexican couple, Señor Edmundo Nóbile (Enrique Rambal) and his wife, Lucía (Lucy Gallardo). As the evening winds down, for some inexplicable reason, none of the guests leave. No one's preventing them from getting their coats and heading to their respective abodes. Days pass, and the guests grow unruly and uncivilized. Buñuel offers no explanation for the group's paralysis. Are they just slaves to bourgeois respectability? Could be. What's clear is the characters are locked in an endless loop of unproductive behavior. Like the hero of Harold Ramis's *Groundhog Day,* all they need to do is recognize these patterns to jump off that treadmill—or in the case of *The Exterminating Angel,* leave the living room. Like the Dunder Mifflin conference room, the door to Señor Nóbile's mansion is wide open. But no one uses it.

I can't resist a quick sidebar about Buster Keaton, who sometimes seems trapped by the actual film frame itself. Noted for his startling agility, we often see Keaton sprint at superhuman speed, but if the camera tracks beside him, the effect is of someone running in place, furiously moving and going nowhere. If there's a better image of the universal dilemma of feeling stuck in a vicious cycle, please let me know.

We laugh at Michael Scott because we feel superior to him, but we laugh at the Dunder Mifflin staff trapped in the conference room because, perhaps, we are them. We all struggle against lives of quiet desperation. We may have the keys to our own cells, but like the POWs of Stalag 13, we often choose confinement over freedom. Characters trapped by cultural conventions, stuck in tiny cubicles, ambushed by boring coworkers, mired in dysfunctional relationships, replaying a pointless script over and over again—it's possible, of course, for all of them to get out of that loop. To make a shift. To walk out of the conference room.

But it wouldn't be very funny, would it?

DESIGNING A FLUID MASTER

Why is the long take, in which action unfolds without a single cut, so alluring to filmmakers? Directors and cinephiles love to argue the merits of famous long takes, the more extravagantly staged the better. Is the three-minute-and-twenty-second tracking shot in Orson Welles's *Touch of Evil* more glorious than the three-minute-and-five-second Steadicam tour of the Copacabana in Martin Scorsese's *Goodfellas*? Are both of these shots outclassed by the deliriously intricate four-minute-and-fifty-three-second opening of Brian De Palma's *The Bonfire of the Vanities*? Does Cary Joji Fukunaga's six-minute tour de force in the fourth episode of the first season of *True Detective* leave them all in the dust? I've found myself trapped in fiery debates about which single-take action scene deserves the crown. Is the hospital shoot-out in John Woo's *Hard Boiled* more breathtaking than the hallway fight in Park Chan-wook's *Oldboy*?

Whether a long take actually reinforces the emotional core of the scene is far less interesting than how flamboyant it is, how complicated the interplay between actors and camera, not to mention the duration of the shot.

What excites film lovers is directorial derring-do, as if the filmmaker is executing an acrobatic feat rather than telling a story. Or juggling. There's no disguising a mistake in juggling. If one of the balls hits the ground, the audience groans, the juggler retrieves the ball and resumes the act. Long-take bravado is about how many cinematic balls a director can keep aloft . . . without a cut.

In the photochemical era, the length of a 35 mm film roll was one thousand feet, which runs about eleven minutes. You could design a fifteen-minute shot, but technically there was no way to achieve it (in 35 mm) before the advent of digital cinema. In his 1948 film *Rope,* Alfred Hitchcock used cinematic sleight of hand to overcome this limitation. The film consists of ten long takes, ranging between five and ten minutes apiece. Hitchcock uses foreground wipes to hide the transitions between shots, effectively fooling the audience into believing the film is comprised of a single take.

Today it's possible to digitally stitch together shots to create the illusion of an uninterrupted take. In *1917,* director Sam Mendes uses visual effects to hide the seams between shots, creating the sensation that we are experiencing the story in real time. Indeed, it's now common to see long takes that are mostly computer-generated—they barely depend on photography at all. Does the lengthy opening shot of Alfonso Cuarón's *Gravity,* in which George Clooney and Sandra Bullock whirl in outer space, even qualify as a "take"?

Semantics aside, the key question is: What makes a long take preferable to staging the action with different camera angles? Would Scorsese's Copacabana scene feel as exhilarating if it were a series of shots? Would the hallway fight in *Oldboy* lose its grandeur if designed as a montage? Would the opening of *Touch of Evil* feel as suspenseful if it didn't unfold in real time? Many directors favor long takes to capture action that, as a carnival barker might say, "must be seen to be believed." Watching Astaire and Rogers perform a thrilling dance in one take, framed from head to toe, is certainly more satisfying than watching the same dance from multiple angles. In this sense, the prison fight in *Oldboy* is not unlike an Astaire and Rogers number. In the scene, the story's hero, Oh Dae-su (Choi Min-sik), is attacked by no less than a dozen guards, but Dae-su overcomes them all, even with a knife stuck in his back. The battle takes place in an extremely narrow corridor, but Park Chan-wook constructed a cutaway set, affording a proscenium-style view of the action. The director frames Dae-su and his opponents in a wide shot and tracks along the corridor as Dae-su lays waste to every single combatant. The camera movement creates the impression of a scroll being unfurled. It's an animated tableau, like an ancient tapestry commemorating a historic battle. The fight is a grueling endurance test for Dae-su, and the absence of cutting reinforces the arduous nature of his effort. The choreography could not be more stylized, but the duration of the shot lends veracity to the action. You are a witness to his perseverance.

Park's composition puts the viewer at arm's length from the action, but many filmmakers use long takes to create an immersive experience. Alejandro Iñárritu wanted *Birdman* to play as an uninterrupted shot to create an intense connection with the hero, Riggan Thomson (Michael Keaton). He was striving for a kind of psychological verisimilitude; indeed, describing his choice, the director has said, "We live our lives with no editing."

Scorsese's Copacabana shot is a peerless technical achievement, but it's memorable because it immerses you in the specific emotional reality of its characters. There are plenty of long takes in which a Steadicam gratuitously slaloms through some labyrinthian space. In *Goodfellas*, the camera movement and the shot's duration completely support the characters' story.

Let's break it down. We follow Henry Hill (Ray Liotta) and his date, Karen Friedman (Lorraine Bracco), as they cross West Forty-seventh Street toward the nightclub. They bypass the waiting line, descend a stairway leading to the employees' entrance, snake down a long hallway into a busy kitchen, finally making their way into the club proper. The maître d' greets the couple, then dispatches a busboy to place a table near the stage especially for Henry and his date. The camera follows the busboy as he zigzags through the club, table hoisted over his head. Henry and Karen reenter the shot and take a seat. A complimentary bottle of wine is delivered, prompting a pan to reveal the gifter, Mr. Tony, and his cronies, all of whom raise their glasses to Henry. As the couple settles, we hear the master of ceremonies announce the night's headliner, and the camera pans to reveal "King of the One-Liners" Henny Youngman.

Much of the shot trails behind Henry and Karen, but emotionally it puts you firmly in their shoes. You feel their exhilaration, particularly Karen's—this is her first time at the storied nightclub, and her date is being treated like the mayor. The aggressive camera move also highlights Henry's elation. Showing off for Karen, he's practically giddy. His criminal career is on the upswing, and the shot feels like a victory lap for him. One can cite longer takes with even more daunting challenges, but this one earns its renown because the emotional content and the technical feat are in perfect alignment.

Four years after *Goodfellas* was released, NBC premiered the medical drama *ER*. The long take quickly became part of the show's visual language. The producers of *ER* actively encouraged directors to stage "oners," to complete whole scenes in one shot, often encompassing long stretches of dialogue by a host of characters. Needless to say, the Steadicam never rested—that is, the Steadicam operator never rested. A hospital emergency room is a high-energy workplace, and the show's house style—long takes and constant camera movement—created a uniquely immersive experience. The oner seemed tailor-made for multiple events occurring simultaneously, the camera careening from one interaction to the next, giving viewers a chance to catch up with all the major characters in a single brushstroke. For television, it was visually bold and, from a production standpoint, very time-efficient. Other ensemble dramas quickly followed suit, and soon it was typical for directors to cover pages of dialogue in a oner, or—to cite a phrase in common parlance, a "walk-and-talk." We've seen innumerable scenes in which characters spout exposition— "laying pipe"—while walking with great determination, the camera gliding in front of them, its movement supplying a kind of ersatz intensity in the absence of any real drama.

As a fledgling filmmaker, you may find extended takes

enticing but don't have the means to accomplish them. A Stea-dicam might not be in your budget. You may lack the amount of track needed to do a marathon dolly shot. You cannot afford the time to rehearse and shoot a three-minute tour of the Copacabana. But that doesn't mean you can't design a long take that's both dramatically organic and visually compelling, even for a scene that consists entirely of intimate dialogue. First things first: let's adjust our nomenclature. Instead of *oner,* which for me connotes a kind of brawny bravura ("We pulled it off in a oner!"), let's substitute the phrase *fluid master.* (I give full credit, by the way, to Gyula Gazdag, artistic director of the Sundance Directors Lab, for introducing me to this useful designation.) *Fluid master* keeps the focus on the dramatic components of a scene. What are the beats? How do they develop? How does the dynamic shift between the characters? If you're directing a dialogue scene between two people, set in a confined space and not, say, a sprawling emergency room, most would opt for traditional coverage (e.g., over-the-shoulder shots, close-ups). Imagining the same scene as a fluid master, however, you can employ every conceivable angle and image size . . . without a single cut.

Orson Welles does this very thing in *The Magnificent Ambersons,* a film that eight decades on continues to yield fresh riches, especially if you want to learn about staging. (Full disclosure: I "borrow" Welles's blocking ideas as often as humanly possible.) There's a three-page exchange between a pair of characters in *Ambersons* that's simple and instructive. It's a model of how to take a nominally static scene and turn it into a nimbly choreographed, single-take gem.

Here's the setup. Twentysomething George Minafer (Tim Holt) is enraged to discover that the townspeople of Indianapolis (a small town at the turn of the century) have been gossiping about his mother, Isabel Amberson Minafer (Dolores Costello), spreading a rumor that Eugene Morgan (Joseph Cotten) is pursuing the recently widowed Isabel. The scandalous implication is that Isabel welcomed Eugene's wooing before her husband's passing. George confronts one of the purported gossipmongers, his next-door neighbor Mrs. Johnson (Dorothy Vaughan). Here, from the shooting script, is the scene:

```
INT. MRS. JOHNSON'S HOME—DAY
The front doorbell is ringing insistently.
Mrs. Johnson hurries to it and opens the
door, admitting George.

          MRS. JOHNSON
     Mr. Amberson—I mean Mr. Minafer.
     I'm really delighted.


          GEORGE
          (in a strained loud voice)
     Mrs. Johnson, I've come to ask you
     a few questions.


          MRS. JOHNSON
          (becoming grave)
     Certainly, Mr. Minafer. Anything I
     can—
```

GEORGE

I don't mean to waste any time,
Mrs. Johnson. You were talking about
a—you were discussing a scandal
that involved my mother's name.

MRS. JOHNSON

Mr. Minafer!

GEORGE

My aunt told me you repeated this
scandal to her.

MRS. JOHNSON
                (sharply)
I don't think your aunt can have
said that. We may have discussed
some few matters that've been a
topic of comment about town—

GEORGE

Yes! I think you may have! That's
what I'm here about, and what I
intend to—

MRS.JOHNSON
                (crisply)
Don't tell me what you intend, please.
And I'd prefer it if you wouldn't make
your voice quite so loud in this
house, which I happen to own.

                    GEORGE
I can't stand this!

                  MRS. JOHNSON
I had a perfect right to discuss
the subject with your aunt. Other
people may be less considerate.

                    GEORGE
          (viciously)
Other people! That's what I want to
know about—these other people! How
many?

She doesn't answer.

                    GEORGE
How many? What?

                  MRS. JOHNSON
What?

                    GEORGE
I want to know how many other
people talk about it.

                  MRS. JOHNSON
Really, this isn't a courtroom
and I'm not a defendant in a libel
suit.

> GEORGE
> (losing control)
> You may be! I want to know just who's dared to say these things, if I have to force my way into every house in town, and I'm going to make them take every word of it back! I mean to know the name of every slanderer that's spoken of this matter to you and of every tattler you've passed it on to yourself. I mean to know—
>
> MRS. JOHNSON
> (rising)
> You'll know something pretty quick! You'll know that you're out in the street. Please to leave my house!

George stiffens sharply—bows and strides out the door.

George, arrogant and pugnacious, assumes Mrs. Johnson will buckle under his assault, but she squares up to him and holds her own. George's reproach completely backfires, and the unflappable Mrs. Johnson shows him the door.

Let's come up with a traditional shooting plan. We know George's goal: he intends to accuse Mrs. Johnson of spreading scurrilous gossip. We are effectively telling the scene from George's perspective, so a logical choice would be to open with George's point of view of Mrs. Johnson as she appears at her front door. To reinforce the sense that we're telling George's story, perhaps we add a *moving* POV shot as George enters Mrs. Johnson's drawing room. If we're clever, George can enter *his own* POV and turn to face Mrs. Johnson.

Now the two characters butt heads. The conventional and by no means inelegant choice would be to stage their confrontation in a series of increasingly tighter shots, the better to mirror the rising conflict between them. In the editing room, these pieces enable you to control the tempo of the scene and highlight specific performance moments. You have the ability to delete a line or two. You may decide to shift perspective from the belligerent George to the besieged Mrs. Johnson, giving her words and reactions more weight in the tussle. This is something you can only do if you have shots to manipulate.

In staging the scene, perhaps Mrs. Johnson moves to evade the pestering George, who demands she divulge the names of all the neighbors with whom she's spoken. Is it an evasive move? Maybe Mrs. Johnson slips past him to gather her strength for the next sally, in which she sternly reminds George that's she not on trial.

A conventional shot list would include a pair of close-ups as the scene reaches its climax. George, frustrated by Mrs. Johnson's lack of contrition, announces his intention to root out every slanderer in town. His overreaction deserves a tight close-up. For her part, Mrs. Johnson basically tells George to get the hell out of her house. An equally tight close-up of her would be welcome. Again, the change in image size mirrors the rising intensity of their contretemps.

Yes, it's a standard-issue approach, seven or eight shots, enlivened mainly by George's *moving POV* as he marches into Mrs. Johnson's house, and a bit of choreography as they spar, culminating with a reliable pair of close-ups as the pot reaches a boil.

What Welles does is take every one of the shots just mentioned and combine them into a seamless, fluid master. There's nothing showy or conspicuous about his staging; in fact, when I first watched the scene (it runs just under eighty seconds), I assumed there were cuts. What delights me about this deftly designed shot is that it required no special toys or visual effects. All that was needed was a bit of ingenuity.

In place of complementary angles, Welles continually re-positions his actors so that key lines are always delivered to camera. He does begin the scene with George's moving POV as he strides into the room. When George levels his accusation at Mrs. Johnson, the angle favors him, as seen over her shoulder. At this point their dance begins, with George and Mrs. Johnson trading places within the frame, circling each other, advancing and retreating. The choreography is not arbitrary; indeed, each move seems tactical—a parry here, a riposte there. Camera movement is minimal, but as their argument heats up, George and Mrs. Johnson move closer to the lens.

It's unforced, effortless, yet fully designed. All the angles and image sizes you'd expect in traditional coverage are here, but the director has woven them into one smooth shot.

Welles transforms what could have been an inert ex-change into a sly pas de deux. Each move underscores the power shift between George and Mrs. Johnson. The camera does nothing striking; yet there's a musicality in the way the actors interact with the lens. I repeat—this is not a shot that calls attention to itself, but there's a little master class in staging to be found here, and the result is graceful. Needless to say, not every scene should be executed as a fluid master, but even with a scant amount of time, inadequate equipment, and a skeleton crew, you can take the most unassuming scene and produce a jewel.

RECOGNIZING YOURSELF

The day *He's Just Not That into You* was released on DVD, I went to my local video store, excited to see my ninth feature on display. By the way, asking a video store employee to direct you to one of your own titles could be perilous. In the heyday of home video, staffers were known for their fervid, unsolicited opinions. The young woman I spoke with that afternoon, however, was a fan of the film, except she wasn't sure where to find it. "Is *He's Just Not That into You* under drama or comedy?" she asked a fellow staffer, who wasn't sure either. It turns out copies of the DVD had been placed in both sections. No one was quite certain where it belonged, which I took as a small triumph. My hope was to make a film that behaved a little differently from what was expected of the genre. But which genre? *He's Just Not That into You* deals with romance, but it doesn't feel like a rom-com; indeed, it eschews many tropes of romantic comedy. The story features scenes of real heartbreak, but it's hardly a romantic drama in the tradition of classics like Leo McCarey's *Love Affair*. What is it, exactly?

He's Just Not That into You began its life as an offhanded remark in the writers' room of the HBO series *Sex and the City*. As writer Liz Tuccillo describes it, the mostly female staff routinely drew inspiration from their own experiences, "our personal love lives weaving in and out of the fictional lives we were creating in the room." On that day, one of the writers was dissecting the mixed messages she was getting from a guy.

Everyone weighed in on the matter, among them writer Greg Behrendt, a consultant whose principle job was to offer a straight-male point of view on the show's plot lines. As Liz recalls, Greg's prognosis was simple: "Listen, it sounds like he's just not that into you."

After concurring that Greg had a point, the staff developed a story exploring this theme, which resulted in the episode "Pick-a-Little, Talk-a-Little" (written by Julie Rottenberg and Elisa Zuritsky). This little truth bomb also inspired Liz Tuccillo and Greg Behrendt to pen a self-help book entitled *He's Just Not That into You: The No-Excuse Truth to Understanding Guys*. To say this book struck a chord with the public is a major understatement. Taking a tough-love approach to its mainly female readership, Behrendt and Tuccillo catalog the innumerable excuses women make for the men in their lives or the ones they desire. The book covers everything from how women rationalize inattentive men ("But he's got a lot on his mind") to excusing a commitment-phobe ("He's just not ready"). For many, it was a refreshingly blunt wake-up call.

When *He's Just Not That into You* was published in 2004, Hollywood was not in the habit of turning self-help books into movies. For instance, there is no feature film based on such stalwarts of the genre as Dale Carnegie's *How to Win*

Friends and Influence People. The conventional wisdom was that people don't want to be lectured to at the movies.

Audiences want to escape their problems, not be reminded of them. And female viewers definitely don't want to be told they're wasting their lives making excuses for disappointing men, right? Well, producers Nancy Juvonen and Drew Barrymore thought otherwise. Their debut collaboration, *Never Been Kissed,* was a crowd-pleasing romantic comedy starring Drew as an insecure twenty-five-year-old who yearns for love. To adapt Behrendt and Tuccillo's advice book, Juvonen and Barrymore enlisted their *Never Been Kissed* screenwriters Abby Kohn and Marc Silverstein, but this time the goal was markedly different—namely, to bring to the big screen a book with no characters and no plot.

Kohn and Silverstein's solution was to create a theme-and-variations structure. The theme: we all need to stop making excuses for people who aren't interested in us. We need to read interpersonal signals better. The screenplay follows nine characters whose lives intersect. Some are guilty of misreading messages, while others send signals that are mixed or blatantly dishonest.

When I cracked open the screenplay, I expected a buoyant ensemble comedy along the lines of *Love, Actually.* Instead, I was surprised to find a story filled with rejection and misery. At one point or another, every character—male and female—suffers rejection. In her introduction to the book, Tuccillo argues that facing the awful truth will free you: "We're taught that in life, we should try to look on the bright side, to be optimistic. Not in this case. In this case, look on the dark side. Assume rejection first. Assume you're the rule, not the exception."

My second reaction was that I wish I'd read the script in college, when I wasted far too much time pining after people who never gave me the time of day. Plus, the message of the story, that we need to decode signals more accurately, extends far beyond the realm of romance. In my work life, I often find myself making excuses for someone's glaring indifference. Here's a typical scenario. I pitch a project to a studio on, let's say, Thursday. "We'll get back to you soon," the executive in charge announces at the end of the meeting. Friday comes and goes, but, hey, it's only been twenty-four hours. The executive no doubt needs the weekend to mull over my project. Monday comes and goes but, hey, the studio's big release tanked over the weekend and everyone's in damage-control mode. Tuesday comes and goes, but, hey, that's the day the studio holds its staff meetings. The week drags on, I get nothing but radio silence, and my excuses for the nonresponse grow more and more tortured: "Clearly, there must be a death in the family. I'm sure I'll hear something on Monday." In so much of life, we cling to the hope that we're the exception, not the rule. But what's the alternative? To assume rejection at every turn? Is the glass always half-empty?

Kohn and Silverstein's script offers no fantasy solution to the problems its characters face. There's no call girl with a heart of gold who gets swept off her feet by a wealthy corporate raider. Love does not magically triumph over class, race, religious, or ideological barriers. In fact, the only barriers are internal. To varying degrees, all nine characters have a talent for denying the obvious. A few recognize what's standing in their way. Most don't. And Kohn and Silverstein pull no punches. As one character declares, "If a guy is treating you like he doesn't give a shit—he doesn't. No exceptions." Does this sound like dialogue from a frothy romantic comedy? I think not, and that's what appealed to me.

Meeting with Drew Barrymore and Nancy Juvonen, I made a simple pitch: the measure of success for the picture is whether or not you recognize yourself in all the characters. To accomplish that, we need to abandon the idea that there are any heroes or villains in the story. Everyone is yearning for a meaningful connection, and everyone is flawed. Even a character who makes an ill-advised choice does so for perfectly good reasons. The script explores—*exposes* might be a better word—people at their most vulnerable, at their neediest. The big challenge, I suggested, is to not shy away from behavior that will make an audience cringe in embarrassment. (In the following chapter on test screenings, I will detail viewer reaction to the single most cringe-inducing scene in the film.)

Needy people, as we all know, can try a person's patience. Once I had a colleague who pored over a one-word text message from a potential date for hours, trying to rationalize and even defend what was obviously a rejection. And a curt one at that. Well past midnight, having polished off a bottle of wine, my coworker drafted innumerable replies, discarding one after another until finally sending the most problematic one. Immediately regretting the decision, she spent the remainder of the night drafting a follow-up, designed as a disclaimer, in the vain hope of neutralizing the original, bungled message. Shuffling into work the next morning, my red-eyed associate cried on my shoulder about the entire misspent night, then asked me to rate all the messages considered but not sent, while clinging to the hope that an encouraging reply would arrive shortly.

Here's how *Webster's Dictionary* defines *pathetic*: "Having a capacity to move one to either compassionate or contemptuous pity." Many characters in *He's Just Not That into You* move one to pity, but first among equals in this department is Gigi, who fancies Conor, a guy who couldn't care less about her. After their one and only date, Gigi repeatedly excuses Conor's failure to call her. Finally, she takes matters into her own hands and, like my colleague, composes an ill-advised message. Reading from her notes, she leaves the following on Conor's voice mail:

>   GIGI
>   (into phone)
>   Hey, Conor. It's Gigi. I just
>   thought, I hadn't heard from you
>   and, I mean how stupid is it that
>   a gal has got to wait for a guy's
>   call anyway, right?

Unable to read her own handwriting, she
ad-libs the rest:

>   GIGI (CON'T)
>   I mean, we're all equal, right?
>   More than equal—more women are
>   accepted into law school now than
>   men, and we do better in those

```
police simulations where you can
mistakenly shoot innocent people—I
mean I don't know if you saw that
Dateline—but women practically
have penises now, right?
        (beat)
Well, call me. This is Gigi. Call me.
```

When I first read this scene, I wanted to take Gigi by the shoulders and scream, "Wake up, you idiot!" Circling back to *Webster's*, I knew my challenge was to make sure that the audience wasn't moved to "contemptuous pity" by Gigi. It's appropriate for viewers to find her exasperating, as long as they also root for her to come to her senses.

Here's the setup of the story: Gigi (Ginnifer Goodwin) is smitten with Conor (Kevin Connolly), who has little interest in her. Conor is madly in love with Anna (Scarlett Johansson), who has little interest in him. Anna falls for Ben (Bradley Cooper); unfortunately, he is a married man. Anna asks her best friend, Mary (Drew Barrymore), for advice. Mary poses the question: "What if you meet the love of your life—but you already married someone else? Are you supposed to pass them by?" This spurs Anna to pursue Ben, who cheats on his wife, Janine (Jennifer Connelly). Janine works with Beth (Jennifer Aniston), who lives with Neil (Ben Affleck). Neil loves Beth but has no interest in marrying her, forcing Beth to end the relationship. Just outside this matrix is Alex (Justin Long), who tutors Gigi about men—specifically, about the danger of misreading signals from a guy who is "just not that into you." Rather than heed his advice, Gigi mistakes Alex's tutelage for romantic interest, which leads to heartache.

Directing a film with nine main characters, the first and most daunting task is to make sure each of their stories is equally engaging. Not everyone has the same amount of real estate in the film, but certain themes (e.g., how to weather rejection) are shared by all. For me, the key was to find a distinct part of myself in each of the nine, to trace a line between each story and a specific event in my life. Whether grossly misreading a gesture, overthinking the obvious, sending a garbled signal to avoid telling the truth, or failing to notice when someone *was* into me, I managed to peg each story to some misstep of my own. When I talk about approaching the scene from the inside out, this is what I mean: putting myself in each character's shoes. Walking their walk.

We've all seen ensemble films in which everyone's on the same page except one cast member, who seems to be performing in another film altogether. How do you make sure nine actors with very different strengths and acting styles cohere into a seamless unit? Jennifer Connelly, for instance, is famed for her compelling work in such searing dramas as *Requiem for a Dream,* while Jennifer Aniston is among the most gifted comediennes of any generation. They're both remarkable, but their energies could not be more dissimilar. How do you strike a tonal balance between the two? Justin Long has wonderful improvisation skills and loves to play fast and loose with the script. Ginnifer Goodwin, on the other hand, is classically trained (she studied at the Shakespeare Institute in Stratford-upon-Avon and London's Royal Academy of

Dramatic Art). Playing fast and loose with the script is not how she operates; in fact, her copy of the script was meticulously color-coded and filled with notes about her character's arc, backstory, and motivation from scene to scene. They share more screen time than anyone else in the ensemble, so their chemistry was critical. Ginnifer and Justin's first scene together, to be quite frank, was a bit of a mess. He would ad-lib his lines (very funny ad-libs, by the way), and she would respond with her scripted dialogue, which increasingly made no sense. After a few takes, both were supremely frustrated. As so often happens, the two actors weren't available to rehearse during preproduction. Had they been, we would have explored ways to blend their distinct styles. Instead, we had to figure it out with the clock ticking and a crew getting more and more impatient. Rather than framing it as an impasse, I put the situation in a positive light, saying it gave each actor a chance to exercise creative muscles they normally didn't use. But, I added, let's first work with the scene as written, uncover the meaning of the words, before substituting words of our own. The advice worked, and the relationship between Gigi and Alex quickly came to life.

Here's another challenge: you want the characters and their dilemmas to be as relatable as possible, but how do you pull this off with actors who are among the most glamorous people on the planet? The female cast has graced the covers of such fashion magazines as *Vogue, Elle,* and *Allure.* They are routinely included on lists of the most beautiful women in the world, and two male cast members were named *People* magazine's Sexiest Man Alive. (Admittedly, one of them earned this distinction two years after the film's release.)

How do you tell actors to tone down their natural beauty? And why would you want to for a story that deals in no small part with sexual attraction? The word I kept in mind was the one I used during my first meeting with the producers: *recognition.* I told each actor that I wanted viewers to recognize themselves in these characters, and that it was vital to look as natural as possible. I'm hardly the person to give anyone makeup tips, but everyone agreed to deglamorize for this story.

The challenge to keep it real extended to all aspects of the picture. Cinematographer John Bailey created a look that's rich and textured, but never slick or glossy. Close-ups are vivid but always feel grounded in reality. The faces of the stars don't exist on some ethereal plane, disconnected from the world (think of Lee Garmes's or Bert Glennon's photography of Marlene Dietrich).

Everyone feels like someone you know, someone like yourself.

Makeup, hair, and lighting aside, what ultimately kept things real was each actor's connection to his or her role. Remember, all nine characters were drawn from maxims in a self-help book, and they could have easily felt generic—stick figures designed to make a point. Here's a passage from the book that clearly inspired the story line of Neil (Ben Affleck) and Beth (Jennifer Aniston):

> Every man you have ever dated who has said he doesn't
> want to get married or doesn't believe in marriage, or
> has "issues" with marriage, will, rest assured, someday
> be married. It just will never be with you. Because he's

not really saying he doesn't want to get married. He's saying he doesn't want to get married to you.

Jennifer Aniston's portrayal truly struck a nerve with viewers, but it wasn't because she was playing an idea, a variation on the "he's just not that into you" theme. Nor was she playing an everywoman. Her connection to Beth was specific. And personal. Likewise, Scarlett Johansson embodied Anna's many contradictions in ways that were so truthful I felt as if I'd known this woman forever. As a yoga instructor, Anna radiates a sense of balanced energy; on the other hand, her emotional life is completely out of alignment. Jennifer Connelly's portrait of Janine rouses such compassion; I find myself simultaneously rooting for her to save her marriage *and* walk away from her philandering husband.

Ginnifer Goodwin's uncanny ability to project the crazy workings of Gigi's mind, Drew Barrymore's talent for taking a character with a modicum of screen time and making you feel like she's your oldest and best friend—there wasn't a weak link in this chain. Everyone brought their A game—that is, everyone brought their messy and flawed humanity to the table.

That video store I mentioned at the outset no longer exists, of course. I believe it's now a gluten-free doughnut shop. If it were still around, I might suggest they designate a new section: Human Comedy. Many of the films I most admire would live on those shelves, and I'd be happy for *He's Just Not That into You* to join their company.

TOTALLY UNRELEASABLE

Put down your pencils. Your ten weeks are up. As all feature filmmakers know, ten weeks is a sacred stretch of time during postproduction. It's the DGA-mandated period during which a director assembles his or her cut—the "director's cut." Producers and/or financiers may try to worm their way into the cutting room, but you are within your rights to bolt the door and explore your footage in privacy. There may, of course, be a tactical reason for sharing a work in progress with producers or financiers, but during this time, you set the rules. Per the guild, for ten weeks your cutting room is a protected space.

When the clock runs out, however, things can get pretty turbulent. You are bombarded with opinions and suggestions. For many studio executives, it's a point of pride to generate a monstrously exhaustive and fussy set of notes. Multiple executives will no doubt have conflicting ideas. To complicate matters, the executives often farm out the nitpicking to their respective underlings. At a certain point, it's impossible to know whose notes are whose. Yet all of this pales in comparison to the most time-honored and painful indignity a director must endure: the market research screening.

By all rights, a director should welcome the opportunity to preview a film, to try out different scenes and get a gut feeling about how the story plays. Sadly, a market research screening often becomes a battleground on which the studio and filmmaker fight for control of the cut. The battlefield, of course, is far from level.

The studio financed the film and foots the bill for the research screening. The researchers may pay you lip service, but they report to the studio. Their job is to let the studio know if it has a salable product—and, if not, how it can transform the product into something salable.

When it comes to the ordeal of market research, there are three categories of directors:

1 An elite group of *auteurs* with the power to skip the process altogether.

2 A slightly larger, though still exclusive, group that submits to the process but has the clout to disregard the results.

3 The rest of us.

Modern market research for feature films was born in the late 1970s, with the founding of the National Research Group, but one finds progenitors of modern testing as far back as the silent era. Indeed, Harold Lloyd deserves mention for helping to open this Pandora's box. For his 1928 feature *Speedy*, the ever-resourceful silent comic created a grid to measure audience laughter. He called it the Speedy Lafograph. The grid's x-axis represented the film's eighty-one-minute length. That axis was subdivided into ten-minute intervals, and within each interval Humorous High Spots were enumerated. In one sequence, for example, Speedy (Lloyd) spends Sunday afternoon with his girlfriend at Coney Island. At one point, a live crab falls into Speedy's pocket and proceeds to create havoc. Among the gags delineated on the graph are "Crab bursts first balloon" and "Crab pinches lady." The y-axis measured the intensity of each laugh. Lloyd divided laughter into six categories: Titter, Chuckle, Laugh, Outburst, Scream, and Screech. At one screening of *Speedy*, there were no Humorous High Spots that generated a screech from the test audience. The only gag producing a scream occurs sixty-eight minutes into the film; at that point in the story, a fight breaks out between a gang of thugs and various shopkeepers, each armed with implements from their places of business. A laundry-man uses a flat iron to scorch the rear ends of several goons, and if we can trust Lloyd's Lafograph, the level of hilarity surpassed Outburst, peaking at Scream. I consider that rarified air for any gag, by the way. I would love to have heard Lloyd parse the difference between Scream and Screech. Perhaps the latter was just an aspirational category.

Lloyd's Lafograph is quite charming compared to the contemporary research process, in which a dizzying amount of data is collected and analyzed. Needless to say, every mass-produced item undergoes some testing. Before Frito-Lay foists a new flavor of Dorito upon the world, you can be sure that the flavor undergoes a vigorous set of trials. Reading the ingredients on a package of Doritos attests to what an epic process it must be to finalize a flavor. Indeed, the satirical newspaper *The Onion* once ran the following headline: DORITOS CELEBRATES ONE MILLIONTH INGREDIENT. But a studio-produced feature film has nothing in common with a cheese-flavored tortilla, right? Yes, both are consumer products, but surely there's a world of difference between a story point that needs clarity and a tortilla chip that could use more hydrogenated cottonseed oil. Well, not from the studio's point of view.

THE SCREENING

In the not-too-distant future, researchers will probably use a microchip implant to monitor the serotonin level of viewers during a preview. At present, here's how a typical market research screening unfolds. Civilians are recruited to attend the preview based on a generic synopsis of the film. A moderator introduces the film, reminding the audience they're watching a rough cut: the music is temporary, the visual effects are temporary, the color is unbalanced, and sound effects are missing. Not long ago, in the celluloid era, the moderator also instructed viewers to disregard scratches on the print. As the lights dim, many directors are inclined to leave for the nearest restroom, to chain-smoke and/or throw up. During the screening, junior executives from the studio are imbedded within the audience, texting to one another. "I knew that line wasn't funny." Or "Did you see that? Another walkout." I cannot overstate how unnerving the whole experience is.

Think of the most grueling torture devices of the Middle Ages, then add one. The Rack. The Wheel. The Knee-Splitter. The Head-Crusher. The Market Research Screening.

THE DATA

After the screening, the audience remains to fill out a questionnaire. Among many things, the survey asks viewers to rank characters from favorite to least favorite. Often, the villain of a story is the least liked of all, which naturally creates confusion. An unlikable villain is what you want, right? If the villain is the least favorite, does that mean the character is poorly drawn?

Hannibal Lecter could not be more riveting, but he hardly fits the conventional definition of *likable*.

The survey includes questions about specific elements (setting, comedy, music, ending, pace). Finally, the questionnaire asks you to give the film an overall rating (Excellent, Very Good, Good, Fair, Poor). The Total Highly Favorable number, a combination of Excellent and Very Good ratings, is the number often bandied about by entertainment folk. If you overhear someone at a restaurant declare, "The film scored a 94," he or she is touting the Total Highly Favorable number—that is, 94 percent of the audience rated the film either Excellent or Very Good. Now, that ratio might be wildly lopsided: 2 percent Excellent, 92 percent Very Good. In that case, converting those Very Good marks into Excellent ones is a conundrum that turns many executives into nervous wrecks. The search for anything that will shift those numbers (e.g., add a popular song, tighten the pace, shoot a new scene) can become obsessive and quixotic. Executives conveniently forget that viewers are more likely to apply the word *excellent* to films of an edifying nature (e.g., *Schindler's List, 12 Years a Slave*) than a genre film. An audience may howl with delight at a crude comedy about losing one's virginity, but few will leave the theater proclaiming, "Wasn't that film excellent!"

One question completes the survey: Would you definitely recommend the film? Or probably recommend it? The distinction between *definitely* and *probably* is of supreme importance to studios. At a test screening of a comedy I directed, *The Beautician and the Beast,* 45 percent of women twenty-one years old or older said they would definitely recommend the film, while 38 percent of the same age group said they would probably recommend it. Predictably, there was much hand-wringing and deliberation about how to move those probable endorsements into the definite category. By the way, 78 percent of women *under* twenty-one said they would definitely recommend the film, but for studios, the holy grail is to produce something that is equally loved by all segments of the audience—all four quadrants (men, women, boys, girls); in other words, every sentient being with the means to buy a ticket.

One dubious assumption of the "probably vs. definitely" construct is that your most important reaction to a film occurs moments after the final credits. I cannot tell you how many films I thoroughly enjoyed in the moment that left no impact on me whatsoever. By the time I reached the parking lot, the film was a distant, if pleasant, memory. On the other hand, I've seen many films—commercial films—that confounded me upon a first viewing but lingered in my mind, haunting me for days or weeks. Those became the titles I heartily recommended to one and all.

The questionnaire has a space for viewers to offer comments about the film, giving everyone a chance to lob their rotten tomatoes. These comments can range from amusing to appalling. Sometimes both at once. If you test a film in the greater Los Angeles area, you'll no doubt get opinions from industry-savvy moviegoers. It doesn't matter how many times the moderator reminds viewers that the visual effects are temporary, VFX-obsessed cinephiles will single out every unfinished shot for derision. At each test screening of the rescue adventure *Big Miracle,* about three California gray whales trapped off the northernmost tip of Alaska, the moderator noted that our computer-generated whales were far from finished. Nevertheless, survey cards were filled with astute comments like, "The whales look stupid" or "No one will ever believe those are real whales." In fact, the finished whales were so credible that many people singled out the underwater whale photography for praise, despite the fact there was no photography whatsoever—the images were completely computer-generated. At test screenings in Los Angeles, a healthy number of audience members either work in show business or have parents who do. At a preview of my sophomore effort as a director, the screwball comedy *Vibes,* one eleven-year-old boy volunteered the following comment: "Totally unreleasable." I'd love to find out what became of that youngster. For all I know, I'm probably working for him now.

THE FOCUS GROUP

The surveys are collected and the crowd disperses, with the exception of twenty viewers randomly selected to form a focus group. The moderator leads the discussion, but a studio executive may preemptively ask the moderator to pursue a particular line of inquiry. For example, the studio and the director may be at loggerheads over a "problematic" scene. Without leading the witness, the moderator might subtly guide the discussion toward the studio's point of view. As a director, you sit at a discreet distance behind the focus group, totally helpless as the moderator urges nonprofessionals to dismantle your efforts.

As with any group dynamic, a focus group has leaders and followers, performers and wallflowers. Invariably there are people who really enjoy the sound of their own voice. During the focus group discussion after a screening of *He's Just Not That into You,* one young man said, "I thought this was going to be funny, like a Judd Apatow movie. His movies are great." There were murmurs of agreement, and I had the distinct feeling the more reserved focus group members simply clammed up. Maybe they thoroughly enjoyed my film, but no one wanted to challenge this wise guy. The situation reminds me of a favorite *Peanuts* comic, in which Charlie Brown, Linus, and Lucy are lying on a hill, looking at clouds.

"If you use your imagination," Lucy says, "you can see lots of things in the cloud formations . . . What do you think you see, Linus?"

"Well, those clouds up there look to me like the map of the British Honduras on the Caribbean," Linus observes. "That cloud up there looks a little like the profile of Thomas Eakins, the famous painter and sculptor . . ."

"That's very good," commends Lucy. "What do you see in the clouds, Charlie Brown?"

"Well," the now-deflated Charlie replies, "I was going to say I saw a ducky and a horsie, but I changed my mind."

This perfectly captures what often occurs in a focus group. The loud and/or erudite rule. But a well-informed or well-spoken viewer is not necessarily a storyteller. It's hard enough for professionals to give precise feedback about a story, let alone a random group of moviegoers. The moderator often poses questions that the test group is not really qualified to answer. "Does the music help the story?" is one such query. In theory, if the audience is completely absorbed by the story, they won't be aware of the music at all. And if there is a recognizable musical element—a hit record by Adele, for instance—each viewer's response to it will be highly personal and not germane to storytelling. If a focus group member wearing a Megadeth T-shirt raises his or her hand and says, "I hate that Adele song," how is that remotely meaningful? That viewer no doubt prefers such tender ballads as "Tornado of Souls" and "Symphony of Destruction." For the studio, a lone dissenter can cast doubt on a viable creative choice. The Megadeth enthusiast won't say, "Adele's not my favorite, but I understand how the song moves the story forward."

INTERPRETING THE DATA

The next day, no sooner have you recovered from the screening than a summary report arrives, filled with data and analysis. Most market research summaries begin with a disclaimer, something to the effect that the data gathered from audience surveys are not predictive of box office success. Research groups stress that their findings are not useful to gauge the "want-to-see" level for a particular film. The findings are purportedly useful in analyzing "playability"—that is, how well a film satisfies the audience that's presumably interested in seeing it. In other words, a test screening of *Mulholland Drive* for an audience of children will not generate useful data, though who wouldn't want to read survey cards for a David Lynch film written by kids?

As with all polling data, market research can be interpreted in a variety of ways. We've seen countless politicians cherry-pick data to advance their agendas, while turning a blind eye to evidence that undercuts their goals. Studio executives often latch onto certain statistics that support their preconceived notion of how a film should play, while dismissing data that's, well, inconvenient.

Summaries often blur the line between reporting facts and prescribing changes. *He's Just Not That into You* was designed to mix comedy and drama. It purposefully didn't follow the romantic comedy playbook. We did not intend to wrap up story lines neatly; indeed, more than one ends unhappily, and we were well aware that this mix of tones would be a challenge for viewers. We also knew it would distinguish the film from a standard-issue romantic comedy.

The most controversial story line concerns the married couple, Ben (Bradley Cooper) and Janine (Jennifer Connelly). Feeling restless in the marriage, Ben begins an affair with Anna (Scarlett Johansson). At one point, they rendezvous at his office for an afternoon tryst. Their lovemaking is interrupted by a knock at the door—it's Janine. Ben quickly stows Anna in a closet, then opens the door for his wife. Janine hopes to rejuvenate their love life, and she's made this surprise visit to propose . . . an afternoon tryst in his office. It's an absurd situation, and Ben has little choice but to make love with his wife while Anna remains stuck in the closet. The goal of the scene is to put the audience in an uncomfortable position. We're rooting for Janine to restore her marriage, but we can't help but feel pity for Anna, forced to overhear their lovemaking. At the first research screening, many audience members felt that Anna was getting her just deserts for coming between a married couple, and a close-up of Anna hidden behind the closet door, looking quite devastated, polarized viewers. As you might imagine, a vast majority of the audience—male or female—took a dim view of adultery, and when viewers singled out this plot line as their "least favorite," it's hard to say whether they were casting a vote against adultery or taking issue with the story line for aesthetic reasons.

Researchers seized upon the close-up of Anna, and the dissension it provoked, as evidence that the story line wasn't "playing well." The fact that viewers had clashing opinions of Anna's predicament was seen as a negative. From the studio's point of view, it's always better to have unanimity within an audience, and the research analysis reinforces this in none-too-subtle ways. The second preview of *He's Just Not*

That into You featured many editorial changes—among them, the deletion of Anna's close-up in the closet. Despite many refinements (e.g., better pacing, additional music), the researchers placed much of the credit for the film's improved performance on the decision to remove that close-up. From the summary report: "The excision, from the previous cut of the movie, of the strongly disliked shot of Scarlett Johansson in tears in Ben's office, listening in misery to him having sex with his wife, may be part of the reason for the increased enjoyment of *He's Just Not That into You*." Needless to say, this is a purely subjective observation; in fact, it made me wonder whether the researcher wasn't letting his or her own life experience color the analysis.

Screenwriters Abby Kohn and Marc Silverstein created a scene that unsettled viewers. It succeeds by making you squirm. But the market researcher guards against anything that pushes the audience out of its comfort zone. If not literally in league with the studio, the researcher nevertheless promotes a play-it-safe attitude—namely, viewers like what's familiar. Regarding the sex scene in Ben's office, the summary has more to say: "At the same time, however, the perception among some moviegoers of a discordant mismatch in tone, which was most *explicitly* exemplified by the particular shot [Anna in the closet], was nonetheless still present and problematic for some people, who simply are put off by a very serious and downbeat adulterous conflict that ends in unhappiness for all concerned in what is otherwise an uplifting and optimistic (though unquestionably grounded in real life) romantic comedy." Rather than frame the adulterous story line as a refreshing challenge to viewers, one that expands our

sense of how a romantic story should behave, the researchers cast it in a completely negative light. Moviegoers reacted
exactly as we hoped they would, but the summary essentially
warned against any story line that flew in the face of typical
expectations. More insidiously, the summary recommended
that the film's playability would improve if the story line had
less screen time, if it were relegated to a subplot. From the
researcher's point of view, *playability* means one thing: the
audience is pleased, not provoked. I'm happy to report we ig-
nored that suggestion.

I was responsible for another sex scene that polarized test
audiences, this time for the Showtime Network. Test screenings for a television pilot have a peculiarly Orwellian aspect
to them. Viewers are segregated by gender and herded into
two adjoining theaters. Each seat has a dial knob installed
in the armrest. If you turn the knob in one direction, it signals pleasure or approval; in the opposite direction, it's basically an electronic jeer. Adding a surreal touch to the process,
the researchers, network executives, and creative team can
watch the viewers' faces through a pair of two-way mirrors,
one for the male audience and one for the female. Meanwhile, above the mirrors hangs a large monitor broadcasting
a live feed of the audience's dial responses as the pilot plays.
The dial responses are displayed on two parallel lines, one for
each gender.

The pilot in question, which I produced but did not direct,
was a razor-sharp satire on modern mores as seen through
the eyes of an angst-ridden advertising man named Thom
Payne (Philip Seymour Hoffman). In the story, Payne has
the vexing task of creating a new advertising campaign for

the Keebler Cookie Company. The provocative scene is a literal nightmare in which Payne dreams of having sex with Ma Keebler, the matriarch of the Keebler elves. It's as outrageous and disturbing as you might imagine. Philip Seymour Hoffman having sex with a cartoon grandmother was not to everyone's taste.

Watching the faces of both test groups, I was stunned. The entire male contingent laughed uproariously. Their female counterparts, however, watched in silent disbelief—it was like the initial reaction to *Springtime for Hitler*. The female dial response didn't just hit rock bottom, it sank below the graph. To my surprise, the Showtime executives were delighted by the contentious reaction. In the parlance of television folk, this was a "watercooler moment"—that is, something to be discussed and debated around the watercooler at work. When a junior executive wondered whether Philip Seymour Hoffman having sex with an elderly elf would make him unlikable to viewers, the president of the network coolly replied, "Likability is overrated."

If anything, the dial test, during which viewers render judgments in real time, brings us full circle, back to Harold Lloyd's eerily prescient Lafograph, measuring mirth on a moment-by-moment—or gag-by-gag—basis. One can imagine Lloyd poring over the Lafograph data, pondering ways to convert those Screams into Screeches. I wonder if Lloyd, in his storied career, ever came up with a gag that produced a bona fide Screech from the audience. All I can say is that, having suffered through more than a few market research screenings, I could easily demonstrate one for him.

TOO CLEVER BY HALF

To cast a spell on the audience, to create that wondrous suspension of disbelief, it's necessary to hide your craft, to prevent viewers from peeking behind the curtain. That's certainly what I was taught in film school. Narrative filmmaking should be seamless. From the time the lights go down until the final fade-out, the audience should remain blissfully unaware of your handiwork. In other words, do not advertise the seams lest you break the spell you've so delicately cast.

If a character glances at the camera, if a microphone dangles into frame, if a focus pull is clumsy, or if the camera moves in some flagrantly unmotivated way, the general consensus is that viewers will be distracted, their investment in the story hampered by the sudden awareness that there's a whole crew of people outside the frame making a film.

Let's consider each of the aforementioned "sins." Characters have been looking directly at the camera, staring right down the barrel of the lens, ever since the final shot of Edwin S. Porter's *The Great Train Robbery* of 1903. In that singular shot, one of the train bandits, played by Justus D. Barnes, aims his six-shooter at the camera and fires point-blank at the audience. Far from breaking the spell, my hunch is that more than a few untrained moviegoers ducked under their seats in terror. As we've discussed, there's a great tradition of screen comics breaking the fourth wall, interrupting the action for a wisecrack to the audience, and viewers seems none the worse for the wear. Does this mean the rules of engagement are more relaxed when it comes to comedy? If a character in a weighty drama unexpectedly turns to the camera, moviegoers would be "taken out" of the experience, right? Well, hold that thought.

For some, no sin is more egregious than a sloppy focus pull. Let's say you're watching a musical scene—the ballet sequence from *An American in Paris,* for instance. It's abundantly clear that nothing takes place on a real Parisian street. Everything is stylized to the nines, with nary a nod to reality. The backdrops look like paintings by Toulouse-Lautrec. The artifice could not be more glaring, but nothing intrudes upon the action to remind you of the filmmaking process. The ballet ends with the camera pushing dramatically toward a rose in Gene Kelly's hand. If the camera operator mistimed the focus pull, and the rose suddenly went fuzzy, that would surely botch the moment, wouldn't it? Viewers would be uncomfortably aware of the technical aspect of the shot. Even within the artificial world of the scene, that kind of flub would be unforgivable. But can you imagine a shot in which a mistimed focus pull is used for creative effect, and actually enhances your emotional involvement?

If you're watching a film version of *Romeo and Juliet,*

and the moment Romeo appears at Juliet's balcony a microphone dips into shot, my guess is most viewers would find this laughable. And disruptive. The last thing the audience should be thinking about is the dialogue recording process. We want to focus on the two doomed lovers and their plan to marry the following day. Perhaps Romeo's costume features an Elizabethan ruff, and a lavalier microphone is cleverly hidden in its frill. What if Romeo cheekily dismantles his clip-on microphone to have a truly private conversation with his beloved? What insane director would sanction such a thing? Not only would it deprive us of Shakespeare's words, it would eliminate sound altogether. This is guaranteed to take the audience right out of the scene, correct?

Lastly, there have been plenty of camera moves throughout cinema history that boldly announce themselves as camera moves. Here are two very different examples. In Abel Gance's 1927 epic *Napoléon,* we meet fourteen-year-old Napoléon Bonaparte at a French military academy. The students stage a snowball fight to resemble a military campaign, and at one point, Abel Gance catapults the camera through the air as if it were a snowball. What does this image represent? A snowball's point of view? Needless to say, a snowball cannot see. My film school instructors would scoff at a shot that calls such conspicuous attention to itself. (By the way, the snowball's POV may be the tamest thing in this delirious scene.) From the sublime to the ridiculous, in Robert Stevenson's 1961 film *The Absent-Minded Professor,* Fred MacMurray plays a chemistry teacher who creates a crazily elastic substance he dubs "flubber." In one scene, the villain of the story, played by Keenan Wynn, is pushed from a second-story balcony, but because he's wearing flubber-coated shoes, he proceeds to bounce repeatedly off the ground. Stevenson devises a bouncing point-of-view shot—the camera rockets away from the pavement, then quickly drops, all at nausea-inducing speed. Granted, it is a motivated camera move—it's literally Keenan Wynn's point of view, but the shot doesn't simply call attention to itself. It screams. Still, is it possible for such a muscular camera move to actually deepen our involvement, even as it trumpets its own cleverness?

I want to examine four cinematic moments that, by all rights, shouldn't work. Based on everything we were taught, they should disrupt our suspension of disbelief by foregrounding the filmmaking process. These four directorial choices should ostensibly take me out of the experience; instead, they make me all the more engrossed.

MONIKA'S GAZE

Ingmar Bergman's twelfth feature, *Summer with Monika*, is a story of young love. Coquettish, eighteen-year-old Monika (Harriet Andersson) and earnest nineteen-year-old Harry (Lars Ekborg) meet and fall for each other. Harry's a stockroom boy at a porcelain warehouse, constantly bullied by coworkers. Monika works at a produce market, where she suffers sexual harassment on a daily—if not hourly—basis. The two rebel, quitting their jobs and fleeing Stockholm to a remote island for the summer. Their idyll is short-lived. Monika gets pregnant, and though she chafes at the thought of returning to civilization, Harry's desire for domesticity wins the day. A hasty wedding follows, after which a baby girl, June, arrives. Parenthood is a joyless bore for Monika, who blames Harry for getting her pregnant. While Harry is away on business, the restless, impetuous Monika has an affair with a man she meets at a café. Harry returns early and catches Monika with her lover. Their marriage promptly unravels, the unrepentant Monika departs, and the story ends on a gloomy note, with Harry raising their child on his own.

Bergman shoots the story in a naturalistic, if occasionally gritty, style. Life in Stockholm feels stagnant and somber. The sun can't quite penetrate the fog that blankets the city. A stray dog here, a pair of penniless street musicians there. A desolate cul-de-sac. Bergman definitely has the Italian neorealist playbook in his back pocket. The staging is simple, camera movement minimal, and the performance style nontheatrical. In short, there's nothing splashy about Bergman's storytelling. As a result, nothing prepares us for a shot that occurs one hour and twenty-two minutes into the film.

After Harry leaves on business, we find Monika at a café, sitting in a booth across from a man. Bergman begins close on the man's hands as he drops a coin in the café's jukebox—we cannot see his face. Bergman pans to reveal Monika in the booth, framed in profile. The man takes his seat off-camera. As he leans into frame to light her cigarette, we catch a glimpse of his face. Do we recognize him? Was he one of Monika's tormentors at the greengrocer? Monika takes a drag off her cigarette, then turns directly to the camera, gazing at the lens for quite a long time. The camera pushes toward her, and Bergman dims the café lights, isolating her in a dark limbo. No dialogue. End of scene.

Summer with Monika wasn't widely celebrated when it first opened in 1953; indeed, in the United States it was re-edited and released as an exploitation film, with the ridiculous title *Monika, the Story of a Bad Girl!* The film was not on anyone's radar, but in 1958 Cahiers du Cinéma critic Jean-Luc Godard wrote a rhapsodic reappraisal, singling out the shot in question: "One must see *Summer with Monika,* if only for the extraordinary moment when Harriet Andersson, before making love with the man she has already thrown out once before, stares fixedly into the camera, her laughing eyes clouded with confusion, and calls on us to witness her disgust at involuntarily choosing hell over heaven. It is the saddest shot in the history of the cinema."

Who is Monika looking at? And how do you characterize that look? Perhaps she's provoking the audience, as if to say, "I dare you to judge me." We have been gazing at Monika for nearly ninety minutes, often prancing naked along the edge of the sea. Now she returns our gaze with a laser-sharp challenge: you think you know me, but you don't. Or, as Godard suggests, maybe it's a look of self-loathing. Monika, poised to make a choice she knows is wrong, turns to us for support and understanding.

Far from being a "distancing effect," the image invites us inside Monika's thought process. Breaking the fourth wall supercharges our engagement with her. A novelist can use words to describe her moral conundrum, a playwright can fashion a monologue to express her interiority, but Bergman puts the pen right in the viewer's hand. Monika's stare-down with the audience forces our participation. Instead of "This makes me aware I'm watching a movie," my reaction is: "I know exactly what you're feeling, Monika."

"THAT WASN'T JUST SOME WOMAN."

If Bergman transformed a teen romance into a meditation on finding one's place in the world, in his 1967 film *The Graduate*, Mike Nichols elevated the soapy tale of an illicit affair into a biting satire of middle-class morality. He did so, in part, by creating images full of visual wit, among them the iconic shot of Dustin Hoffman framed in the crook of Anne Bancroft's bare leg. There are plenty of images, camera moves, and transitions in *The Graduate* that fall squarely into the "too clever by half" category. They're sly and cocky. You can almost hear Nichols saying, "Boy, aren't I something." One of these shots, however, confounds me by the emotional punch it packs. Again, by all rights, it should be a detriment to the scene. It flies in the face of a bedrock rule of image-making—namely, that a close-up should be in focus. For me, the shot actually amplifies the emotion of the moment, even as it points to the mechanics of filmmaking.

The plot so far: recent college graduate Benjamin Braddock (Dustin Hoffman) has a unique problem: after striking up an affair with a married woman, Mrs. Robinson (Anne Bancroft), he falls in love with her daughter Elaine (Katharine Ross). Mrs. Robinson (does she even have a first name?) is naturally incensed at discovering she's been replaced by her daughter as the object of Benjamin's affections. Furiously, she orders Benjamin to stop seeing Elaine; moreover, she's prepared to divulge the affair to her daughter if Benjamin doesn't submit to her demand. Fearing Mrs. Robinson will make good on her threat, Benjamin beats her to the punch, cornering Elaine in her bedroom to make his confession. Elaine is initially confused by Benjamin's anguished need to reveal the identity of his lover; then she turns to find her mother lurking in the bedroom doorway, guilty as sin.

To set the mood, Nichols stages a tempestuous exchange between Benjamin and Mrs. Robinson in an actual tempest. Benjamin huddles in his car outside the Robinson house during a downpour. He's waiting for Elaine and is shocked when a rain-soaked Mrs. Robinson climbs into the passenger seat. She levels her threat, at which point Benjamin bolts from the car, running through the blinding rain into the house, with Mrs. Robinson fast on his heels.

Benjamin surprises Elaine in her room—she's half-dressed, not quite ready for their date. He's frantic, and with Elaine's back to the bedroom door, he comes clean. "That woman," he begins. "That older woman that I told you about? The married woman? That wasn't just some woman." Puzzled, Elaine asks, "What are you telling me? Benjamin, will you just tell me what this is all about?" Elaine is framed in close-up, and now her mother slinks into view behind her, just outside the doorway. A critical point: Elaine is photographed in close-up using a long lens. She is crisp while Mrs. Robinson is soft, even though she stands a mere two feet behind Elaine. Benjamin says nothing, his eyes now glued on Mrs. Robinson. Following his gaze, Elaine turns to face her mother, and the shot naturally shifts focus to Mrs. Robinson, shame written across her face. After a painful beat, Mrs. Robinson skulks out of frame, and Elaine turns back to Benjamin. We naturally expect a rack focus to Elaine's face, so we can clearly gauge her reaction. But Nichols directs the camera operator not to refocus, and for what feels like an eternity, Elaine is a complete blur. Finally, as the truth sinks in that her boyfriend and her mother were lovers, Elaine's face slowly comes into sharp focus.

At such a peak emotional moment, why obscure Elaine's face? Wouldn't it be more effective to let Katharine Ross simply play the moment, rather than use a camera trick to mimic her dawning awareness? For me, and I'll allow that I may be in the minority, this very self-conscious choice adds to the gravity of her realization. All of Elaine's illusions—about her parents' fidelity, her boyfriend's sincerity, and people being true to their word—have been obliterated in one fell swoop. Elaine's face coming into focus is the fog lifting on her new reality. People lie. Parents disappoint. Nothing is what it seems to be. Life's not pretty.

"SHE SAID NO, BY THE WAY."

Surely, the BBC series *The Office,* created by Ricky Gervais and Stephen Merchant, is not germane to a discussion about shots calling attention to themselves. After all, the show continually reminds viewers of the filmmaking process. Characters routinely glance at the lens or address the documentarian behind the camera. As an added self-referential twist, the show's feature-length epilogue, entitled "The Office Special," takes place after the finished documentary has been "broadcast," and focuses on the characters dealing with their new status as "reality stars." Having said that, one of the most heartbreaking moments in the entire series is staged in a way that, in theory, should wreck the emotion of the scene. And it does the opposite.

Over the course of twelve episodes, Tim Canterbury (Martin Freeman), an employee at the Wernham Hogg Paper Company, has carried a torch for office receptionist Dawn Tinsley (Lucy Davis). Unfortunately, Dawn is engaged to one of the company's warehouse workers, the arrogant, violence-prone Lee (Joel Beckett). Needless to say, we eagerly root for Dawn to come to her senses and call off the engagement. We also root for mild-mannered Tim to get up the nerve to declare his feelings to Dawn. In the twelfth and final episode, he takes action. The stakes are particularly high, as Dawn is poised to move with her fiancé to Florida.

The shot in question begins as a typical "talking head" interview with Tim. Faced with Dawn's imminent departure, Tim tries to put a good face on the situation, but his pain is evident:

> When I asked Dawn out, I didn't ask her out. I asked her out . . . as a friend. I felt sorry for her because she was having trouble with Lee at the time. It was no—it wasn't like that. Under different circumstances, sure, something may have happened, but she's going away now, and you can't—you can't change circumstances.

As if struck by his own pitiful words, Tim suddenly leaps from his seat. The camera operator, totally unprepared, clumsily tracks Tim down a long corridor, where he finds Dawn at her reception post. Tim asks for a private word, and the two step into an adjoining conference room. The door closes, and our view of them is partially obscured by venetian blinds. Tim then reaches into his shirt and detaches his lavalier—his clip-on microphone, and abruptly all the sound cuts out. No room tone. No crowd murmur. No background noise of any kind. Just . . . nothing.

We see Tim and Dawn's exchange but hear not a syllable of it. The angle favors Dawn, and we scrutinize her face, looking for a sign that his declaration is reciprocated. They share a hug. It's more than polite, but far from romantic. Tim emerges from the room and heads back to his desk, the shot still starkly silent. It's hard to discern from his body language what transpired. Tim takes his seat, reactivates his lavalier, lifts the tiny microphone to his lips, and casually announces, "She said no, by the way."

By throwing a character's face out of focus, Mike Nichols runs the risk of putting the audience at arm's length from his story. In an equally bold move, Stephen Merchant and Ricky Gervais shine a light on the sound-recording process itself. It would have been enough for Tim and Dawn to confer behind a closed door—viewers would easily accept not being able to hear them.

Reminding the audience that Tim wears a clip-on microphone makes the shot self-reflexive, and the blankness on the soundtrack would be radical in any context, let alone a tender moment between the romantic leads of a television comedy. But I would argue the business with the microphone only deepens the pathos. Tim's attempt to control the action, to prevent the documentary team from eavesdropping on him at this crucial juncture, when he risks everything for love, is all for naught—it's no defense against a simple no from the woman of his dreams. If Godard considers Monika's gaze to be the saddest shot in the history of cinema, I feel that Tim Canterbury reattaching his lavalier is among the saddest moments in the history of television.

LEAVING THE STATION

Like *Summer with Monika*, Federico Fellini's 1953 feature *I Vitelloni* is a coming-of-age story set against the sea, in this case an unnamed coastal town along the Adriatic, possibly a stand-in for the director's hometown of Rimini. The title *I Vitelloni* literally means *slabs of veal*, appropriate for a story about five tender "calves," aimless young men committed to doing as little as possible with their lives. There's the flirtatious Fausto (Franco Fabrizi), the wannabe actor Riccardo (Riccardo Fellini), the intellectual Leopoldo (Leopoldo Trieste), the tender Alberto (Alberto Sordi), and, finally, there's Moraldo (Franco Interlenghi), who observes his friends' immature antics with detachment. A dreamer, he yearns to be elsewhere.

Fellini stages the adventures of his layabout quintet in a highly naturalistic style. Eight years earlier, the director established his neorealist bona fides as the coauthor of Roberto Rossellini's *Roma Città Aperta*, a quintessential example of this Italian film movement. He would later become famous for his cinematic flights of fancy, but nothing in *I Vitelloni* feels theatrical. Compositions and camera movements are unassuming—that is, until the film's final scene.

Deciding he must break free from the provincial monotony of his hometown, Moraldo packs his bag and boards a train. It's not clear where the train is bound. The station boy, Guido (Guido Martufi), who admires Moraldo, asks where he's going. "I don't know," Moraldo replies. "I'm leaving." Not satisfied, Guido presses Moraldo to explain. "Didn't you like it here?" the boy asks. Moraldo has no answer, and the train pulls away. As it picks up speed, Moraldo looks off at the city he's leaving behind and thinks of his four best buds: Fausto, Riccardo, Leopoldo, and Alberto. They are, he imagines, sound asleep. Fellini cuts to a shot of each of them, but in a startling break from the film's unobtrusive style, the camera dollies past each slumbering friend, as if Moraldo's train were passing through their respective bedrooms. To reinforce the effect, we hear the clatter of train wheels as the camera glides past each bed.

Clearly, we have left the station on many levels, including a stylistic one. It's as if Fellini is bidding a wistful adieu to the strictures of neorealism. This short montage doesn't represent Moraldo's literal point of view. Trains do not pass through apartment buildings. Can a camera movement have the function of a simile? The camera dollies through the bedroom *like* a hurtling train. This series of shots, different from anything we've seen in the previous one hundred minutes, certainly calls attention to itself for sheer cunning. But does it throw an unnecessary curveball into the final minute of an otherwise realistic story?

Conventional wisdom says yes, but I feel these four dolly

moves underpin the sadness of Moraldo's departure in a way that four static shots could not. Yes, a montage of fixed shots would imply that Moraldo is thinking of his friends, but the camera movement tells the story of Moraldo *in the act* of leaving his old life behind, the "train" whisking past each sleeper underscoring a sense of finality.

Moraldo knows he will never see these friends again. Doesn't Franco Interlenghi's acting convey this feeling? Of course, but the feeling is heightened by the sort of self-aware camera move our teachers warned us would sandbag a scene.

I don't mean to disparage my old film production teachers, though they were a crotchety bunch. They were simply passing along conventional wisdom, the main tenet of which is to conceal your craft. As a director, it's helpful to have these maxims under your belt, all the better to know how and when to discard them.

The four moments discussed are, for me, *not* too clever by half. They are good examples of flying in the face of the expected. I often wonder how committed these directors were to their nervy choices. Did Ingmar Bergman shoot an alternate close-up of Harriet Andersson not looking into the lens? Did Mike Nichols get a take of Katharine Ross in proper focus? Did Merchant and Gervais do a "safety" version of the scene in which Martin Freeman does not reveal his clip-on microphone? Did Federico Fellini hedge his bets and film four standard-issue shots of Moraldo's posse? As a director who admires such daredevilry, I certainly hope not.

FEAR OF MUSIC

It has been variously attributed to musicians as diverse as Frank Zappa and Thelonious Monk, but the consensus remains that comedian Martin Mull coined the quip, "Writing about music is like dancing about architecture." The feeling that music, instrumental music in particular, resists literal interpretation also inspired a memorable 1977 *Saturday Night Live* skit entitled, "Listening to Great Music." In the sketch, John Belushi plays the pompous host of a music appreciation program. Introducing Wagner's "Ride of the Valkyries," Belushi says:

> Wagner often writes music which seems to evoke a sort of suggestion of place, of things. So, as I play the record, you try to imagine for yourself images which appear before your brain from the music. Okay? Just imagine . . .

The piece begins, and as the brass announce the entrance of the Valkyries, Belushi describes the images Wagner's music conjures for *him*. As you might guess, those maidens of Norse myth are nowhere to be seen:

> Horses! Horses! Ah, people! Mountains! Snow! Landscapes! A horse! The sky! A field! A big show with lots of horses! A lot of people going into the show, some trying to get in for free. Ah, but they can't!

His interpretation gets even nuttier:

> Ah! Rainbows, waterfalls . . . ooh, there are two people who meet and fall in love! And immediately they fly to Hawaii. Oh, they want to get married, but they can't! Because the father doesn't approve of the marriage . . .

The stubborn notion that instrumental music is innately nonrepresentational was shared by no less than Igor Stravinsky: "I consider that music is, by its very nature, essentially powerless to express anything at all, whether a feeling, an attitude of mind, a psychological mood, [or] a phenomenon of nature." Is that true? For example, is there nothing intrinsically sad about a minor triad? Are we just culturally conditioned to feel a certain way when we hear that chord?

Whether or not you agree with Stravinsky, his diatribe underscores how dicey it is for directors to make clear their musical desires to a composer. With rough cut in hand, you need music to accomplish the very thing Stravinsky argues it's incapable of doing—namely, express *a feeling, an attitude of mind, a psychological mood, a phenomenon of nature.* No wonder some directors have a fear of music. Is it important for you to have a background in music to communicate effectively with a composer? Absolutely not. In fact, it can be a handicap. Many want to impress a composer with their good taste or musical acumen but fail to get across what a scene actually needs. Indeed, sometimes the best way to communicate with your composer is not to talk about music at all.

As with every aspect of the directing craft, be it working with the cast or conveying a visual idea to the cinematographer, your job is to represent the emotional essence of the story. If you directed a western, and you're eager to give the villain a musical signature, it's not useful to say, "I want a big, thumping bass as the villain walks through town." It's ineffectual and rather insulting to say, "When the villain enters, I want that Ennio Morricone sound." Even asking your composer to give the score a "spaghetti western vibe" merely points him or her in the direction of other music. Better to focus on what's essential: describe the character's makeup and let the composer translate those traits into musical form. Your note to the composer could be as simple as this: "The character is a badass." The villain might be a woman who speaks very little, and you want the score to do the talking. In that case, verbalize your villain's subtext. Just remember that every villain is the hero of her own version of the story. Perhaps your character bears an ancient grudge against the town's sheriff. Maybe she has a legitimate ax to grind, but nurturing that grievance ultimately becomes her downfall. With that in mind, your composer may create a tragic theme: the character may be a badass, but she's also doomed, the victim of an obsession. Again, the typical misstep is to rely on examples of other music ("I want it to feel Mahlerian"). Better to operate from the domain that's rightfully yours: the inner lives of your characters.

For the moment, I want to confine my observations to musical underscore as opposed to popular songs, be they written for a film (e.g., "Raindrops Keep Fallin' on My Head" in *Butch Cassidy and the Sundance Kid*), appropriated by a film (e.g., Tom Cruise dancing to "Old Time Rock and Roll" in *Risky Business*), source music (e.g., the radio station hosted by DJ Mister Señor Love Daddy in *Do the Right Thing*), or "scource"—source music that operates as underscore (e.g., the getaway driver's playlist in *Baby Driver*). Regardless of the musical palette, whether the score features a full orchestra or a solo guitar, whether it's developmental or ambient, you want material that's not just expressive in a generic sense but truly symbiotic with your characters and their situation.

A prop or even a piece of wardrobe can have a musical signature, and what follows is the story of one particular theme of mine and how it grew. To set the scene, I first need to recount a phone conversation I had with my agent.

"Warners has a new project they'd like you to consider," he was excited to report.

"Great," I replied. "What's it about?"

"Four teenage girls who share a pair of pants," he said.

After a long beat, I probably muttered something like, "Huh." To entice me further, my agent added, "For some unknown reason, the pants fit each of the four girls perfectly." To be honest, my heart sank. So this is what my career had come to: four girls and a pair of pants.

Reluctantly, I opened the screenplay *The Sisterhood of the*

Traveling Pants, fully expecting a bubblegum movie. Instead, I got a surprisingly honest look at four teenage girls, each with a compelling emotional journey that unfolds over the course of one summer.

The life issues each faces are quite meaty. To recap: Bridget (Blake Lively), emotionally numb after her mother's suicide, yearns for someone to guide her through the grieving process. The only adult in Bridget's life, her father, is too shut down to help. Attending summer camp, Bridget channels her grief into an inappropriate fling with a soccer coach. Lena (Alexis Bledel), painfully uncomfortable in her own skin, visits the Greek island of Santorini, whose abundant sensuality challenges her to emerge from her shell. Tibby (Amber Tamblyn), who wears her alienation on her sleeve, befriends a thoughtful young girl who is dying of leukemia. Carmen (America Ferrera), a child of divorce, is excited to spend the summer with her father, but her plan is upended when she discovers he's engaged to a woman with three children.

Sisterhood is essentially four coming-of-age stories, and I relished the juggling act it required, making sure the stories were balanced, equally grounded, and engrossing. I was confident each story would have its own musical identity, and working with composer Cliff Eidelman (this was our third collaboration), we traced all four arcs, and he sketched themes to support each one.

The thread tying these four tales together, pardon the pun, is a pair of pants, and Cliff felt it was critical to give the pants a theme. Again, the four friends stumble upon a pair of jeans in a thrift store that strangely fits them all. Unable to find a rational explanation, they decide to share the pants over the course of the summer.

Did the pants really need a theme? Honestly, the idea gave me the jitters. I was afraid of music calling attention to the one aspect of the film people might find ridiculous: a magical pair of pants. *Sisterhood* was hardly a fairy tale, and what would a "pants theme" do other than spread pixie dust over an otherwise truthful and occasionally heart-rending drama? Here was a film exploring themes of death, grief, the breakup of families, and parents in absentia. Tonally, could it also accommodate such a whimsical grace note?

My fear duly noted, Cliff and I began to home in on a theme. We proceeded by a process of elimination. Cliff grilled me about the nature of the pants.

"Are they magical?" he asked.

"No," I replied. "I don't like the word *magical*. It makes me think of trickery."

"Are they mysterious?" he queried.

"Uh, no. I don't like the word *mysterious*. It makes me think of Nancy Drew. We're not making *Nancy Drew and the Mystery of the Pants*."

"Are they mystical?"

"No," I said. "*Mystical* implies a higher order, and there's nothing particularly spiritual about the pants."

"Well," a slightly frustrated Cliff countered, "what exactly does this pair of pants do?"

My answer was hopelessly vague. "When someone wears the pants, something happens."

"You mean, like fate?"

"Yes." I smiled. "That's it. Like fate."

The word *fate* was our gateway to the theme. It had a certain gravitas, invoking the three Fates of Greek mythology: Clotho, Lachesis, and Atropos. Those three Fates weren't exactly in the pants business, but they knew their way around a piece of thread. Clotho spun the thread of life, Lachesis allotted it, and Atropos cut the thread at the moment of death. Greek deities aside, what's important is that I didn't lead by pitching a musical approach to Cliff. I didn't suggest he use a theremin or musical saw to identify the pants. I didn't cite other composers, other movies, or even a particular musical style. Instead, I treated a piece of apparel as if it were a character. In my own fitful way, I tried to imagine how a pair of pants might express itself.

Initially timid about giving the pants a motif, I now embraced the task with zeal. I wondered aloud, "What if the pants could speak? What if the pants had dialogue?" Emboldened, Cliff proposed that we add a vocal element, that we literally give the pants a voice. And with that, all the pieces fell into place. We arrived at a simple theme in which piano and female voices are intertwined, set against a diaphanous texture, and anchored by a drone in the strings. The theme floats with possibility while staying tethered to fate. We used the theme, with slight variations, at many points throughout the story. Often it signals the moment a character takes charge of her own destiny. At other times, it signals the moment when destiny intervenes on behalf of a character, paving the way to emotional growth. The theme does its work in a quiet, unassuming way, but it fortifies the framework of the film with real muscle: the audience feels it, even if they're not conscious of what they're hearing.

Again, the way to fire your composer's imagination is to dig into the emotional particulars of a scene rather than describe the musical surface you want. You will invariably disagree about where a cue should begin or end, or whether the arrangement should be dense or spare. A cue may be rapturous but wrong for the character. An arrangement may be wonderful but not robust enough to support the action. A cue that begins early may inadvertently tell the audience too much. Of course, a scene may best be served by no music at all.

Too many people, directors included, assume that films and television shows *need* music. There are endless examples of stories that are simply slathered with underscore and/or pop songs. As a result, a musical idea with real punch gets lost in the wall-to-wall wash. A lot of directors grow impatient unless there's a constant pulse pushing their story forward. Too many forget that quiet can be riveting. And don't think of quiet as an absence. Whether in a comedy or drama, quiet is a powerful storytelling tool. There's a truism that comedies require peppy, jaunty music. You wouldn't know that from watching *The Office.* For all of its nine seasons, there wasn't one note of underscore. Indeed, quiet moments—dead air—became a hallmark of the show. Alfonso Cuarón's *Roma* certainly has its share of source music from car radios and record players, but there is no musical underscore in the film whatsoever, and some of its most powerful moments are refreshingly wordless, hushed, and music-free. The bulk of Luis Buñuel's filmmaking oeuvre is marked by the lack of music.

For Buñuel, the absurdity of human behavior is best served dry, with no music to cushion his surrealist sting.

Studios and networks, ever anxious about dwindling attention spans, may demand a musical blanket, often in the form of pop songs. If I suffer from film music anxiety, it stems from endless battles with financiers intent on plugging popular music into films. In *Sisterhood,* Cliff Eidelman's orchestral score works in tandem with an album's worth of pop music. Unfortunately, the decision to include a pop song is often driven by factors that have absolutely nothing to do with telling a good story. On more than one occasion, a studio asked me to bury a song in the background of a scene, rendering it audible enough to justify inclusion on a soundtrack album.

Trust me, I'm not cranky about pop music. Ever since Bill Haley and His Comets' "Rock Around the Clock" graced the opening credits of John Huston's *The Asphalt Jungle,* film directors have embraced and/or wrestled with hit tunes to help tell stories. We've all seen films that feel like mere excuses to generate a soundtrack album. There are, however, great examples of using a familiar song to create rich emotional overtones, to really supercharge a scene.

Pop music can provide context for a period film. Hearing a childhood favorite emanating from a character's car radio will no doubt evoke personal memories. Think of the plethora of period-specific tunes in *Once Upon a Time in Hollywood.* A song from a bygone era may also provide ironic commentary. In the Tarantino film, Charlie Manson's trio of murderous girls, chauffeured by henchman Tex, rolls toward the iconic Cielo Drive to the strains of "Twelve Thirty (Young

Girls Are Coming to the Canyon)" by The Mamas and the Papas, a buoyant song that was hardly written with homicidal hippies in mind. Louis Armstrong's 1967 hit "What a Wonderful World" is used to darkly ironic effect in *Good Morning, Vietnam,* with lyrics like "The colors of the rainbow so pretty in the sky" set against images of napalm raining down upon a Vietnamese village. (For hairsplitters, the story is set in 1965, so the Armstrong hit is not technically period-specific.) Many directors see no need to be period-appropriate at all. Jean-Philippe Rameau and Bow Wow Wow rub elbows in Sofia Coppola's *Marie Antoinette,* while the eponymous hero of *Django Unchained* gallops across the Old West to Jim Croce's 1973 hit "I Got a Name."

Pop songs often provide a summation statement at the end of a film. On the heels of Trent Reznor's intense, ambient score, *The Social Network* concludes with The Beatles' "Baby, You're a Rich Man." One could argue that the film's message hardly needs restatement in the form of a song, but there's no denying that a Lennon-McCartney tune lends authority to that message. Pop songs can amplify a character's mood or intensify the situation, and often the lyrics seem tailor-made for the moment. Harry Nilsson's "Jump into the Fire" warns that living on the edge will not free your soul. It's the perfect accompaniment to bleary-eyed, cocaine-addicted Henry Hill frantically setting up a drug deal in *Goodfellas.* There are song scores in which one singer-songwriter acts as a kind of troubadour, providing musical narration (e.g., Aimee Mann in *Magnolia,* Cat Stevens in *Harold and Maude,* Kimya Dawson in *Juno*). On rare occasion, that musical troubadour will be an on-screen presence (e.g., Stubby Kaye and Nat King

Cole in *Cat Ballou*, Jonathan Richman in *There's Something About Mary*).

The danger of using a familiar song is that it triggers such specific associations (e.g., a romantic breakup) that it pulls the viewer right out of the scene. On the flip side, there are examples of pop songs whose meanings are now inextricably linked to their usage in one film. For moviegoers of a certain generation, it's impossible to hear Q Lazzarus's "Goodbye Horses" and not shiver at the thought of Buffalo Bill in *Silence of the Lambs*. And I'm hardly alone in feeling that razor-toting Michael Madsen in *Reservoir Dogs* ruined "Stuck in the Middle with You" forever.

Your approach to pop songs should be no different from underscore. Whether working with a songwriter who's penning a tune for your film or riffing with a music supervisor about favorite records, the key is to keep everyone focused on the heart of the scene. If Marie Antoinette is bopping down the halls of Versailles, Annabella Lwin squealing, "I want candy!" needs to make some emotional sense, right? And, frankly, a musical sugar rush seems like the perfect choice for a monarch who felt her peasants' problems would go away if they only ate cake.

THEY NEED YOUR BLOOD

"What would you like to be when you grow up?" asked Mrs. Metcalf, my third-grade teacher at Blessed Sacrament School. One by one, each of us stood to answer the question. Some had given the matter much thought. The freckle-faced boy in the front row practically shouted, "I'm going to play outfield for the Cardinals." A pretty blond girl beside me was equally decisive: "I'm going to be a nun." Now, it was my turn. I was neither an athlete nor the class clown; I wasn't an egghead, and I certainly wasn't cut out for the priesthood. But I had my answer ready. I blithely informed the class, "I plan to be a film critic." My announcement was met with blank stares from everyone. Frankly, what was I thinking? For starters, what sort of boy refers to a movie as a *film*? I may as well have been wearing a smoking jacket. Second, the concept of critic as a profession was too remote for this bunch. My teacher narrowed her gaze, waiting for me to change my answer to something recognizable. And useful. But I stuck to my guns.

I promise I wasn't lording over the class with my urbanity.

Simply put, as a boy who spent the lion's share of his allowance at the movies, I came to realize there were a lot of interesting films that would never play in Belleville, Illinois. The handful of film books at the Belleville Public Library confirmed there was a universe of modern cinema to which I had no access. I pored over these texts, reading about art films from Europe and Japan. Several of the books were anthologies of film reviews, and thus began my obsession with cinematic tastemakers. If I couldn't see a film, I could at least find out what Pauline Kael or John Simon or Stanley Kauffmann or Penelope Gilliatt or Andrew Sarris had to say about it.

My father taught dentistry at Southern Illinois University in Edwardsville, and during the summers I would accompany him to hunker down in the stacks of the SIU library, surrounded by back issues of *Film Quarterly* and *The New Yorker*. My peers memorized sports stats. I memorized reviews. I wolfed them down. Not able to view the films in question, I didn't always comprehend what I was reading, but I was enthralled with the idea of trumpeting a performance, a scene, or a directorial flourish. And I was equally riveted by a snotty dismissal of a film, an actor, or an entire director's output. I snickered along with every Pauline Kael zinger. What fun to skewer a worthless director! If this be the sport of aesthetics, play on!

In college, I found like-minded souls who were happy to imbibe gallons of coffee and debate the merits of not films themselves but reviews of films. Was Pauline Kael too harsh on *Shoah*? Is she too easy on Brian De Palma? In my cockeyed brain, I nurtured the illusion that directors and reviewers were all part of the same club, everyone chummy and convivial. It never occurred to me to put myself in the shoes of some poor, maligned director. If Pauline Kael did trash a De Palma film, he would no doubt concur with her assessment and promise to make amends with his next effort, right?

All of this came to an abrupt halt when, as a professional director, I found myself at the business end of a particularly brutal review. I won't dignify the reviewer by revealing his name, but, weirdly, I felt betrayed. These were my people, and they let me down. Before going further, let's take a moment to distinguish between two species: the critic and the reviewer. Criticism, at its best, moves beyond questions of good taste to broader issues of aesthetics and ethics. Reviews are basically consumer reports that reflect a narrow sense of whatever qualifies as good taste at that moment. For the first time, it dawned on me that reviewers were basically entertainers themselves. And let's face it, nothing is more entertaining than a mean-spirited put-down.

The night before my second feature *Vibes* opened, my then girlfriend Marisa and I eagerly waited at the newsstand across from Canter's Delicatessen for the *Los Angeles Times* to arrive. When the truck pulled up and the vendor unloaded the morning edition, I suddenly had a bad premonition and asked Marisa to do the honors of peeking at the review. She flipped through the pages and silently read. Then, with no discernible expression on her face, she replaced the issue in the rack and said, "I think we should go home now." What transpired over the next twenty-four hours was an onslaught of spiteful notices, an outpouring of venom from the majority of the country's reviewers. It felt like a coordinated attack—were all these people in cahoots with each other? How could it be that my goofy, unassuming comedy generated so much hate? Over the following days, colleagues steered clear of me, as if I'd contracted something contagious: don't get near Ken, unless you want to be mercilessly panned. The film died a quick death, one "friend" suggested I consider a new line of work, and a few acquaintances actually defended the reviewers, as if I were due some sort of karmic comeuppance. Being vilified in public, of course, has one salutary aspect: it clarifies who's in your corner and who's not.

As was customary in the pre-email world, the studio sent me photocopies of every heartless review, and the massive stack sat on my desk for days, taunting me. What was I to do with this compendium of malice? Should I sift through the pile in search of a few charitable crumbs? Should I ceremoniously set it on fire? There is a celebrated fiction writer who reputedly pins negative notices to a telephone pole and uses them for target practice. At first, I tucked the reviews in a box, filing them away for another century. *Someday,* I reasoned, *I'll open the box and just laugh at all that viciousness, its power to sting me long since extinguished.* But I couldn't do it. I couldn't ignore the box. It was a hex upon my house. After considering various dramatic means of disposal, I finally opted for the recycling bin.

I then commenced an informal research project; I surveyed the creative people I knew to find out how they dealt with bad notices. More than a few swore by Friedrich Nietzsche's adage, "That which does not kill us, makes us stronger." By the way, I also heard this line attributed to Nietzsche: "A critic is like a wasp. It doesn't mean to hurt you. It just needs your blood to live." I was surprised how many people felt that the best defense against bad reviews is to simply grow thicker skin. If you can't stand the heat, get out of the kitchen, right? Sticks and stones, right? There was a contingent that took a relativistic approach: if you believe the good ones, you have to believe bad ones, too. For this group, reading every review, from the pitiless pan to the ardent rave, would somehow make you more objective about your work.

After conducting my survey, I came to one unambiguous conclusion. Creative people have a remarkable ability to remember, almost word for word, their worst notices. I once met a director I greatly admired, and I singled out a particular film for praise. The director just shook her head and launched into a recitation of one execrable review she received. It had been years since the film's release; nevertheless, she could quote savage passages from a single review. Those words, I realized, were stuck on her personal hard drive. If there had been glowing notices, they were hidden in a remote corner of her mind. I spoke with an established playwright who recalled a cruel wisecrack made by a critic decades earlier. *What's the point of growing thick skin,* I thought, *if you can't purge all this critical bile from your system?*

During my tenure on *The Larry Sanders Show,* I directed an episode that confirmed this observation. Entitled "Off Camera," the episode featured film reviewer Gene Siskel playing himself. Among the costars was John Ritter, also playing himself. In the story, written by Peter Tolan, both are guests on the show within the show. Ritter gives Siskel the cold shoulder when they meet backstage. When Siskel confronts him about his chilly manner, Ritter admits he's

bitter about the piss-poor review Siskel gave his performance in Blake Edwards's comedy *Skin Deep*. Here's how
the scene unfolds:

> GENE SISKEL
> Hi. Gene Siskel.

> JOHN RITTER
> John Ritter.

> GENE SISKEL
> I know.

> JOHN RITTER
> I know you know. I've heard you
> talk about my work on your show.

> GENE SISKEL
> Good things, I hope.

> JOHN RITTER
> (flatly)
> Not really.

> GENE SISKEL
> Oh.
> (thinking)
> Oh. The Blake Edwards movie, what
> was it . . . ?

JOHN RITTER
"Skin Deep."

GENE SISKEL
Oh, right. Well, you know . . .
that scene with the glow-in-the-
dark condom, that was funny.

JOHN RITTER
You know what? I don't care. I
don't listen to critics, it's not
constructive, I don't care.

GENE SISKEL
Okay, but come on . . . you must
have a subjective eye. It wasn't a
very good movie.

JOHN RITTER
It did very well in Europe. All I
know is . . . I put a great deal of
energy into it, then I turned on
my television set and had to listen
to you saying I "seemed distracted
by what was going on during the
movie . . . and after a while I
became a bore." I don't need
that.

                    GENE SISKEL
                    (amazed)
          You know, I think those were my
          exact words. That was what . . .
          five years ago? You remember it
          that well? And you're the guy who
          doesn't listen to critics?

Off-camera, the enraged Ritter throws a punch at Siskel. True Chicagoan that he is, Siskel returns the favor by striking Ritter in the face. When we next see Ritter, he's nursing a bloody nose in the green room. Having suffered at the proverbial hands of Siskel myself, it was a vicarious thrill to watch Ritter lose his cool. Having said that, the salient point belongs to Siskel: negative reviews lodge themselves in your brain. And those words take on a life of their own.

Around this time, I heard an anecdote about a powerful writer-director, someone with carte blanche to make any kind of film he wanted, an artist with studios literally at his beck and call. This director, I was told, was petrified of reviews. He went so far as to avert his eyes from blurbs in newspaper advertisements. He routinely tossed the unopened Arts and Leisure section of *The New York Times* into the trash, rather than risk exposure to punditry of any kind. I was truly shocked to learn that someone with complete control over his creative endeavors was still a raw nerve when it came to reviews.

Maybe thick skin is overrated. Why subject yourself to all those slings and arrows? Wouldn't it be smarter . . . to duck? So, I made the decision to go cold turkey; I would no longer read reviews of my work. The way to exert power over reviewers, I decided, is to not have their words in my head. If I live to be one hundred years old and never know what so-and-so wrote about my work, so much the better for my mental health. Besides, any positive review will never be as glowing as the one in my imagination, and I can easily pen a more insightful pan of my work than a so-called professional.

I mentioned my moratorium to friends, and many were skeptical that I could pull it off. And, yes, as with all self-imposed health regimes, I fell off the wagon more than once. Some insisted, "Don't you want to hear when people say nice things about you?" In my experience, even a rave will contain one word that can trip you up completely. "Veteran director Ken Kwapis . . ." *Veteran? How old do they think I am?* "A big improvement over his last effort . . ." *And that's supposed to make me feel good?* A kindly relative once urged me to read a rave review; unfortunately, she didn't actually read past the opening paragraph. That's when the reviewer produced his stiletto.

I confided to my father that I was on a review-free diet, and he said I was being obtuse. His attitude was, "Get with the program." He argued that critics had a certain authority and it was my duty to pay them heed. In addition to teaching, my father was a practicing oral surgeon, and I challenged him to recall any negative notices he'd ever received. "No one writes a scathing review of a molar extraction!" I exclaimed.

Over time, my prohibition became easier to maintain, and

it expanded to include reviews of other directors' work—in particular, reviews of directors I know personally. Professional jealousy is a virus found in every walk of life, but it seems particularly virulent in the entertainment world, where careers rise and fall willy-nilly, sometimes wiped out by a mere tweet. It's easy to envy the success of your peers or gloat when they stumble, and I'm far from immune, which is one more reason I keep the taste-making machinery at a distance. Another benefit to being oblivious to critical consensus is that it has sharpened my own critical thinking skills, forced me to be more precise about how I respond to a film or series. I know many people who leave a movie theater and simply regurgitate the review they read before buying a ticket. I know . . . because I was one of them. Why would you want anyone to do your critical thinking for you, especially someone whose livelihood occasionally depends on using a poison pen?

Now, I'm not naive. When releasing a film or series into the world, it's impossible to remain truly uninformed about which way the winds are blowing. The morning my film *License to Wed* opened, I awoke to find an email from a trusted producer. The subject heading read, "Fuck The New York Times." I didn't feel it necessary to open that email. On the plus side, a disparaging review of *License to Wed* provided a teaching moment for me as a parent. My fourteen-year-old son, en route to school, heard a radio announcer lambast the film and was startled that anyone would speak ill of his father. A classmate heard the same caustic comment and, displaying great sensitivity, remarked, "Your dad's film must really suck." That such snarky people even existed was new and troubling for my son. The two of us had a heart-to-heart, less about the review and more about the monumental challenge of not letting other people define you. The short version of our conversation went something like this: "I'm proud of the film," I said.

"But what if people don't like it?" he asked.

"I can't control what people think, but I don't have to listen to anything they say," I replied. "What I can control is the filmmaking process itself. And if the process is creative and inspiring, I call that a success."

Our discussion inevitably turned to a much bigger menace than galling reviews. People paid to write rude things about movies, we decided, are small potatoes compared with that universe of vitriol available on the internet. I can't imagine how profoundly disconcerting it must be to grow up in an age when anyone can post anything about anybody without attribution or consequence. My advice to my son: "Sometimes the healthiest thing to do is simply . . . not know."

TENACITY

Today I had nothing to do but traverse four middling mountains over seven miles of well-marked trail in clear, dry weather. It didn't seem too much to ask. It was hell.

—Bill Bryson, *A Walk in the Woods*

I want to circle back to our earlier chapter about how to take a meeting, whether a pitch meeting with a financier or a job interview with a potential employer. What I neglected to discuss is coping with disappointment after the meeting doesn't go your way. Studio and network executives don't let you down gracefully; in fact, in the "ghosting" era, they often don't pay you the courtesy of a proper pass. After not getting the job, it's easy to frame the interview as a failure. I've wasted a lot of energy dissecting every beat of an unsuccessful meeting, second-guessing each word of the pitch document I'd worked so hard to create. "It wasn't meant to be" is one refrain we all repeat. It's easy to dwell in defeat and forget that many factors led to the decision not to hire you, most of which had nothing to do with you. No amount of experience makes it easy to pick yourself up and move forward. But somehow you do. You put one foot in front of the other and start up the hill again.

When I received the call about meeting Robert Redford to direct *A Walk in the Woods,* based on Bill Bryson's memoir, I knew this would be no ordinary job interview. To date, Redford had forty-two features as an actor under his belt, and it was tough composing a pitch with the shadows of Sydney Pollack, George Roy Hill, Alan J. Pakula, Arthur Penn, and Michael Ritchie looming over me. As a director himself, Redford had nine features to his credit, the first of which earned him an Academy Award for Best Director. Add to that the fact that he essentially changed the face of independent filmmaking in America, and you can understand what a tough task this was going to be. What could I say that would convince Robert Redford that I was the right director for a story about two old guys who decide to walk the 2,100-mile Appalachian Trail?

My strategy was to keep things personal. Rather than try to outclass the towering talents who came before me, I decided to do the unthinkable: be myself. After sitting down with Redford in his modest Santa Monica office, I opened my pitch with an anecdote about my father-in-law, Ray, who decided to celebrate his seventieth birthday by climbing Mount Kilimanjaro. Many people felt it was a thoroughly insane idea and urged Ray not to do it. Mount Kilimanjaro may be the most user-friendly of the great peaks, but it's still 19,341 feet above sea level, the highest freestanding mountain in the world. Ray was in good shape, but there was a lot of anxiety on the home front as he embarked for Tanzania to make the seven-day trek. "At the end of the week, he reached the top," I told Redford as

I pulled an 8×10 photograph from my satchel. "Here's what he looked like at the summit," I said, handing him the picture. Against a cloudless sky, my father-in-law stands near a rickety wooden sign that reads: "Congratulations! You are now at Uhuru Peak, Tanzania, 5895M." His hands are thrust in the air. His mouth is open; it appears as if the camera captured him mid-roar. There's a slightly crazed look on his face, a look of defiance, as if thumbing his nose at all the naysayers. "Perhaps he's thumbing his nose at death," I added as a throwaway, trying not to sound portentous. "It's like he's looking death in the face and saying, 'You're not getting me yet!'" Redford smiled and nodded.

After that, I dove into the subject of male friendships—specifically, the challenge of sustaining friendships over the long haul. In Bryson's memoir, the author and his childhood pal, Stephen Katz, haven't seen each other for decades, and their paths could not have been more divergent. In my pitch, I described a few of my male friends as "some of the most emotionally disconnected people I know." But I added, "These are guys I love." I made two observations about my male friends. First, we have an uncanny ability to go for years and years without seeing one another, then cross paths and pick up the conversation exactly where it was left. Second, we are quite content to argue about a trivial matter for our entire lives. Are The Stones better than The Beatles? Is Larry Fine funnier than Curly Howard? (I know many who would insist this is no trivial matter.)

I then shifted gears to the project itself. Below is a breakdown of my talking points, with a thumbnail summary of each:

Theme: The journey is more important than the destination. The main characters, Bill Bryson (Redford) and Stephen Katz (Nick Nolte), fail in their quest to complete the hike but emerge as better men in the process.

Hero's arc: Bill Bryson has written bestselling books about a vast array of subjects, but he has overlooked the most important one: himself.

Stakes: The stakes in the story are high, but not obvious. Bryson and Katz are in the autumn of their lives, and if they don't achieve some clarity on this trip, some understanding about themselves, then the adventure is for naught.

Tone: There are many existential road movies like Wim Wenders's *Kings of the Road* and Monte Hellman's *Two-Lane Blacktop*. I see *A Walk in the Woods* as a comic journey with those same serious undertones. In other words, it's not a Hope and Crosby road movie but more akin to Michael Winterbottom's *The Trip*. In that film, Steve Coogan and Rob Brydon traverse northern England, reviewing restaurants. They devote much of their time to topping each other's jokes, but seem incapable of connecting emotionally. For me, it's a sad story about men failing to dig beneath the surface. I suggested that *A Walk in the Woods* is both funny and elegiac. As Bryson and Katz take stock of their lives, reviewing roads taken and not taken, they move through a once-idyllic world that is increasingly degraded.

Visual Style: There are three main characters in the story—Bryson, Katz, and the trail itself. Bryson writes of the woods, "I discovered an America that millions of people scarcely know exists." Visually, the film can introduce that America to viewers. The biggest challenge, I told Redford, is how to make two guys plodding through the woods feel dynamic, funny, and, at times, thrilling. The action of the story, by definition, is repetitious. Tedious, even. To create variety, our visual approach to walking should change as our characters' inner journey deepens. Initially, when the walk is arduous, the men grouse and keep their noses to the ground, and our view of the woods should be just as claustrophobic. As they rediscover their friendship, they are better able to appreciate the beauty around them, and our view of the trail opens up accordingly.

Sound: The sonic textures along the trail can give the picture unexpected production value. The sound of the woods should be specific to time of year, time of day, and the precise stretch of trail Bryson and Katz are traveling. For instance, the birdsong one hears in Georgia is not the same as Tennessee. The jazzlike improvisations of the brown thrasher, the state bird of Georgia, could not be more different from the trill of the pine warbler, which you hear along the Tennessee section of the trail.

I finished my pitch by suggesting ways to punch up a few scenes, one of which made Redford laugh. That buoyed my spirits, and I left the meeting with a spring in my step. Personal. Confident, but not cocky. No clunkers. I felt good.

Two days later, I learned that Redford chose another director for *A Walk in the Woods*. Upon hearing the news, I did what anyone who's been passed over for a job does. I beat myself up. What did I do wrong? Did I say too much or too little? I reviewed my pitch document from top to bottom. Was it too personal? Perhaps it was a mistake to lead off with anecdotes about my own life. Who wants to hear about my complicated male friendships? Obviously, not Redford. Maybe I didn't dress casually enough. That spiffy sport coat no doubt sent the wrong signal—namely, that I wanted the job too much, that I was needy. I should have worn running shoes instead of my old brown dress shoes. Yes, that's it. Running shoes would have made the difference. Or should I have worn hiking boots? Were my notes on the script too pedantic? Maybe I sounded like a schoolboy presenting a term paper ("The central theme of *Huckleberry Finn* is . . ."). I replayed the meeting in my head ad nauseam. Did I misread Redford's laugh? Was it merely a titter?

After torturing myself for the better part of a day, I came to a surprising conclusion. I liked my pitch, and if I had it all to do over, I'd take the same approach. The notes were solid, the personal stories important, and the sport coat was, well . . . it was me. Hey, you could do a lot worse than spend an hour with the Sundance Kid. I tucked my pitch document into the missed opportunity file, put my dress shoes in the closet, and was about to toss the script into the recycling bin when I thought, *Maybe I should just hang on to this for a little while.*

Six months later, I was sitting at my desk in a low-grade funk, debating the best way to procrastinate, when my manager called. "Redford just fired the director of *A Walk in the Woods*," he excitedly reported. "And he wants to meet you again." Needless to say, I was wholly unprepared for this. "When does he want to meet?" I asked.

"In an hour," my manager said.

"I haven't even showered," I protested.

"It's a movie about walking the Appalachian Trail. You don't need to shower," he replied.

As I carelessly threw on some clothes, a worry seized me: Was I putting on the same outfit I'd worn at the first meeting? I stared at those old brown shoes. Wearing them again would be a terrible move, right? It would conclusively demonstrate that I have no sense of style. On the other hand, it might send the signal that, as a creative person, I'm too focused on what really counts (the project) to care about such piddling matters as my appearance. I opted for the latter rationale, made my way across town, sat down with Redford, and, to my complete surprise—I swear this is the absolute truth—he was wearing the same brown shoes as I was. Once I got over the shock of our matching footwear, I launched into my pitch. One week later, I was on a plane bound for Georgia to begin scouting locations for *A Walk in the Woods*.

The hardest part was coming to terms with the con-stant dispiriting discovery that there is always more hill . . . Each time you haul yourself up to what you think must surely be the crest, you find that there is in fact more hill beyond, sloped at an angle that kept it from view before, and that beyond that slope there is another, and beyond that another and another, and

beyond each of those more still, until it seems impossible
that any hill could run on this long.
　　　　　　　　　—Bill Bryson, *A Walk in the Woods*

Roget's Thesaurus has many synonyms for the word *shuffle*. There's *shamble, straggle,* and *pad,* among others. None of these accurately describes Nick Nolte making his entrance for our first meeting. To say that every footstep required effort is an understatement. It was like a mountain range scuffing its way into the room. As I quickly noted, Nolte was in perfect shape for the role of Stephen Katz, Bryson's long-lost friend— that is, he was perfectly out of shape. Bryson and Katz had a falling-out during a youthful trip to Europe, and as Bryson tells it, "After our summer in Europe, Katz had gone back to Des Moines and had become, in effect, Iowa's drug culture. He had partied for years, until there was no one left to party with, then he had partied with himself, alone in small apartments, in a T-shirt and boxer shorts, with a bottle and a Baggie of pot and a TV with rabbit ears." Faced with Nolte's utterly shambolic presentation, I thought, *The man has been preparing for this role for years.* My second thought: *There's no way in hell Nolte will be able to walk up a hill, let alone do so for multiple takes, spouting pages of dialogue along the way.* Even as we shook hands, my mind was in damage-control mode: Do I need to hire a stunt double . . . for walking?

There wasn't one day during our thirty-four-day schedule that I didn't worry about Nolte keeling over during a scene. When Bryson and his wife, Catherine (Emma Thompson), greet Katz at the commuter airport in Hanover, New Hampshire, Katz makes a frantic beeline for a vending machine, where he buys a package of powdered doughnuts. He stuffs them into his mouth as if his life depended on it. In fact, it does, as Katz explains:

> KATZ
>
> I've got to eat something every hour or so or I have, what do you call it . . . Seizures?

> BRYSON
>
> Seizures?

> KATZ
>
> Took some contaminated phenylethylamines about ten years ago—totally jacked my system.

Take after take, Nolte inhaled the doughnuts. It's not easy to pronounce the word *phenylethylamines*, let alone with a mouthful of dough, not to mention a face covered in white powder. None of this felt like acting. I truly believed that once upon a time Nolte took contaminated phenylethylamines, and the only way he would survive the scene was by gorging doughnuts. It was Emma Thompson's first shooting day, and she couldn't get through a take without breaking into laughter. Then, she pulled me aside. "Is he going to have a stroke?" she asked, trying to stifle her giggles. Redford's performance in the scene was spot-on, but again, I wondered if any acting was involved. Was this Bill Bryson having second thoughts about inviting this human train wreck on a monumental hike? Or was this Robert Redford watching his costar scarf down doughnuts and thinking, *What the hell have I gotten into?*

On the trail, however, Nolte surprised me with his sheer grit and perseverance. It was clear that his emotional connection to Katz was very deep. Katz's eagerness to prove to his successful and prosperous pal that he's not a complete fuck-up resonated with the actor, and Nolte's need to express himself in this role won my heart. Having said that, he wasn't happy about trudging up a muddy hill, weighed down with a backpack, for six or seven takes. One day, in complete frustration, Nolte put me in a headlock. It was an affectionate gesture, mind you, but a headlock nonetheless. By the way, Nolte played defensive end for his college football team, a fact I recalled while rubbing my neck later that day. During one lengthy scene on the trail, I watched Nolte fight his way up a steep stretch while our Steadicam operator nimbly led the way, walking backward while carrying a camera suspended from a cumbersome stabilizing rig. All I could think of was the Little Engine That Could, chanting, "I think I can, I think I can," while pulling the train up the mountain. It was then that the real subject of *A Walk in the Woods* hit me: tenacity. A word I didn't use in my pitch, it now struck me as the watchword of the entire picture. In the book, Bryson describes his very first encounter with a hill: "I trudged perhaps a hundred feet up the hill, then stopped, bug-eyed, breathing hard, heart kabooming alarmingly. Katz was already falling behind and panting even harder. I pressed on." Why? Why press on? Many complete the 2,100-mile hike, and Bryson singles out several who deserve a place in the Chutzpah Hall of Fame: "One man hiked it in his eighties. Another did it on crutches. A blind man named Bill Irwin hiked the trail with a seeing-eye dog, falling down an estimated 5,000 times in the process." What kept Bill Irwin going? It's hard to pick myself up after a bad job interview. He did it 5,000 times.

As I've noted, perhaps too often, the entertainment business can be quite punishing. A career as a film and/or television director is an unending series of hills. And given the odds against anything getting made, realizing your dreams requires a mad sort of pluck that has no logic. I know filmmakers who have labored years and years to get their projects made. I count myself among them. Beyond every hill is more hill. If I were given the task of creating a new awards show for filmmaking (just what the world needs, right?), instead of a golden statuette of a stylized knight holding a sword, I would design one based on Sisyphus, smiling as he pushes that boulder uphill for eternity. The award would only be given to filmmakers who are still trying to get their projects off the ground. Actually making the film would disqualify you.

Bringing *A Walk in the Woods* to the screen was an uphill climb for Redford. One imagines that an actor-producer-director as celebrated as he would have no problem getting any film made, let alone one based on a popular book. But *A Walk in the Woods* suffered a string of setbacks, and it was Redford's doggedness that carried the day. Redford optioned Bryson's 1998 memoir to develop as a vehicle for Paul Newman and himself. Remarkably, it would have only been the third pairing of these titans. Two films, *Butch Cassidy and the Sundance Kid* and *The Sting,* cemented Redford's and Newman's place in the pantheon as an iconic screen duo. Newman was very involved in the script's development (he pitched one rather salty line of dialogue that remained in every subsequent draft, and Nolte memorialized Newman's contribution with gusto).

Unbeknownst to most people, Newman was battling lung cancer at the time, and as the disease got the upper hand, he finally called Redford to bow out of the project. "I just don't think I'm going to be available," Newman said to his friend.

After Newman's death, Redford put the script on the shelf. He simply couldn't imagine making the film with anyone else.

Four years later, Redford directed the political thriller *The Company You Keep;* he also played the lead role of a 1960s militant on the run from the FBI. Redford cast Nolte in the role of a fellow radical from the Vietnam War era. They had never before worked together, and the collaboration proved so satisfying that Redford decided it was time to revisit the Bryson project. Given these auspices (Redford, Nolte, bestselling title), how difficult could it be to find a backer for *A Walk in the Woods*? Well, surprisingly difficult. With studios narrowing the scope of their output, a small, character-based tale about old friends reconnecting could not find a place at the table, one increasingly occupied by comic book heroes and animated characters. Directors came and went, as did various financiers, and by the time Redford enlisted me, the funding for this indisputably American story was coming from South Korea. *A Walk in the Woods* had become *The Little Film That Could.* Needless to say, having created the Sundance Institute, Redford knows more than a bit about little films that could. The film festival he founded in 1978 is nothing if not a celebration of the intestinal fortitude required to bring your story to life, the resilience needed to cope with innumerable setbacks, be they as dispiriting as a meeting that doesn't go your way or as devastating as the death of your costar.

Every Saturday night during the shooting of *A Walk in the Woods,* Redford and I had dinner to discuss the following week's work. I brought my script and placed it on the table, but I never opened it. Not once. Instead, I listened as Redford waxed nostalgic about a career that spanned over half a century. He often circled back to his earliest days as an actor. He was twenty-four when he portrayed a Nazi with a conscience in the *Playhouse 90* production of Rod Serling's drama *In the Presence of Mine Enemies,* but listening to Redford's lively reminiscence, you'd think he'd played the role last week. Over the course of these wonderfully rangy dinners, a theme emerged. Redford didn't regale me with tales of debauched Hollywood parties. And he never touted his many triumphs. Instead, each story focused on a problem to be solved, an obstacle to negotiate, a hurdle to overcome. Whether aiming to make the most of a bit role on CBS's *Route 66,* trying and failing to persuade an elusive Elia Kazan to direct *All The President's Men,* or fighting to create a forum where independent filmmaking voices could emerge, Redford relished the uphill climb. I was tempted to ask, "Why do you keep going? What do you still need to accomplish?" If anyone deserved to rest on his laurels, I thought, it was Redford. But during these dinners, he answered the question without my ever asking it. Every anecdote reinforced the same point: the process was much more compelling than the outcome. It was the striving, not the achievement, that excited him.

One overcast morning, we were shooting deep in the Georgia woods. On the schedule was a short, transitional scene in which the brainy Bryson lectures Katz about the demise of the American chestnut tree. As they hike, Bryson observes, "Just fifty years ago, one in four of these trees would've been an American chestnut." Given Redford's passion for environmental conservation, he might have been happy with a ten-page monologue about the tragedy of the American chestnut, felled by a fungus imported from Asia at the turn of the last century. While we were setting up the camera, Redford wandered off the path, heading down a ravine. I watched from a distance as he stood quietly in a grove of oak trees. I approached slowly, not wanting to disturb his reverie. What was he thinking? Perhaps he was preparing for the scene, putting himself in Bryson's shoes, contemplating those chestnuts holding fast against a blight they had no means to repel. No amount of tenacity would save the chestnut. Redford brushed his hand against the bark of a majestic oak that could easily have been a hundred years old. It was very still, and it suddenly occurred to me that all the ups and downs of this crazy job were worth enduring just to stand here and watch Redford enjoy this solitary moment in nature. He turned and caught me looking at him. "We're ready to shoot," I called. Redford nodded. "Let's go," he said, and we started back up the hill.

HUMANS WERE INVOLVED

"I can't do it! It's impossible!" cried the harmonica player, throwing up his hands in frustration. He looked around at his fellow musicians, nearly sixty in number, assembled at a venerable Hollywood scoring stage to record the music for *Sesame Street Presents: Follow That Bird*. A few of the players smiled in sympathy as the harmonicist resumed his complaint. "There are just too many notes. I can't hit them," he moaned.

At the podium was the score's coauthor Lennie Niehaus, a renowned jazz saxophonist turned film composer who collaborated with Clint Eastwood on no fewer than fifteen pictures. He no doubt concurred with the harmonicist, and the obvious solution was to take a break and simplify the harmonica melody in the cue. Lennie looked over his shoulder at the recording booth, where his colleague Van Dyke Parks sat at the controls. "What do you think, Van Dyke?"

Now, before I get to Van Dyke's reply, introductions are in order. Van Dyke Parks, composer, arranger, singer-songwriter, and dazzling raconteur, had been a musical hero of mine since I stumbled onto his debut LP, *Song Cycle,* at my local record shop in the early 1970s. His music is lush, whimsical, unruly, beguiling, joyous; to me, it has a singularly holistic quality. I invited Van Dyke to score *Follow That Bird* and was over the moon when he decided to come aboard. His exuberant style was perfect for the story of Big Bird's journey of self-discovery.

The musical cue that so flummoxed the harmonica player accompanies a scene of Big Bird walking down a country road that seems to go on forever. To create a rural feeling, Van Dyke composed a playful melody for a banjo. Then, he added the harmonica, playing in unison with the banjo. Needless to say, you can fingerpick a banjo much faster than you can play a harmonica. By writing the parts in unison, Van Dyke saddled the harmonicist with an extra degree of difficulty.

I was seated in the booth near Van Dyke, awaiting his verdict. From the orchestra, the harmonicist once more pleaded his case. "Van Dyke, there are too many notes. I keep making mistakes." Finally, Van Dyke leaned into the microphone and said, "That's okay. Mistakes are okay. In fact, mistakes are important. That's how we let people know that humans were involved."

The studio musicians laughed, the harmonicist shook his head, and things got back on track. But I was dumbstruck by Van Dyke's throwaway remark. I quietly mulled it over for the remainder of the session and have carried it with me like a mantra to this day. Humans were involved. Getting the notes right is less important than the *effort* to get the notes right. A robot can perform the notes perfectly. A computer can render an immaculate image. We can remove a blemish from an actor's face, eliminate shadows under his eyes, and tuck in his tummy. A machine can execute a camera move without a glitch. We can groom every shot, vacuum every speck, digitally scrub away every stain, but in the process, we will have missed the point entirely. Getting it right is irrelevant. It's the struggle to get it right that makes us human. As Robert Browning wrote, "Ah, but a man's reach should exceed his grasp / Or what's a heaven for?" The spectacle of that reach is what I want to capture on film.

A student recently asked me to sum up my process as a director. I told her that I strive to create an atmosphere that welcomes surprises, that embraces the unexpected, that celebrates the occasional misstep, that honors flaws of all kinds; in short, I want to stand behind the camera and make sure there's something alive going on in front of it, something recognizably human.

ACKNOWLEDGMENTS

Marisa Silver is my North Star, and she gave me the courage to embark upon this journey. Reynolds Anderson, Alexandra Beattie, Rick Berg, and Robert Dimitri gave me incredible feedback along the way. Jordan Lonner and Byrd Leavell were true believers before I typed a single word. For his astute editorial counsel, I am indebted to Michael Homler. For their wisdom about the directing process, I want to thank Robert Redford, Michelle Satter, Gyula Gazdag, Ilyse McKimmie, and all my fellow advisers at the Sundance Institute Directors Lab. For moral support, I want to thank Valerie Weiner, Rebecca Benenati, Debra Cohen, Loreni Delgado, Deb Kaye, Gregg McBride, Jim Masri, Toni Profera, Bruce Dolin, Barbara Hall, Val Almendarez, Jeremy Butler, Daphne Dentz, Nicole Dubuc, John Bailey, Christine Sacani, Leslie Maskin, Howard Rodman, Treva Silverman, Brian Duchinsky, David Kramer, Don McGlynn, Larry King, Rina Dokshitsky, and Colman deKay. I am grateful to my sons, Henry and Oliver, for calling me on all my bullshit. Finally, I want to thank Paul Brenner for keeping me sane throughout the writing of this book; and Brian Hohlfeld, my partner in crime since this whole adventure began.

INDEX

ABOUT THE AUTHOR

Mark Schafer

KEN KWAPIS is a director of motion pictures and television. He has directed eleven feature films: *A Walk in the Woods*, *Big Miracle*, *He's Just Not That into You*, *License to Wed*, *The Sisterhood of the Traveling Pants*, *Sexual Life*, *The Beautician and the Beast*, *Dunston Checks In*, *He Said, She Said* (codirected with Marisa Silver), *Vibes*, and *Sesame Street Presents: Follow That Bird*.

Kwapis helped launch nine television series, among them *The Larry Sanders Show*, *The Bernie Mac Show*, *The Office*, *Outsourced*, *Happyish*, and *#blackAF*. He also directed episodes of numerous shows, including *Freaks and Geeks*, *Malcolm in the Middle*, *Santa Clarita Diet*, and *One Mississippi*.